THE BOUNDARIES OF

CITIZENSHIP

RACE, ETHNICITY,
AND NATIONALITY
IN THE LIBERAL STATE

JEFF SPINNER

THE JOHNS HOPKINS UNIVERSITY PRESS
BALTIMORE AND LONDON

© 1994 The Johns Hopkins University Press
All rights reserved. Published 1994
Printed in the United States of America on acid-free paper
03 02 01 00 99 98 97 96 95 94   5 4 3 2 1

The Johns Hopkins University Press
2715 North Charles Street
Baltimore, Maryland 21218-4319
The Johns Hopkins Press Ltd., London

Library of Congress Cataloging-in-Publication Data
will be found at the end of this book.
A catalog record of this book is available from the British Library.

ISBN 0-8018-4812-1

To Cathy Cohen,
Regina Freer,
Kim James,
and Jocelyn Sargent

CONTENTS

PREFACE

ON A TRIP to Israel a few years ago, I saw a short film produced by the government that was meant to instill pride in Israel among its Jewish citizens. It showed a tired but proud young soldier arriving home for the weekend. After greeting his family, he made his way toward his bedroom, where he fell asleep on his bed. His younger brother peered into the room, watching his brother sleep. Slowly walking into the room, the little brother looked upon his older brother and the gun beside him with great admiration and a little jealousy. He then tried on his brother's boots, hoping that he was big enough to be an Israeli soldier. The boots were too large, but the younger brother obviously could not wait until he became old enough to join the army, where he too could wear army boots and shoot a gun. The admiration of the boy for his older brother was touching; the nationalism displayed in the film was stirring, but this nationalism can also be troublesome. Only some people can be full members of the Jewish state; non-Jews are outsiders. It is hard to see how equal rights can be given to all members of a state that is supposed to be the national home of one particular group of people. I thought that there were good reasons for the existence of a Jewish state, but the message of this movie bothered me. Didn't the history of the oppression of the Jews justify a Jewish state? Wasn't the maintenance of national identities something to applaud? Before answering these questions, I realized that the dilemma of nationalism I saw overseas was, in some ways, similar to dilemmas of my own that I experienced in the United States.

I came into this world as a citizen of the United States and as a Jew. I grew up with a strong Jewish identity, an identity in which I take considerable pride. It is an identity, however, with which I often struggle. At home I was taught to distinguish between Jews and non-Jews, that there were differences between these two groups, differences that ought to play an important part in my life. Where I lived and went to school, whom I befriended and dated, were all supposed to be guided by questions of identity. At school, however, I was taught that everyone is equal. Distinctions based on cultural heritage, which is often hard to see, seemed to conflict with this idea of equality. If we all are equal, why should I seek to live near and become friends with people who have a certain ethnic identity? If we all are equal, why should cultural heritage make a difference among people? Yet I take pride in my Jewish identity.

The maintenance of ethnic and national identity, I concluded, requires a certain exclusiveness. Groups must distinguish between members and non-members if they are to continue to exist. Sometimes the boundaries between groups are voluntarily drawn by group members, but other times these boundaries are forced upon people. Although Jews often choose to retain their identity, they have also been marked out as separate and subordinate. Jews are an ethnic group in the United States and a national group in Israel, but they were often considered to be a racial group in other times and places. Racial groups are sometimes cultural groups but are situated hierarchically in a society. Some racial groups have power, while others do not. When people who have political power think of themselves as members of a superior race, members of the subordinate race often find themselves oppressed. This hierarchy often reinforces group identity. Indeed, racial identity is often a vibrant identity. When anti-Semitism declines, Jewish identity becomes precarious. There is nothing like a good dose of anti-Semitism to help maintain Jewish identity (except when this anti-Semitism leads to the massacre of Jews). Is group identity, I wondered, best maintained under conditions of oppression and hierarchy?

This is a troublesome possibility if the maintenance of group identity is an important value. I began to think of how dominance and subordination are connected to issues of identity. I wondered if exclusiveness, which seems so important to maintain particular identities, could accord with the idea of equality. I questioned whether there was room in a liberal democracy for cultural differences. Although this project began very personally, it has moved beyond my own identity. My interest here is in the political implications of group identity and how the cultural identity of citizens is affected by the liberal state. To examine these issues, I discuss Black Americans, the Amish, American Jews, French Canadians, and other groups in this book.

My discussion of these groups is, in many ways, a discussion about boundaries; the maintenance of distinct cultural groups is predicated to a large degree on the maintenance of boundaries between groups. Liberal citizenship and liberal equality, however, work to break down boundaries. Some groups are distinct because of their subordination; other groups are distinct because of their voluntary partial withdrawal from mainstream society into patriarchal and hierarchical communities. Because liberalism fights against inequality and subordination, it combats some of the boundaries between groups. Many cultural practices are inegalitarian and so are incompatible with liberalism. Unfortunately, liberalism is not always as effective as it should be in breaking down the barriers that keep some groups subordinated; it needs to develop better ways to combat racial hierarchies. Under conditions of liberal equality, different cultural identities can flourish in the private sphere; however, liberals often exaggerate the autonomy of the private sphere from other spheres in society. Consequently, they exaggerate the extent to which distinct cultural identities actually flourish in the liberal state.

The private sphere is affected by other spheres in society; the demands on liberal citizens in these other spheres make it hard, but not impossible, for distinct cultural identities to thrive in the liberal state. Liberalism enables, and sometimes encourages, members of different groups to share in each other's cultural practices. To the extent that cultural practices are shared, cultural diversity will exist, but the connection of these practices to particular ethnic cultures will often be murky. Liberal citizens with a variety of cultural heritages will partake in the cultural practices of others. As liberalism breaks down boundaries, it transforms cultural identity.

It is precisely because liberalism works toward breaking down boundaries that some groups in liberal societies become nationalistic and push for their own state; a state of their own will help them maintain their distinct identity. Nationalism, however, poses a severe challenge to liberalism. Liberals can weakly support one tenet of language-based nationalism, that which enables people to become citizens by learning a particular language. Yet there will probably always be tensions between nationalism and liberalism, just as the interactions between liberalism and other forms of group identity will always produce tensions. In the following pages I hope to highlight these tensions and shed some light on matters of race, ethnicity, and nationality in the liberal state.

As I finish this book, unexpected events have eased some of the dilemmas I felt while in Israel a few years ago. The signing of the Israeli-Palestinian agreement brings the hope that the conflict between these two peoples may come to an end. This good news is tempered, however, by the decimation of the Bosnian people in the early 1990s. The Bosnian people, who created a peaceful pluralistic society, have been the victims of organized rapes and gruesome and senseless killings. The world has done little to stop this genocide; it has not even given the Bosnians the means to defend themselves. The Bosnians may get a rump state—a state hardly worthy of the name—but not until after too much horrendous damage has been done. The sad irony of writing a defense of pluralism as this society is destroyed has not been lost on me. The countries of the world, including the liberal democracies, may speak of human rights and pluralism, but their words were all too cheap for the Bosnians.

Being a friend of mine these past two years or so has not always been easy. At some point, I've collared most of my friends and quizzed them on their cultural identity. In fact, many acquaintances of mine—some of whom I barely know—have found themselves subjected to a barrage of questions on the same subject. Most people cheerfully humored me by answering my queries. I thank all of these people, who are too numerous to name here, but the help that some people gave me deserves special mention. Gary Shiffman spent hours arguing and discussing with me most of the ideas that appear in the following pages. He also pointed out how embarrassed I'd be if certain arguments I initially wanted to make actually appeared publicly under my name. Gary tirelessly read several drafts of each chapter, noting time and time again the flaws in my arguments. My only complaint is that he did not always time his vacations around my deadlines. William Coleman lent me his expertise on Quebec by reading chapter 7. Rebecca Bratspies, Jean Cahan, Cathy Cohen, Michael Combs, David Imbroscio, Jonathan Simon, Jocelyn Sargent, Ron Spinner, and Elizabeth Theiss-Morse all read one or more chapters. Elizabeth Anderson, Michael Dawson, Douglas Dion, Eric McKee, Don Herzog, Edward Rosenbaum, Arlene Saxonhouse, and Bernard Yack read the entire manuscript, often reading more than one draft of each chapter. I greatly appreciate their patient comments. Rogers Smith also read the entire manuscript under a tight deadline, just before it had to be sent off to the publisher. The book is better because of his thoughtful comments. I presented parts of this project to the law faculty at the University of Nebraska-Lincoln, to the political science faculty at the University of Nebraska-Lincoln, and at the 1992 and 1993 annual meetings of the Midwest Political Science Association. I benefited from the questions and comments of these audiences. I am also grateful to Henry Y. K. Tom for shepherding this book through Johns Hopkins University Press with remarkable grace and speed.

This book was originally written as my dissertation at the University of Michigan, where Don Herzog served as the chair of my committee. Don encouraged me to develop my own scholarly interests and style, while also steadily pointing out where I could improve my arguments. His advice, encouragement, and good humor made it possible to get through graduate school and write this book. The Horace H. Rackham Graduate School at the University of Michigan helped me with timely financial support. I thank my family as well; many of the issues I discuss here first arose for me as I was growing up. It was the strong beliefs of my parents and brother and sisters about being Jewish in America that spurred me to examine and revamp my own ideas about liberalism and cultural identity. My rich family life gave me the strength and security to examine the strong cultural identity with which I grew up. I look forward to the days when Elyza and I will watch our children work through many of these issues in their own way.

I dedicate this book to four remarkable women: Cathy Cohen, Regina Freer, Kim James, and Jocelyn Sargent. I learned more about race, identity, and political theory from our conversations than I could from any book; just as important, their warmth and encouragement carried me through many frustrating days while working on this project.

THE BOUNDARIES OF CITIZENSHIP

CHAPTER 1

INTRODUCTION

IN 1848 GERMAN LIBERALS established the Frankfurt Parliament, which, they hoped, would unite a liberal Germany. They invited liberal dignitaries from all over their nation to take part in the parliament. One of them, František Palacký, declined their invitation, saying, "I am not a German— at least I do not feel myself to be one. . . . I am a Czech of Slavonic blood, and with all the little I possess and all the little I can do, I have devoted myself for all time to the service of my nation."[1] Palacký proclaimed his identity to be Czech, not German, and this identity, he said, had important political implications. He did not want to be a member of just any state, but a particular one. He wanted no part of a German state or of German citizenship. He wanted membership in a Czech or, at the least, a Slavic state.

Palacký is not unique or unusual. Many people in today's world make political claims based on their membership in different racial, national, or ethnic groups. Often, these different groups clash with one another. National, ethnic, and racial divisions are sometimes antagonistic and result in bloodshed; they often break up states; in some states, people receive privileges or are dominated based on their group membership. People notice— and act on—cultural differences all the time. Yet these divisions, which have been prominent since the French Revolution, have haunted liberals (and others) since the first half of the nineteenth century.[2]

Liberalism does not ordinarily explain or justify the existence of particular states, nor does it recognize the existence of different national, racial, or ethnic groups. The focus on individual rights in liberal theory often leads liberals to ignore the challenges posed for liberalism by cultural groups. Although some liberal theories are based on consent of the governed, rarely do these theories explain why specific states should exist. The individuals in Locke's state of nature are all very nearly the same; Kant's categorical imperative makes the same demands on everyone. Because these individuals and the situations they face in the state of nature are so similar, all liberal states ought to be similar. It is hard to find justification for a Germany, a France, and a Britain in the classic liberal texts—for liberal states with different cultures, practices, and norms. The classic liberal texts give us little reason to believe that the German state of nature is much different from the English version. The rationality of people in England is the same as that of those in France. If states are so similar, why not have just one state? Some liberals, thinking exactly this, argued that eventually people would overcome their petty differences, leading to the creation of a world government. L. T. Hobhouse, for example, argued: "In ethical truth, there is only one ultimate community, which is the human race. . . . To organize it is now the duty of the statesman."[3]

Few people, though, are holding their breath, waiting for this creation. Quite the contrary: many people in liberal (and nonliberal) states consider themselves to be members of all sorts of groups and are not about to give up these attachments. Indeed, many liberals have ignored not only the differences between states, but also the cultural differences between groups in states. Some of these groups are the familiar voluntary associations that Locke discusses in his *Letter Concerning Toleration,* but racial, ethnic, and national groups, which are crucial to the identity of many people, are not quite the same as voluntary associations. We cannot join any ethnic group we want: I cannot simply announce that I've become a Chinese American. And when we have the requisite qualifications to join a group, we still might not be able to choose whether we want to identify with the group. Sometimes our identity is foisted upon us: Alfred Dreyfus was convicted of treason because he was Jewish, even though he was an assimilated Jew who cared more about France than about Jews. We can resign from our racquetball club or even our church, but it is not quite the same to resign from our racial, ethnic, or national group.

Some states assume that their citizens are homogeneous or enough so that issues of identity can be safely ignored. Other states are more purposefully nationalistic and argue that only members of a specific nation should be part of their state or that only members of their nation can have first class citizenship. This homogeneity, however, is belied by the living arrangements of the modern world: most states are a polyglot collection of different races, ethnicities, and nationalities. People may be members of a state but feel part of (or be forced into) different racial, ethnic, or national groups. This brings to the fore the following questions: What does it mean to be a citizen and a member of a group? What should the political implications of these groups be? How should the liberal state respond to those citizens who have an identity imposed on them? How should the arrangement of states be affected by these groups?

Liberal theory does not explicitly answer these questions. My aim is to try to fill this gap in liberal theory in three ways. First, I explore the effects of liberalism on identity. Second, I argue how liberalism should and should not change to account for identity. Third, I examine the strategies used by cultural groups to maintain their identities in liberal society. Moving freely between these three connected projects, I address two different audiences: members of racial and ethnic groups in liberal states and liberals. I want to convince these members that liberalism has something to offer them; that, in fact, liberalism is a better political theory for them than are the alternatives. I am less sanguine about convincing nationalists of their need for liberalism; instead, I hope to work out a compromise between nationalists and liberals. Liberalism needs to recognize and respond to some of the claims of groups, which may mean reworking some parts of liberal theory. Some tensions between group identity and liberalism, however, cannot be fully worked out. Indeed, liberals should avoid embracing some versions of cultural pluralism. Nevertheless, liberalism can account for racial, ethnic, and national groups.[4]

Liberalism

Liberalism is a political theory that is concerned with giving people power over their own lives and an equal say in how the government is run. Liberty and equality are two important aspects of liberalism. Liberal citizens should have the liberty to pursue their plans and projects; each citizen should have equal opportunity to do so. Liberals argue against the hereditary rights of people to rule over others; they disavow the authority of state officials to arbitrarily take the property of citizens or put them in jail. Religious differences, liberals argue, are not cause for differential treatment by the government. Indeed, liberals favor religious toleration, an independent judiciary, and liberty of thought and expression. Concern with arbitrary and tyrannical government led liberals to support the idea that government should be run by elected and accountable representatives. Liberals typically call for debate and discussion about politics by citizens and their representatives. Liberals want to protect the individual from state tyranny, yet liberals also want the state to protect the rights of individuals from other citizens. At the basis of most liberal theories are the same concerns: that individuals be protected from tyranny and that all individuals be accorded equal rights. Liberals do not reject the importance of religion, nor do liberals dismiss the importance of different groups in people's lives. But liberals are generally suspicious of according some sort of political or legal status to groups.

Although most liberals might agree that liberal citizens have equal rights to pursue their plans and projects—as long as they do not harm others—the way in which this is accomplished is hardly straightforward. Many liberals, for example, argue over the role of the state. How much should the state help people pursue their plans and projects? If the state does get involved, will it actually make people's lives worse rather than better? I won't settle these questions here and won't defend or justify the ideas of equality, religious toleration, or individual rights. Instead, I will show how these ideas affect cultural identity and how liberalism should change to accommodate racial, ethnic, and national claims. I will also explain what I mean by the liberal ideas of individual rights, equality, and toleration. I will defend one particular version of liberalism while arguing against others.

My focus on liberalism is twofold: I look at the demands that liberalism makes on its citizens, and I use liberal theory as a standard of judgment. I judge the practices of both those in power in the liberal state and those members of cultural groups that fight for equal citizenship by the tenets of liberalism. Liberalism promises equality to all citizens. What does this equality mean for members of ethnic and racial groups? Do members of mainstream culture prevent this promise from being realized? How should changes be made, in both liberal theory and practice, to better realize the liberal goal of equality? As I ask these and other questions, I move from liberal theory to practice in the following pages. Consequently, I often refer to the practices of the United States and other Western states that fit, perhaps loosely, in the liberal tradition. I move from theory to practice and from practice to theory to examine each and to use each to criticize (or complement) the other.[5] I scrutinize, for example, the meaning of liberal toleration by looking at the Amish and Hasidic Jewish communities. I look at the theory of liberal identity by exploring the life of a victim of racism. By looking at specific practices, I sometimes argue that certain liberal principles ought to be revised. Other times, I argue that these practices violate important tenets of liberalism; in these instances, it is the practices that ought to change. Examining how liberal theory plays out in practice can give us a richer understanding of liberal theory—it can help point to liberalism's strengths and its failings. By looking at liberal practice and specific cultural groups, I also explore the limits that liberalism places on cultural pluralism, as well as the advantages liberalism accords members of cultural groups.

The states that I discuss are, besides liberal, also democratic. Yet one can be a liberal without being a democrat (and one can be a nonliberal democrat). Some Enlightenment liberals, for example, shied away from democracy and flirted with the idea of "enlightened" despotism.[6] As liberalism has developed, however, most liberals have also embraced democracy because they often see democratic institutions as an important guard against tyranny. If government must be responsive to the people, as it should be in a democracy, then it is less likely to oppress them. To be sure, sometimes democratic majorities pass illiberal laws; there are times when majorities want to ignore the liberal rights of minorities. Liberals are often suspicious, however, of the alternatives to democracy. Although putting considerable power in the hands of an unaccountable sovereign may allow the sovereign to protect the rights of her subjects, it also may allow the sovereign to crush their rights as well. This possibility has led many liberals to believe that democracies are more likely to protect the rights of their citizens than are nondemocracies, although there is no assurance that democracies will always do so. To protect against the possibility of majorities passing illiberal laws, the liberal state should try to teach its citizens the principles that are necessary to support liberal institutions to make sure that democracy does not overrun liberalism. Jefferson explained the connection between education and liberal democracy: "Every government degenerates when trusted to the rulers of the people alone. The people themselves therefore are its only safe depositories. And to render even them safe their minds must be improved to a certain degree."[7]

Liberalism is partly about giving people a stake in government and educating them to use this stake wisely. It is also a theory of institutional arrangements. Liberalism is often seen as a map dividing the world into two spheres, the public and the private. In the private realm, people can join the groups they want, amuse themselves as they wish, and generally pursue their life plans and projects as long as they do not harm others. In public, these private choices are not supposed to matter. In public, all citizens are supposed to be treated equally: liberal citizens should not be discriminated against in public settings based on their identity. Political equality means that all citizens, formally at least, have the same political rights, regardless of their identity or group membership. All citizens can run for office and vote; they have free speech, the right to assembly, and so on. In public institutions, the standards of nondiscrimination ought to apply. In the private realm, however, people can discriminate. And it is in the private sphere that cultural identity can flourish—or so goes the conventional liberal argument.

This argument is disingenuous because the public/private distinction is not as simple as many liberals (and nonliberals) portray it. Instead of dividing society into two parts, the public and the private, liberals ought to recognize explicitly a third realm: civil society. (The idea of civil society has been around since Locke, but its meaning is often obscure.) If liberal equality is to be realized, the principle of nondiscrimination cannot apply only in the public sphere but should apply also to the institutions that make up civil society—institutions like corporations, colleges, and stores—as many laws in the United States already do.

Some liberals insist that liberty means that people should be allowed to associate with whomever they want in private and that most of the institutions of civil society should be considered private. But this view of liberty is unequal: it means that some people will have more liberty than others. We know from the history of the United States that pervasive discrimination against members of some groups means that these members will be less than full citizens, unequal to those citizens who do not face discrimination. By looking at the history of race in the United States, it is easy to see that the educational, economic, and political opportunities enjoyed by first class citizens are typically denied those who face discrimination in civil society. The liberal goal of liberty should not mean that some people can enjoy liberty at the expense of others. Liberalism is supposed to fight against tyranny, not justify it. When liberty is not conjoined with equality, some people will have very little liberty.

Although many of the institutions of civil society have public functions and so should have to adhere to the public norm of nondiscrimination, liberals should not abolish the private realm. It is in the narrow private sphere that ethnic and racial identity can flourish, but two important caveats to this liberal argument must be made. First, the demands of liberal citizenship in the public sphere and in civil society make it hard, although not impossible, for liberal citizens to maintain robust ethnic identities. Many ethnics clamor for equal citizenship, yet folded into equal citizenship is often the unraveling of strong ethnic identities. Although liberal citizenship is often conceived of in terms of participation, the demands of liberal citizenship show up in many, everyday roles. Critics who see liberal citizens as, at best, apathetic voters fail to see how liberal citizenship plays an important role in people's everyday lives. Although liberal citizens may hate members of a particular ethnic group, they are supposed to treat these people equally; in stores, classrooms, or courtrooms, they are supposed to ignore their ethnic backgrounds, even if they want to do otherwise. These demands are not always easy to follow, and they work to break down ethnic boundaries. Ethnic identity may be weakened by liberal citizenship, but this does not mean that ethnicity is destroyed by liberalism. The ethnic identity of some will survive the pressures of liberalism, although this survival will frequently lead to tensions between liberal citizens. It is tempting to say that, with a bit of understanding between different people, ethnic identity can easily flourish in the liberal state. But this would belie the real tensions caused by ethnic (and racial and national) identity, tensions that are not always easily resolved.

The second caveat to the usual liberal argument on cultural identity is this: there are times when racial, ethnic, and national identity should not be thought of as only a private matter. The issue of language quickly puts this liberal argument to the test: states can use only a limited number of public languages, perhaps one or two. A group whose language is not used publicly will find it hard to maintain their language. If a group's language disappears, their distinctive identity may fade. Beyond language, the issue of culture is often a public one because too often members of cultural groups believe that they must give up practices (practices that have nothing to do with language) that are actually compatible with liberalism to conform to a state's implicit cultural norms. Members of a mainstream culture who are in positions of power often pressure others to take on mainstream cultural practices, even though nothing in liberal theory demands that ethnics take on these practices. Laws and rules that discriminate against members of racial and ethnic groups in schools, government, and the workplace should be revised, and members of some groups may have to give up some of their cultural practices if they violate liberal principles.

An important paradox in liberal toleration is that the liberal state must often tolerate illiberal communities, although the liberal state can discourage these communities from treasuring illiberal values. Liberalism is sometimes thought of as a theory of neutrality on the good life: as long as citizens do not harm one another, they ought to be allowed to live as they please. This argument is misleading. I contend that there are certain liberal virtues that are encouraged by liberal institutions. For a liberal democracy to function, at least some of its citizens need to believe in equality (or act as if they do) and to participate in democratic debate and discussion about politics and society. These liberal virtues ought to be developed in children in schools; in public and civil society, these virtues are further encouraged. Although laws can be implemented to ensure that people are treated equally in civil society, liberals cannot rearrange people's lives at home in the name of equality. Encouraging liberal virtues is not the same as mandating that all liberal citizens take them on. Liberal toleration means that some citizens can avoid the liberal virtues, even though the liberal state should make this difficult. My examination of illiberal communities in the liberal state also highlights the problems of strong versions of cultural pluralism: I show the sorts of values and cultural norms that cultural pluralists must defend to be consistent with their principles, values that violate the idea of (liberal) equality and are inimical to democracy. Even as illiberal values should be discouraged in the liberal state, they cannot always be outlawed.

Race, Ethnicity, and Nationality and Liberal Thought

Although liberals tend to focus on the liberty and equality of individuals, it would be strange if liberals never noticed ethnic, national, or racial groups. The treatment of these groups by important liberal theorists, however, has been very brief. David Hume noticed differences in national character in a short essay, but he didn't discuss fully the implications of these differences.[8] There is a brief chapter by J. S. Mill on nationality in *Considerations on Representative Government* and a slightly longer response by Lord Acton.[9] Their brevity means that neither piece goes beyond the issue of nationality and that many of the complexities of nationalism are passed over by Mill and Acton.

Many nineteenth-century liberals, with their views of progress, were quite ethnocentric. They thought that the small, "backward" nations of the world would want to join the more advanced nations. These nations had much to gain and little to lose by doing so. The nineteenth-century German liberals who invited Palacký to their parliament were dumbfounded when he told them that he and other Czechs did not want to become part of a new, united Germany. Who would want to be Czech if he could be German?[10] J. S. Mill expressed a similar sentiment when he discussed France: "Nobody can suppose that it is not more beneficial to a Breton, or a Basque of French Navarre, to be brought into the current of the ideas and feelings of a highly civilized and cultivated people—to be a member of the French nationality . . .—than to sulk on his own rocks, the half-savage relic of past times."[11] It is not hard to see how a vision of a world or European government could follow such a view: the various nations would combine until one, quite progressive nation emerged. Others, like the Italian nationalist Mazzini, argued that, instead of a world government, certain nations would emerge to dominate Europe. In this view, the smaller and less powerful nations would simply fade away.[12] In either case, the problem of nationality was quite tractable. The advanced nations would, in the course of time, swallow up the backward nations. This required little political action (and so little needed to be written on the matter). Because members of the smaller, backward nations would see that it was in their interest to join the larger ones, time would solve the nationality problem.

This view, although ethnocentric, is at least relatively benign; behind it is the hope that all peoples in Europe ought to be able to take part in Europe's progress. Other liberals, however, cannot be credited with such an innocuous hope. Racism clearly blinded some liberals from seeing the heterogeneity of the world. John Jay, in the *Federalist Papers,* for example, applauded America's homogeneity: "Providence has been pleased to give this once connected country to one united people—a people descended from the same ancestors, speaking the same language, professing the same religion, attached to the same principles of government, very similar in their manners and customs."[13] Jay here ignored not only Blacks and Native Americans, but also Jews and all those from countries other than Britain.

Thomas Jefferson had a better view of the United States; he recognized that there were many Blacks living here. Jefferson thought that slavery was an "abominable crime" that should be outlawed, although he managed to hold this belief while owning many slaves. Jefferson argued that a race problem would always plague the United States as long as Blacks remained here; refusing to see Blacks as equals, Jefferson did not see how Blacks and whites could live together peacefully and equally. The best he could suggest was Black colonization. If Jefferson had seen Blacks as equal to whites, he might have spent less time bemoaning our race problem and devoted more of his considerable energies and intellect to solving it.[14]

Recently, in response to critics and to the divisions in American society, liberals have directly discussed race and ethnicity. Recognizing that Black Americans have faced a history of oppression, some liberals contend that the United States needs to redress this history through programs like affirmative action. This program, in typical liberal fashion, focuses on the economic deprivation of Black Americans. Although it recognizes a group, affirmative action is designed to bring Blacks into mainstream society. It is based on an integrationist strategy, intent on reducing the differences among American citizens. If it is successful, there will be no further reason to recognize Blacks as a group. Integration may be the right strategy for Blacks—I discuss this issue further in chapter 6—but this strategy does not recognize that, besides being economically deprived, Black Americans have distinct cultural practices, as do many other peoples in the world. Liberals who oppose affirmative action share much in common with those liberals that support it; they maintain that culture is a private matter. These liberals argue that the state is obliged to ensure that no one faces discrimination but should not take any steps beyond that.

The issues of culture, groups, and identity have barely been discussed by these liberals, although liberal discussion of these issues is increasing.[15]

There is a gap between liberal theory and the world's practices. There are also tensions between liberalism and group identity. The idea of equality is central to liberalism, yet discrimination is integral to ethnic and national groups. Although liberal theory treats everyone the same, people don't treat each other that way. Groups sometimes claim that, to maintain their community and identity, they must discriminate against others. For example, some claim that they need to restrict who can live in their neighborhood or join certain clubs. Ancestry, appearance, and specific cultural practices are all ways by which members are distinguished from nonmembers. If they do not discriminate somehow, these groups argue that they may disappear. Occasionally, minority cultural groups claim that they need special recognition and laws to survive; if the state treats its members as individuals, without seeing them as members of a group, their culture will be swallowed up by the dominant culture. Modern liberal society, with its mobility and large institutions, enables people from different cultures to meet and become friends, lovers, and marriage partners. Some group leaders disapprove of liberalism because they fear that it condemns their group to disappear in a sea of assimilation. Many traditional Jews in eighteenth-century Western Europe, for example, viewed the emancipation of the Jews with trepidation, fearing that many Jews would assimilate into Christian culture, a fear that has been partly realized.

Liberals frequently celebrate the neutrality of the state but rarely note that a certain cultural group controls the state. The United States has been controlled by whites who have not treated everyone as equal, even though this is demanded by liberal theory. When the liberal state claims that group identity isn't a political concern, it refuses to acknowledge or do anything about the members of nondominant groups who are disadvantaged because of their identity. Although liberal equality means that all members of the state should be treated equally, those who have controlled the United States throughout its history have not always followed the tenets of liberalism. People in power here have favored whites over Blacks in many ways. Members of minority cultures complain that to conform to the rules of different institutions means losing a part of their identity; it means becoming like the members of the dominant culture, who establish the rules and set the standards of society.

Many argue that the failure of liberals to recognize groups is a severe and perhaps fatal flaw of liberalism. Refusing to recognize groups, these critics argue, may mean the end of those smaller cultures that exist precariously, or this refusal may relegate their members to the margin of society, to be constant victims of discrimination and racism.[16] Although equal citizenship may be a nice goal, critics of liberalism may say, it is a faraway, probably impossible dream in the liberal state. Liberal theory may say that people should not be discriminated against, but discrimination is rampant nonetheless; only some people benefit from full liberal citizenship. I suspect that some critics of liberalism are sympathetic with its goals: equality of opportunity for everyone, a society with no discrimination, a place where people can construct and pursue their plans and projects in a fulfilling way.[17] But these critics look at the states in the West and claim that for many people in them these goals are, at best, mere dreams. They note the poverty and the racism, the sexism and the violence that pervade these states. If this is liberalism, they want no part of it. Equal citizenship, for example, is wrongly denied to Black Americans.

I do not think that liberals have to accept all current practices in the United States and other Western states in the name of liberalism. Liberals can point out that equality of opportunity does not exist and that not everyone can construct and pursue their life plans in the United States. People are treated differently by the courts and by real estate brokers because of their race and gender. Black men and all women are victims of discrimination in many different social settings. In its rulings on citizenship, the U.S. Supreme Court has not always upheld liberal principles. Sometimes, it has explicitly rejected liberal arguments and endorsed racist (and sexist) conceptions of citizenship.[18] Liberals can criticize these practices and rulings from a liberal point of view, however. Liberals can point out that in a variety of ways the United States and other purportedly liberal states are quite illiberal. Indeed, the liberal tradition is not the only tradition in the United States; civic republicanism and nativism also have a long history in this country and still influence both major political parties.[19] Some people in the United States, for example, want this country explicitly to embrace a particular version of religious values, something that is clearly illiberal. My use of the term *liberal state,* then, is not completely accurate; although I characterize the United States as liberal, much of what goes on here is quite illiberal. Still, there is a strong liberal tradition in the United States, and so I will use it as an example of a liberal state in the following chapters.

We liberals can learn from our critics the ways in which the liberal state is failing its members. If the practices of the liberal state fall short of liberal theory, liberals must do more than criticize the state in the name of liberalism, although this criticism is important. Liberals cannot merely point to specific practices, call them illiberal, and leave it at that. Liberals must accept the possibility that liberalism itself may be responsible for the difficulty in changing these practices. There are at least three related reasons for the failures of liberal citizenship. First, liberals usually rely on persuasion rather than force when trying to change people's attitudes and actions. Although this is certainly a strength of liberalism, it also means that people may (and do) vote for illiberal laws. Second, liberals tend to rely on laws to achieve equality. Citizens who face discrimination can go to court to fight for redress. But if a group of citizens faces constant discrimination, the courts will be of limited help; citizens cannot spend all of their time in court. Third, the liberal tendency to rely on laws sometimes obscures how power works (although some liberals, notably J. S. Mill, are attentive to power). Liberalism does recognize power in some forms; liberals do not want individuals to be forced to live a certain kind of life. But power is not always used in obvious ways by people forcing others to do things against their will. There are social pressures that work to change the way people act. There may be no law preventing anyone from being loud in public, but ethnics who are rather expressive in the way they talk may find themselves receiving many strange and condescending looks from others and change their ways in response.

Despite these problems, it is worth trying to figure out a way in which liberalism can accommodate group identity. To point out flaws in a theory is not to condemn the theory; no theory is perfect, and no theory is flawless. In the absence of a better alternative, the best option is to work on improving liberalism. In chapter 3, I point out how Marxism is ill-equipped to deal with matters of racial, ethnic, and national identity. The most promising current alternative to liberalism, communitarianism, is mostly a critique of liberalism. Communitarians do not (yet) have much of a constructive alternative to liberalism.[20] Those who think that classical liberalism is completely bankrupt will not want to figure out ways to improve liberalism. To them, this is a hopeless project. But I'm not so pessimistic.

Liberalism is not without its strengths. Liberalism has the flexibility to incorporate different modes of analysis. To be sure, liberalism is not infinitely malleable: "Stronger forms of community, deeper, unquestioning, untroubled forms of allegiance (to family, church, clan or class) might embody genuine forms of the good life lost to societies that flourish in a liberal way."[21] Liberalism arose out of the realization that agreement on important issues, like the true religion, could not be reached by many people. Diversity of opinions by people, Locke argued in his *Letter Concerning Toleration,* "could not be avoided" and ought to be recognized and accommodated.[22] John Stuart Mill argued that, despite the tradition of religious tolerance in liberalism, there was still considerable social pressure for people to conform to mainstream lifestyles: "The likings and dislikings of society, or of some powerful portion of it, are thus the main thing which has practically determined the rules laid down for general observance, under the penalties of law and opinion."[23] Although Mill did not usually discuss ethnicity and race, the point translates easily enough. There is pressure in our society for people to leave behind the ethnic markers that make them stand out. Liberals can follow Mill's advice and demand, on liberal grounds, that those who want to retain a rich sense of their ethnic identity and so look "different" should be allowed to do so. The seeds of diversity are already planted in liberalism, although there are important limits to this diversity. Liberals want people to find and express their individuality. They do not want to suppress people's identity; they want each person to flourish in her or his own way. It is the extension of the traditions of religious pluralism and of the liberty to be different to the realm of culture that offers us the best hope to achieve a just plural society. Few other political theories have a similar tradition of allowing much diversity.[24]

I examine race, ethnicity, and nationality to probe liberalism, to find liberalism's strengths and its limitations, and to suggest some of the ways in which it should change. It is possible that the needs of cultural groups and liberalism are incompatible. This may be a reason to eschew liberalism, although it also may be reason to dismiss the claims of these groups. We liberals should be honest about the costs of liberalism; all theories have their strengths and weaknesses. Liberalism cannot accommodate all of the claims of cultural groups. Liberalism may indeed cause the weakening of some identities; when and how it does is something I point out. This is not something liberals should automatically lament. Sometimes, though, liberalism can change to accommodate group identity and the problems facing groups. The needs and claims of these groups can show us some of the current failings of liberalism and point to the changes liberalism needs to make. The solutions to the problems posed by identity are not always neat, and the tensions between cultural groups and liberalism will be with us for a long time, but an amended liberalism offers the best way to accommodate cultural groups.

To argue for a liberalism that is attentive to the problems and concerns of different cultural identities, I draw on the classic liberal texts (particularly those of J. S. Mill and Locke) and those of lesser known theorists, like Horace Kallen, who wrote about cultural pluralism in the beginning of the twentieth century. Unlike many political theorists, I also rely heavily on empirical examples to illustrate my arguments. Because political theorists have rarely discussed cultural groups, I define race, ethnicity, and nationality in the next chapter. Throughout the book I look at many cultural groups. I emphasize four, however, mostly in a North American context: Jews, the Amish, Black Americans, and French Canadians. I examine these groups because of the issues they highlight: ethnicity, a starkly different way of life, race, and language. It is only through an understanding of the actual experiences of cultural groups in liberal democracies that we can learn about and try to resolve the issues raised by them.

CHAPTER 2

THE FORMATION
OF IDENTITY

CORNELIUS MAY, a Creole in Sierra Leone, was the editor and owner of the widely read *Sierra Leone Weekly News*.[1] A man of refined tastes, he attended poetry readings, lectures, musical entertainments, and recitals; he belonged to the Young Men's Literary Association, which tried to "raise" the culture of the "corrupt" youth of Freetown (Sierra Leone's capital). He identified with the urbane and cultured *haute bourgeois*. May saw himself as an educated gentleman who, along with the British, wanted to "civilize" those Black Africans in Sierra Leone who still practiced their "barbaric" social and religious customs. May agreed with the first wave of British colonizers of Sierra Leone who thought that, with the right doses of European education and Christianity, anyone could be transformed into a European gentleman.

By the end of the nineteenth century, however, racism in the colonies had begun to take a new, biological turn. Unlike the first Europeans who had landed in Sierra Leone, an increasing number of Europeans during May's adult life believed that whites were biologically superior to those with a different skin color. Education and Christianity would never be enough to transform the African into the equal of the European, these racists argued. This posed an acute problem for May and others like him. They were thoroughly Europeanized but were told they could never be the equal of a European. They were told that they were *Black*. At first enticed into but then rejected by European society, May and other Creoles reexamined their role in Sierra Leone. They wondered if they had perverted "their 'true racial personality' through indiscriminate Europeanization."[2] They looked at their education, social lives, occupations, dress, houses, food, and hairstyles and saw the imprint of Europeans. They concluded that they had lost the "flavor of their race," and they began an attempt to recover their racial identity by founding a Dress Reform Society. Its purpose was to eliminate the most obvious sign of their Europeanization—Western clothing—as a first step toward their gradual independence from all European customs.

The Dress Reform Society failed after less than a year. The wardrobe its members wore was a cross between European dress and the clothing worn in the African bush. This allowed them to distinguish themselves from the Africans, who they still viewed as barbaric, and the Europeans, who rejected them. Caught between two worlds, May and other Creoles "could neither divest themselves completely of the European world into which assimilation had taken them nor embrace a solely 'African' identity."[3] The new racism had not completely changed May's life. Mobility in the European world was hard but not impossible. May ran a successful newspaper with little interference from the government; he was even a member of several governmental bodies. Although he sometimes questioned the idea of assimilation, he generally held an optimistic, reformist attitude for most of his life. This new biological racism would pass.

Or so May thought until he neared the end of his life. In 1926, while serving his third term as mayor, May was arrested for "conspiracy to defraud the City Council."[4] Denied an appeal and trial by jury and convicted by a European judge who ignored the not guilty verdict of three trial assessors, May was sent to jail for a crime he almost certainly did not commit. May died a short time later after being released from prison for poor health, embittered and disillusioned. The British used the scandal caused by May's arrest as an excuse to abolish the Black-run governing institutions in Sierra Leone and replace them with ones dominated by Europeans.

Cornelius May could not define himself. Although he aspired to become a European gentleman, the Europeans told him that he was a Black African. He could not become a Black African, though, for Black-African culture was foreign to him. May's father had been captured by slave traders when he was about ten; their ship, however, had been captured by a British naval ship that had released the Africans in Sierra Leone, where Joseph May had been raised by English colonists and had taken on English and European values. It would have been extraordinarily difficult for him to have retained any part of his Yoruba culture. He could hardly have been expected to pass the Yoruba culture of his youth on to his son.

Cornelius May was raised by his father in a European world with European values. He was not somehow an African "deep down" in his genes. Denied the opportunity to be a European gentleman, May could not simply choose another identity. He could, as he did, try to reach back into his ancestors' past to find an alternative to the identity he was denied. But this was a difficult process. May could not simply become what his grandfather had been; May lived a very different life, a life that was influenced little by Yoruba culture. Just as May could not become a European, he could not become a Yoruba. Instead, May could have tried to create a new role for himself. He could have tried to blaze a third way, incorporating elements of his ancestors' past with his current life.

Even if a person's life is not restricted as Cornelius May's was, his life shows the difficulty in creating a new identity. May could not automatically divest himself of his European upbringing, regardless of whether he wanted to do so voluntarily or not; it was part of who he was. Although he may have been able to wean himself from this identity, this surely would have involved a lengthy struggle. Racism further strangles the efforts of some to define themselves. It puts limits on what people can and cannot do; it puts some identities out of reach, while offering up other, possibly undesirable alternatives. This poses a particularly acute problem for liberals, who celebrate people's ability to choose their life plans and projects. Not all identities pose such a hard problem for liberalism, yet race, ethnicity, and nationality all constrain in some ways people's ability to choose who they are.

The definitions of racial, ethnic, and national groups shape how people think of these groups; consequently, these definitions shape arguments about them. Unfortunately, some people use the terms *race, ethnicity,* and *nationality* without distinguishing among them. *Ethnicity,* for example, is often a catchword for all three groups. Articles and books may announce their topic as race and ethnicity but fail to distinguish these categories. The massive and influential *Harvard Encyclopedia of Ethnic Groups* includes African Americans, Native Americans, Jews, the Amish, Italian Americans, and others under the rubric of *ethnicity.*[5] The differences among these groups need to be delineated. These terms are sometimes used purposefully; when neoconservatives refuse to separate ethnicity from race, they argue against policies that rest on such a distinction. There are no natural criteria that we can use to define race, ethnicity, or nationality; instead, they are socially constructed. Though many people may define nationality, ethnicity, and race using biological criteria, how these criteria are used depends on the circumstances of a particular society.

The Construction of Identity

To say that race, ethnicity, and nationality are socially constructed means that these groups and the social roles they open up are not naturally part of the world. They are created by people, and what is made up by people can be changed by them. Anthropologists teach us that culture is also constructed by people.[6] What one culture considers abnormal may be quite normal in another culture. But to say that something is socially constructed does not lead to obvious conclusions; although people create a culture, it is not easily changed. Something socially constructed and so not naturally part of the world may be deeply embedded in *our* world. Racial identity in U.S. culture has existed for several hundred years, and, though it may disappear someday, it will certainly persist into the foreseeable future. To argue that race is socially constructed does not decrease its importance, yet the meaning and importance of ethnic identity has changed considerably over the past few decades and will, I think, continue to change.

Communitarians notice that groups exist and that they are deeply embedded in our society. They charge that a major flaw of liberalism is its inability to see people with a rich set of characteristics. Michael Sandel argues that the problem with Rawlsian liberalism is that it demands that "I must be a subject whose identity is given independently of the things I have, independently, that is, of my interests and ends and my relations with others." A person like this, who is "incapable of constitutive attachments," is a person "wholly without character, without moral depth." This account of agency, Sandel charges, is impossible. People cannot be separated from their ends, Sandel claims, because their identities are constituted by their interests and ends. Sandel offers an alternative account of identity, claiming that "agency consists less in summoning the will than in seeking self-understanding." Identity is a project of self-discovery; we have little say about who we are. "The relevant question is not what ends to choose, for my problem is precisely that the answer to this question is already given, but rather who I am, how I am to discern in this clutter of possible ends what is me from what is mine."[7]

Sandel's criticism of liberalism is powerful. Although I disagree with the communitarian conclusions that Sandel draws from his account of identity, liberals need to face up to Sandel's critique. Liberals want people's identity to be self-constructed. Liberal citizens are (supposedly) engaged in the project of self-creation. We choose our attachments, our plans, and our projects; we choose who we are. Certainly, many parts of our identity *can* be changed; sometimes this can be done easily but sometimes only with a tremendous amount of difficulty and time. A person can be a mother, a daughter, a sister, a doctor, an Italian American, a Californian, a political activist, a Democrat, a Dodgers fan, and a classical music lover. She can examine some parts of her life while holding others constant. She can question her role in the Democratic party while attending classical music concerts unthinkingly. A person can remain a wife while reviewing her political commitments, or she can contemplate divorce while continuing her political activism. These changes are not always easy to make, as anyone who has gone through a divorce can testify. Changing one's identity can be a painful process, but sometimes the alternative is much worse.

Yet this liberal picture did not apply to Cornelius May. He could think of himself as a European gentleman only if he refused to see how white European gentlemen rejected him. He tried to see himself as a Black African, but this attempt failed. He could not easily reconstruct himself as somebody else; his life plans were too caught up in a Europeanized world. This picture is surely a problem for Sandel. It is not clear what it would mean for May to discover his identity; if he had lived longer, May would probably have had to carve out another identity for himself, as difficult as this would have been. His self-understanding would almost surely have been impossible for him to maintain had he lived much longer. Sandel's failure here is no reason for liberal cheering; May could not choose just any identity. This project of redefining oneself does not take place in thin air. Racism restricted May's choices, as did his character. He was constituted in various ways, with certain attachments and certain loathings; he had plans and projects, aspirations and dreams. Racism meant that he would have had to reinterpret all of these. But he would have had to reinterpret his own character, not somebody else's, to do so. This project would have been difficult and perhaps impossible.

In the same book where he describes May's life, Leo Spitzer follows the life of Stephan Zweig, an acculturated, cosmopolitan, Austrian Jew who lived in the earlier part of this century. A well-known and respected member of the European intelligentsia, Zweig wrote books and articles that were widely read, studied in German and Austrian schools, and translated into forty languages. With the rise of Hitler, Zweig was "defined from without as a Jew" although he felt little connection to Jews or Judaism. His books were burned and banned in Germany and Austria. His language—German — was no longer his. Forced to flee, Zweig ended up in Brazil, far away from his beloved Europe and the cosmopolitan life he had lived. He continued to have few feelings about being Jewish. In Brazil he noted that "I belong nowhere, and everywhere I am a stranger, a guest at best." In 1940, at age sixty, he and his wife committed suicide. In his suicide note he declared that "unusual powers are needed in order to make a new beginning."[8]

Race

Race defines people as members of groups with different traits. Almost always, these groups are hierarchically established. A group—the dominant group in a society—will define another set of people based on an ascriptive characteristic as a group apart. The dominant group will, in turn, define itself in a particular and superior way. In Nazi Germany, Aryans were on top of the racial hierarchy. They defined several other races, all inferior. The Jews and Gypsies were on the bottom of the hierarchy, although Slavs, Blacks, and others were also below the Aryans. In the United States whites put themselves on top of the race hierarchy and placed Blacks (and sometimes others) below. In South Africa, whites defined several other subordinate race categories: Black, Asian, and Coloured. Typically, the characteristics of each race are set up in opposition to each other. Jews were supposedly cosmopolitan, self-serving, and conniving and so could never be loyal to the German nation. In contrast, Germans were loyal and trustworthy. Black Americans were thought to be lazy, whereas whites were hardworking. Defining the supposed characteristics of one race helps define the other races. Whatever characteristics the dominant group has, the subordinate group or groups are almost sure to have the opposite.

Race is an imposed identity for members of the subordinate races. They are "defined from without" as having distinct (and usually inferior) characteristics. This definition tries to equate culture with biology. Members of the subordinate races are thought to be naturally different because of some supposed biological fact, whereas members of the dominant race are biologically superior. Racists claim that Blacks are lazy, shiftless, and cunning; that Jews are miserly and shrewd; and that Arabs are cleverly dishonest. All Arabs, all Jews, and all Blacks, racists claim, have these characteristics. If they are allowed to mingle freely in society, racists fear that they will endanger the "pure" race. The inferior races, racists claim, must be kept apart. Although some interaction—usually economic—among the groups is sometimes permissible in overtly racist societies, other kinds of contact are not. Intermarriage is usually not allowed; certain jobs and positions in politics are not open to the supposed inferior races. Racists contend that members of the inferior races will undoubtedly cause havoc if given too much power or freedom.

Although racists define race in biological terms, what biological criterion is used to define a group as different, what it means, and to whom it applies are all socially constructed.[9] It is simply not obvious what biological fact is used to define groups. Furthermore, how this supposed fact is interpreted must somehow be decided. Though a biological criterion defined Blacks, this criterion could have been interpreted in other ways.[10] In the United States the line between Blacks and whites has been rigid since the Civil War.[11] Skin color has mattered for Blacks—light-skinned Blacks could sometimes "pass" into white society and often they have more prestige in the Black community—yet whites have usually looked upon all Blacks similarly. When federal and state governments classified people into racial categories, there was rarely a category for mulattoes. People in this country with "one drop" of Black blood have traditionally been viewed as Black.[12] People who look white but have some Black ancestry are often considered Black.

The current dichotomy of white and Black in the United States does not exist in Brazil. In Brazil there are several different categories of skin color which matter.[13] Furthermore, money can "lighten" one's skin color. This is not just a matter of class and wealth; the darker one's skin, the more money is needed to enter many private establishments. To enter places where middle class whites can go, a mulatto needs to be upper class; someone who is dark-skinned will need to be quite wealthy. The darker the skin, the more money is needed to pass as white. Conversely, someone with very light skin but who is very poor is considered black in Brazil.

In the United States, racial categories have been fairly stable since the Civil War, but who has counted as Black has shifted considerably since the great immigration waves of the late nineteenth and early twentieth centuries. The Southern European and Asian immigrants then were thought by many to be inferior to Anglo-Saxons. The differences between the Anglo-Saxons and the new immigrants, it was exclaimed by many hysterical whites, were racial; these new immigrants were not of the same "stock" as the Anglo-Saxons. Frightened whites explained that only trouble was to be expected from these racially inferior newcomers. Some argued that the Anglo-Saxons were strong enough to "absorb" the Southern and Eastern Europeans. Others, however, maintained that the social unrest of the 1880s was proof that this was unlikely. One minister, worried about this strife, saw "anarchism, lawlessness, . . . labor strikes, and a general violation of personal rights such as the Anglo-Saxon has not witnessed since Magna Charta. . . . This horrible tyranny is wholly of foreign origin."[14]

Because the newcomers were not so different from Blacks, many thought they threatened the color line between Blacks and whites. "The color of thousands of them [immigrants] differs materially from that of the Anglo-Saxons," warned one member of Congress. These immigrants faced racial discrimination and segregation when they arrived in the United States. The Italians, typically thought to be the most degraded of the European races (although Jews were thought to be nearly as bad), were not considered to be white by many. "You don't call . . . an Italian a white man?" a construction boss was asked. "No, sir," he answered, "an Italian is a Dago." In one Louisiana town the Italian children were barred from the white schools. In the West, immigrants from China and Japan were seen as a threat to whites. By the early nineteenth century, the "Negro, the Oriental, and the southern European appeared more and more in a common light."[15]

Early twentieth-century whites viewed the Southern European immigrants with such apprehension because they thought that the immigrants would not be able to assimilate into the dominant culture. These immigrants—like Blacks, many thought—*could not* become like whites. There was something in their blood, some whites argued, that enabled only whites to be free; no others had the right kind of lineage to enjoy and protect liberty. If too many came to the United States, liberty here would be threatened, the racists claimed. In 1916 Madison Grant summed up American racism in *The Passing of the Great Race*.[16] He assumed a racial determination of culture; some races were capable of great deeds, and others were not. To the great Nordic race belonged the genius of the world. Happily, said Grant, America had a purely Nordic population in its early days. But immigration brought over hordes of Alpine, Mediterranean, and Jewish hybrids, threatening the old Nordic stock. To save the American Nordic genius, immigration to America had to be halted. A few short years later, with the immigration laws of 1921 and 1924, it mostly was.

When racism is publicly legitimate, it justifies the power that one group has over another. This power, when it first took hold in the United States, did not have much ideological justification; elaborate justifications for slavery began to pour out of the South in the nineteenth century, not when slavery began. As opposition to slavery grew, more vigorous justifications for it emerged. The construction of race in America enabled whites to justify their feelings of superiority over Blacks. It legitimized the power of whites over Blacks.[17] Whites justified the social subordination of Blacks by appealing to race. Even if some whites were poorer than some Blacks, these whites could feel superior to them. Indeed, status can often be a barrier to equality, a barrier that may be harder to see than, say, income or political rights. In the 1930s George Orwell argued that understanding the importance of status was crucial to understanding class-ridden England. The attitude of the lower middle class toward the working class was "an attitude of sniggering superiority punctuated by bursts of vicious hatred." Orwell claimed that accents and manners in England played much the same role as race in the United States: "A shabby-genteel family is in much the same position as a family of 'poor whites' living in a street where everyone else is a negro. In such circumstances you have got to cling to your gentility because it is the only thing you have."[18] Noneconomic markers—accents or skin color—enable some people to feel part of the dominant class, regardless of how little money they actually have.

Unlike the situation in Brazil, Blacks in the United States were told that, whatever else they were, in the eyes of whites and the state they were Black. Regardless of how much money they had, Blacks had to sit in the back of the bus. They could never rise above the category of Black. Most middle class Blacks attained their status through their achievements in the Black community, not mainstream society. They were primarily ministers, doctors, lawyers, and other professionals who served Blacks. Whites could still easily view them as inferior—the law, after all, said they were.

By seeing Blacks as one group, the state mandated and reinforced the view that Blacks are a single racial and cultural group. Societies can be racist, of course, without the formal sanction of the state. There need not be a law forbidding Blacks and Jews from holding certain offices in this country for it to be impossible for them to do so. Whether or not racism is publicly sanctioned, it imposes an identity on people. When people are defined as part of a race, they are defined by the dominant group. It does matter, however, whether the dominant group has the official backing of the state. The role of the state in defining race often plays an important part in determining how and if groups can redefine themselves; when laws classify a group of people as part of a different race, it is nearly impossible for them to redefine themselves. Laws that institute cultural norms make it much more unlikely that those norms will change.

In the United States white racist attitudes were translated into legislation regulating the lives of Blacks. The Jim Crow laws ensured that Blacks could not enter mainstream institutions as equals in many parts of this country. The Black codes after the Civil War restricted the lives of southern Blacks in many ways, but the North was not the land of freedom for Blacks; in all parts of the country, there were legal (and nonlegal) restrictions that applied to Blacks but not whites. Black property ownership was outlawed or restricted in many places, severely limiting the economic opportunities of Blacks. With the *Dred Scott* decision, Black citizenship was disputed; voting rights were taken away from Blacks in many places. The doctrine of "separate but equal" was declared constitutional in 1896 by the Supreme Court in *Plessy v. Ferguson*.[19]

In contrast, immigrants could try to enter mainstream institutions. (This was not always true for Chinese and Japanese immigrants and their descendants on the West Coast. They faced a slew of racist laws designed to limit their opportunities. However, these laws were of shorter duration than were laws affecting Blacks, and some were ineffective.) It helped enormously that few laws in the United States defined Italians and other immigrants as Black; although individual merchants may have refused to hire or serve these immigrants, these actions were rarely backed by the state. Class became more relevant for immigrants; by achieving "middle class respectability," immigrants could become "American." Ethnics could try to lose their accent and dress like Americans; they could try to enter the middle class and become indistinguishably American, something that Blacks could not do. And if ethnics couldn't do all these things, many of their children could and did.

Furthermore, there were fewer restrictions on the ethnic vote than on the votes of Blacks. This meant that ethnics could garner political power. Some politicians tried to gain the support of ethnic communities. The machine politics of many cities enabled some ethnics, particularly Irish Americans, to gain political clout. Even while ethnics faced prejudice, they had some access to the political structure here, giving them some political leverage. This dissuaded some politicians from trying to pass laws that would harm ethnics, making it harder for the state to define ethnics in the same way it defined Blacks. Even in areas where Blacks and ethnics both voted, racism gave white ethnics more political power.[20]

Racist attitudes toward immigrants never enjoyed the same wide support as did racism against Blacks, and, without state backing, it was easier for racism against the immigrants to fade away. The racist view that the immigrants of the great immigration waves were nonwhites and so inferior eventually lost its strength. Many whites argued that these ethnics, through intermarriage and education, could assimilate. There was an important incentive for whites to argue this; millions of immigrants had settled here, regardless of the restrictions of the new immigration laws of the 1920s. If the immigrants were considered Black, white supremacy might be endangered. With the history of a third racial category a distant memory, it would be difficult to define the immigrants legally as something besides Black or white. Immigrants, caught in the middle between Blacks and whites, fought to be accepted by whites. Many whites encouraged this attitude; become like us, they said, and we will accept you. By encouraging assimilation, whites could bolster their strength and numbers.

Italian Americans face much less discrimination than they once did, not because racism has disappeared, but because the definitions of Black and white changed. Italian Americans and other ethnics were initially in the subordinate category but, because this was not legally enshrined, they became part of the dominant group. These immigrants, or, more accurately, their children, ceased to be of a different race and simply became members of a different ethnic group. Not all immigrants and their descendants, however, are free from discrimination. Latinos and Asian Americans often face discrimination in the United States. The decline of discrimination against the immigrants around the turn of the century took several decades; it will probably take at least as long for discrimination to fade for more recent nonwhite immigrants, if it does at all. It's possible that new racial categories will become established in the United States over time. As much discrimination as Latinos and Asian Americans face, however, racism against Black Americans is more deeply entrenched and shows a greater staying power.

Since the state no longer imposes its view of race through legislation, there is now the possibility that American racial categories will break down. As the categorization of many ethnic immigrants has changed, so too may racial categories change. This change, however, if it does occur, will take many years. The effects of the state's attempts to institutionalize the categories of Black and white linger on.[21]

Members of racial groups do not have to simply accede to the categorization they are given by the more powerful; identity for racial groups is not only externally imposed. Racial groups are (like ethnic groups) often cultural groups as well. Light-skinned Black people growing up in the United States might be able to "pass" as white, but if they felt culturally Black they could stop being Black only with great difficulty. Black Americans have some cultural practices that are different from those of whites. Africans obviously had cultures different from those of white Americans and of each other. These cultures did not simply disappear on the shores of the United States. Slaves re-created their African cultures here, adapting them to their new circumstances, while they also took on completely new cultural practices.[22] Race can have not only an external meaning but also an internal meaning. Indeed, race in the United States opens up some possible roles even as it closes off others. The role of the Black minister, a powerful social and political leader in many Black communities, is a role that few whites can aspire to fill. Although race opens up some options for Blacks, many of the more attractive roles in society have been closed off to them.

Although there is often a connection between race and culture, this relationship is not inevitable; race does not strictly map onto culture. The supposed biological makeup of different races does not lead to different cultural values. Cornelius May was culturally more European than African, although he was Black; in chapter 6 I note that parts of the Black-American community and parts of mainstream America are becoming more similar to each other as racism changes. Victims of discrimination, considered to be members of a subordinate race by those in power, may have cultural practices similar to those of their oppressors. Indeed, victims of discrimination sometimes think that if they take on the cultural values of their oppressors they will no longer face discrimination. This strategy sometimes works but often fails. When it fails, when members of a group are continually denied access to the dominant culture, they often develop and maintain their own cultural practices and values.

Ethnicity

Immigration is the key to ethnicity in America; national origin is commonly thought to determine people's ethnicity here. A slightly broader definition of ethnicity is that ethnic groups are communities that base themselves on a sense of group origins and share (or think they share) some cultural attributes. These origins are usually thought to be based on either language or history, although religion sometimes plays an important role. Usually, members of ethnic groups can share in the dominant culture. Irish Americans, Italian Americans, and Polish Americans, by this definition, are ethnics.[23] The day may come when people in California will answer Iowa, Michigan, or Wisconsin when they are asked where their ancestors are from.

The identity of ethnics is not imposed on them by others, as it is on racial groups.[24] Some ethnics were originally seen as a race, however, and at one time their identity may have been imposed on them. Many Italian immigrants did not see themselves as Italian when they came here. They began to immigrate here before there was an Italian state. Even after Italy gained its independence, many Italian immigrants did not think of themselves as Italian; they were Sardinian or Neapolitan or Venetian. Yet the dominant group named and treated them like Italians. (Sicilian immigrants are sometimes distinguished from Italians in the United States.) Similarly, around the turn of the century, most Americans viewed Jews as one group. But within the Jewish community itself there was considerable antipathy between German Jews, who arrived in the United States in the first half of the nineteenth century, and Eastern European Jews, who came later. These two groups of Jews began to identify with each other when others did not treat them as German Jews or Eastern European Jews but simply as Jews. They were treated (disdainfully) as a community and so felt obliged to respond as one.

This forced identity ended for Italian Americans and for Jews as well (though to a lesser degree). Barriers due to their identity eventually fell. The biological makeup of the members of these groups did not alter; their categorization changed. Although their ethnic identity is no longer imposed by others like race, ethnicity can be crucial to someone's identity for cultural reasons. A person's ethnicity (call her Maureen) may be apparent in her cultural practices and in the way she acts; it may be seen in her hand gestures, the way in which she talks and expresses herself, and who she picks as her friends. It may be seen in her views of the country of her ancestors. All of these things, which make up Maureen's ethnic identity, may be part of her self-understanding. She may simply (but strongly) feel Irish American; she could not imagine not being ethnic. Maureen is partly constituted by her racial and ethnic identity. Yet no one *tells* Maureen that she is Irish American. She is not forced to be ethnic. She can interpret her ethnic identity in different ways.[25]

Maureen can try to weave her life so that ethnicity plays an important role for her, or she can decide to do otherwise. The institutions that surround people can create, deepen, or weaken their constitutive attachments. It is not that people simply choose who they are; people choose to become members of some or many of the institutions that help shape their identity (although sometimes people become members of institutions against their will). In a large, pluralistic society like the United States, people are members of many different communities. People can alter their attachments to these communities to change themselves. Maureen can attend an Irish-American church, live in an Irish-American neighborhood, and practice Irish-American traditions. But because the identity of Irish American is not imposed on her, she can also choose to quit her church, move out to the suburbs where there is a polyglot of ethnicities, and ignore Irish-American traditions. In the former case Maureen lives in a way that deepens her ethnic identity; in the latter this identity is weakened. Indeed, she may eventually stop thinking of herself as an Irish American.

Liberals want people to be self-interpreting beings in just the way Maureen is self-interpreting. As Sandel and other critics of liberalism note, no one is without unchosen attachments; no one is without character.[26] Our ethnic and racial identity is not something we choose. Liberals cannot (or should not) dispute this. The arguments between liberals and communitarians are better cast as disputes over how these attachments are formed and changed and what the political implications of these attachments should be. Sandel argues that agency consists of self-understanding. This is only partly true because many people do not completely understand themselves and because people like Maureen can interpret their character in different ways. Her interpretation may change so much that her self-understanding one year may seem rather foreign to her the next year. People's self-understanding can change over time and can be the result of their conscious efforts to change their character.

Sometimes ethnics change their practices and self-understandings because they feel pressure to conform to the standards of mainstream culture;

when this happens, ethnics do not have the ability to interpret their character as they wish. Without minimizing the effects of prejudice on some ethnics, it is important that, compared to members of racial groups, ethnics face few obstacles in society's dominant institutions. Unlike members of racial groups, ethnics have considerable latitude in how they interpret their identity. Ethnics can construct their lives so their ethnic identity is weakened. They can marry someone from a different ethnic group and have children who can then choose to follow the ethnicity of either their father or their mother (or possibly neither). The racial identity of the children of an African American and an Irish American, however, depends largely on skin color.[27] A person with the last name of O'Brien who has dark skin will have a tough time explaining to society that he wants to be thought of as Irish, not Black. He may be asked about his last name, but this is precisely because others wonder how a Black person got an Irish name. A white person with the same last name would go unnoticed.

This is why it is misleading to say there is no majority group in the United States, as Thomas Sowell does and Nathan Glazer implies.[28] To speak only of "ethnic America" suggests that all ethnic groups are equal, which is not so. There is a majority group in the United States, and Blacks are not a part of it. Intermarriage between whites of different ethnic backgrounds is now widespread; intermarriage between whites and Latinos is less common than among white ethnics but seems to be increasing; the rate of intermarriage between whites and Blacks, while slowly rising, is still quite small. Many whites do not seem to understand why Blacks make such a big deal about being Black; these whites see being Black as another ethnic identity. Yet, although a few white ethnics discourage their children from marrying someone outside their ethnic group, this resistance is minor compared to the resistance of many whites to the idea of one of their children marrying a Black person.[29]

Nationality

Defining a nation is notoriously difficult. The prominent historian of nationalism, Hugh Seton-Watson, admits: "I am driven to the conclusion that no 'scientific definition' of the nation can be devised; yet the phenomenon has existed and exists." I think, though, that Benedict Anderson's definition captures the spirit of the modern nation. The nation, Anderson argues, is an imagined political community that sees itself as limited and sovereign. The nation is limited because it does not pretend to encompass the entire world. It is imagined because most of its members will never meet each other, "yet in the minds of each lives the image of their communion." This means that the nation is thought up (imagined) by people. To say it is imagined, though, is not to suggest that it is somehow not real. As Anderson points out, all communities larger than primordial villages of face-to-face contact are imagined: "Communities are to be distinguished, not by their falsity/genuineness, but by the style in which they are imagined." It is imagined as a community because, though it may have deep inequalities, the nation is always conceived as a "deep, horizontal comradeship."[30] Something must be shared among its members so they can imagine themselves as a community, so they can feel this comradeship. Language, history, and culture are the common elements in nationhood, though there may be others.

Ethnic communities are also imagined in the way that Anderson describes. National claims are so much more explosive than ethnic claims because the former are tied up with claims to a certain piece of land and a desire for some form of political autonomy. Members of the nation argue that they have a right to self-determination. This claimed right can often result in bloody conflicts. When two groups claim the same piece of land, the potential for violence is quite high. Zionism and Black nationalism show that an aspiration for a specific piece of land may be enough to get a nationalist movement off the ground. If this aspiration is continually frustrated, however, the nationalism may weaken considerably. Land and sovereignty support each other; nations claim that a certain piece of land is "theirs," and so the people who make up the nation should have some sort of political control of it.[31]

Land and the claims of sovereignty are important ingredients of nationality but not ethnicity. It is too easy to marvel at the relative peace between ethnic groups in the United States when comparing them to ethnic groups in other places if one does not see the differences between ethnic and national groups. Lawrence Fuchs confuses ethnicity and nationality in the very first sentence of his book on race and ethnicity in the United States: "Ethnic diversity a nation does not make, and separatist movements are a source of tension in many multiethnic nations: Sikhs in India, Basques in Spain, Tibetans in China, Albanians in Yugoslavia, Shiites in Lebanon, Estonians in the Soviet Union, the French in Canada, and others." Fuchs also notes "an extraordinary paradox" in the world, that "in dozens of nations . . . ethnic diversity was perceived as a threat to national unity. But in the United States, ethnic diversity was celebrated as a feature of American national unity."[32] Sikhs, the Québecois, the Basques, and others argue that they are not part of the Indian, English Canadian, or Spanish nations. They are, they proclaim, their own nation. They do not consider themselves part of a "multiethnic nation" and would almost certainly be offended by Fuchs's characterization that they are. They want to maintain their own identity and be separate from the dominant nation. They do not share (and do not want to share) in the dominant culture, as ethnics do. Ethnics want to integrate; nations want to separate. Many Sikhs do not want to be part of an Indian India. They argue that they should be granted the right of self-determination in the Punjab. The Punjab, many Sikhs argue, is for Sikhs, not Hindus. Because Hindu Indians argue that the Punjab is part of India, there is conflict between these two national groups. Some Basques want to establish a Basque state on land that is now part of Spain; some Québecois want a sovereign Quebec state in Canada. These claims over the same land are a formula for conflict.

The claim that a particular group is a nation and so has the right to govern a large area is the cause of much violence between nationalities. Although both ethnicity and nationality are based on a common sense of historical origins, nations argue that their historical claim to a piece of land gives them the right to political sovereignty. This formula for conflict is not restricted to countries beyond the United States. Disputes over land in the United States have led to many conflicts between Native Americans and other Americans, disputes that are far from over.

In contrast to national groups, ethnic groups rarely claim that a certain piece of land is theirs. Few Irish Americans argue that Boston or New York is the ancestral homeland of their ethnic group and that this group alone deserves political control over the city. Ethnics here *left* their land to come to the United States.[33] When compared to conflicts between nationalities, ethnic conflicts are unsurprisingly rather tame.

Contested Meanings

These three categories (race, ethnicity, and nationality) are not mutually exclusive, nor do they include other categories like language or religion. Blacks are a racial group, yet there are also Black nationalists. The move to replace *Black American* with *African American* is, at least in part, a move to put African Americans on the same level as white ethnics.[34] Just as white ethnics have an ancestral home, so do Blacks. Black cultural roots are from Africa, leading them to be culturally different from white Europeans and their descendants. Racism and nationalism also sometimes directly play off each other. Many people have defined the United States as a white nation. Blacks, because of their skin color or blood, could never be equal citizens of the nation (and the state), some contended. Many whites, especially in the North, argued that Blacks and whites could never get along as equals, so Blacks ought to return to Africa. Colonization as a solution to this problem was quite popular in the nineteenth century. Liberia was born out of attempts to put this idea into practice.[35]

Victims of racism often disagree on how they should conceive of themselves, resulting in bitter debates. Though racism may restrict people's identity, they typically have room to form their own self-conceptions and fight for their realization. The split in one family illustrates the two typical responses to racism. "Take, for example, the case of two brothers, well known in Brixton . . . one becoming a successful local businessman and marrying an English wife, the other developing a strong commitment to Garveyism and radical black politics. The first habitually spoke London English with a Jamaican accent; the second, Jamaican patois."[36] The first brother wants to think of Blacks as an ethnic group; the other thinks of Blacks (in England, at least) as a nation.

Black nationalists hardly feel the need to argue that they will not be accepted into white society. Here are the words of one Black man:

> White people have always been crying over us half the time and telling us we should be proud to be American the rest of the time. I don't care what they do. I just wish they wouldn't go around braggin' about doing the things which they never did and never will do until we can make 'em. I get tired of that one-nation-under-God boogie-joogie. We are ourselves. We are our own nation or country or whatever you want to call it. We are not no one tenth of some white something! That man has got his country and we *are* our country.

The same man explains why he could never feel part of the American nation: "I'd be a fool if I thought that army was our army. If it's my army and guard and navy and all that, will you tell me why it was shooting at me here a few years ago? If anybody can be the President, why all them dudes look like they do?"[37] Denied the right to define themselves, Black's claim to nationhood can be seen as an attempt for them to become self-interpreting. Given political autonomy, they will not be marked as inferior by others. In such a society, people can define themselves in the same way ethnics can.

The distinctions between the categories of race, ethnicity, and nationality are not always so clear. Despite the overlap of these categories in practice, they are analytically useful. There are important political differences between being an Irish American, a Black American, and a Native American, differences that these categories capture. To talk about Irish Americans and Black Americans in the same way is to blur crucial differences between the two. The formation of identity in the United States has been overwhelmed by the distinction between Blacks and whites. Unfortunately, these dichotomous categories fail to capture completely the identity of many people in the United States, particularly Latinos and Asian Americans.

Clashes of cultures in contemporary America often involve Asian Americans, yet it is difficult to characterize Asian Americans as a group. The term itself is probably misleading, for Asian Americans are quite disparate, ranging from fifth generation Japanese Americans to first generation refugees from Cambodia and Vietnam to highly educated immigrants from India. Instead of looking at all of the Asian-American communities here, I discuss one community that has been in America for about a hundred years, Japanese Americans.[38]

Although much of the experience of Asian immigrants here has been different from that of other ethnic and racial groups, the patterns in the different Asian-American communities do duplicate those of other ethnics in important ways. Asian Americans (if the Japanese-American example will be replicated by other Asian-American communities) are a combination of racial and ethnic groups. They seem to be moving steadily from the former to the latter, although discrimination against Asian Americans will undoubtedly continue for many years.

Like Chinese Americans, Japanese Americans faced considerable discrimination here, culminating in their internment during World War II. Before the war, laws aimed at denying Japanese Americans the right to own land (many were farmers) were passed in several states on the West Coast. Japanese immigrants could not receive American citizenship. There were also attempts to establish separate schools for Japanese-American children, but these attempts usually failed. Job discrimination was rampant; many highly educated second generation Japanese Americans could not get jobs in businesses owned by whites.[39] All of this changed after World War II, when government leaders tried to ease tensions between whites and Japanese Americans. During the war, the rapidly growing West Coast cities had attracted many Blacks and Latinos, so the "Japanese-American problem" seemed minor in comparison. The younger generation of whites seemed less prejudiced than their parents; white organizations emerged to help the inmates of the camps get reestablished.[40] Finally, many Japanese Americans wanted to fit into American society as quietly as possible and did what they could to accomplish this goal.

Since the war many Japanese Americans have integrated into mainstream American society. This is not to say that Japanese Americans no longer face discrimination. Surely many do. Furthermore, as long as economic tensions between Japan and the United States remain, Japanese Americans (and probably all Asian Americans) will face at least some prejudice from other Americans. But this discrimination no longer restricts

Japanese Americans as it once did; it certainly pales in comparison to the discrimination faced by American Blacks. Time and again sociologists have found that third generation Japanese Americans do not differ very much from other Americans in the friends they choose, the organizations they join, or the values they have. Some Japanese Americans do stay in the Japanese-American community and live lives that are distinguishably Japanese American, but they are increasingly the exception in the Japanese-American community.[41] Although many Japanese Americans face discrimination, they can increasingly weave their lives and interpret their identity in the same ways as do other ethnics. Perhaps the best indicator of this is the amount of intermarriage between Japanese Americans and other Americans. Intermarriage can occur only in a climate of relatively little prejudice; furthermore, there must be enough cultural similarity between the two spouses for the marriage to take place. Approximately a third of all Japanese Americans have intermarried, and the percentage increases with each generation.[42]

CHAPTER 3

THE DEMANDS OF
LIBERAL CITIZENSHIP

"ONE MUST REFUSE everything to the Jews as a nation, and give every-thing to the Jews as individuals. . . . It would be repugnant to have a soci-ety of non-citizens in a state and a nation within a nation." So announced Clermont-Tonnerre, arguing for the emancipation of the Jews in the French Constituent Assembly after the French Revolution.[1] The assembly spent a considerable amount of time debating Jewish emancipation, yet fewer than fifty thousand Jews lived in France at the time of the revolu-tion. The agenda of the assembly was quite crowded; they could easily have skipped over an issue that affected relatively few people, like citizen-ship for the Jews, as some assembly leaders urged. Despite its obscurity, however, the issue of Jewish citizenship kept reappearing in the assembly. Its reappearance was not an indication that the assembly cared so much about the Jews; the debate was less about Jews than it was about French citizenship. Who could be a French citizen? What were the qualifications and requirements of citizenship? Deciding on whether Jews could be citi-zens was a way of determining the nature of French citizenship.

Before the French Revolution, the *ancien régime* had been corporate and particularistic; individuals were recognized as members of different legal groups. A tailor needed the protection of his guild, the priest had his reli-gious order, and Jews were recognized as members of the Jewish commu-nity. French Jews, in fact, had some privileges, with a political status

33

greater than that of most peasants. For the most part, the Jewish community prospered at the pleasure of the French kings.[2]

After the French Revolution, however, the corporate bodies lost their standing. When discussions of emancipation arose, a debate over the identity of the Jews emerged: was the Jewish community like other corporate bodies, or did the Jews constitute their own nation? Those who argued against granting the Jews full citizenship maintained that the Jews were a different nation. The differences between Jews and the French in language, dress, marriage, and religious rituals, they maintained, were proof of this. They were a different people with a host of different practices that set them apart.

If the Jews were a nation, they surely could not be part of the French nation, for how could they then act in the French national will? Obviously, they could not; one could not have two primary sets of loyalties. And so they should not, if they were their own nation, receive citizenship. But Clermont-Tonnerre's argument won the day. If Jews were recognized as individuals, not as a nation, then they could be included in the French nation. It was assumed that the Jews would conceive of themselves as French citizens who happened to be Jews, not as part of a separate, Jewish nation. They could be Jewish at home, but that was not a matter of public concern. French in public, Jewish at home: that was the formula.

And this is, to a considerable degree, the liberal formula. Richard Rorty, in a rather typical liberal comment, says that issues of culture and identity should "simply be ignored for purposes of designing political institutions." The individual, not the group, is the primary political actor in the liberal state. Individuals are obligated to obey the state's laws; they can ignore the dictates of their ethnic group if they wish. Liberals do not argue that groups should not exist; they merely say that these groups should have no political standing. Individuals vote for their representatives; groups do not send representatives to the legislature. In the liberal state the individual is "identified and treated by the law not as a member of a particular group but simply as a citizen. Ethnic labels . . . have no place [in politics], although any individual would be free to live according to his own cultural practices without either interference or subsidy."[3]

The argument that culture and identity are merely private matters about which liberalism has little to say is, however, too quick. By relegating groups to the private sphere, liberalism affects the identity of group members, something that few liberals recognize.

Jewish Emancipation
and the Jewish Question

Before emancipation, Jews had to obey the government of the Jewish community.[4] Life in the Jewish community was not always benign. The powerful leaders of the Jewish community sometimes overtaxed the poorer members of the community while denying these members a voice in the community's decision-making apparatus. This often caused resentment among many poor Jews, who sometimes complained that the leaders of their community were tyrannical. Moreover, the leadership of these communities often strictly enforced the religious doctrines of Judaism. Although many Jews followed Jewish law willingly, those who worked on Saturdays or ate nonkosher food were usually punished. A wide diversity of lifestyles in the Jewish community was not encouraged. Occasionally, the desire for more diversity was expressed in widespread "revolts" against the dry, austere Jewish leadership. In the sixteenth and seventeenth centuries in Eastern Europe, several false messiahs arose, inspiring thousands of Jews; in the eighteenth century the Hasidic movement arose, rebelling against traditional Jewish leadership.

Resentful Jews did not have to rebel; they could simply leave the community. But the cost of leaving was heavy. It meant that they could no longer be Jewish. For the most part, Jewish and Christian life in the Middle Ages was starkly divided. Jews had no choice but to identify fully with the Jewish community. The wide gulf "between Jew and gentile [meant] that there could be no question of divided identity."[5] One could not live in one community and have social relations with people in the other. Leaving the Jewish community meant leaving one's family, friends, and residence behind and adopting the religion of the state. Those who left had to find an occupation in this new, foreign environment. Leaving would mean a complete change of identity, a change that the vast majority of Jews undoubtedly could not conceive of making. For most Jews, leaving their community was not an acceptable option. Jews did not face only oppression in their community. The hungry and destitute were cared for by the community. People were surrounded by their friends and family in the community. Being Jewish was important for many. Resentful Jews did not want to abandon their community. They wanted it to be more responsive to their needs. Even if their needs were unmet, most stayed in the community.

With emancipation, Jews had much more freedom to interpret their Jewish identity in their own ways. No longer could Jews be punished for violating Jewish laws as they were interpreted by Jewish leaders. Some emancipated Jews simply stopped being "practicing Jews." Others remained Jewish in nontraditional ways. Jewish emancipation meant that Jews no longer had to answer to the Jewish community. As French (or German or British or U.S.) citizens, Jews had a legal obligation to answer only to the state. No longer confined to the ghetto, Jews found their way into many of society's dominant institutions. This was not always easy, and obstacles to integration still exist.[6] Since the Second World War, however, Jews in many Western countries have increasingly found society more open to them, particularly in the United States. The result of liberal citizenship is that Jewish identity is relegated to the private realm. The rights to vote, run for public office, and engage in public debate about issues that affect everyone in the political community are granted with citizenship.

This formula allows Jews to remain Jewish. Liberal political emancipation allows Jews to remain separate if that is what they choose. Karl Marx argued that, by not insisting that the Jews join the larger community, emancipation and liberal citizenship showed themselves to be deeply flawed. In "On the Jewish Question," Marx said that political emancipation represented great progress over feudalism, but he maintained that political emancipation is limited. It does not emancipate people; it merely shifts the focus of oppression from the public to the private realm: "Thus man was not liberated from religion; he received religious liberty. He was not liberated from property; he received the liberty to own property. He was not liberated from the egoism of business; he received the liberty to engage in business."[7] Marx argued that those who celebrated the political emancipation of the Jews did not care about the Jews' *human* emancipation. Before emancipation, there was no division between church and state in France; religion was often a state affair. Shifting religion from the public to the private realm does not liberate people from religion, Marx argued. "Thus the state may have emancipated itself from religion, even though the immense majority of people continue to be religious." The problem of liberal emancipation is that it "leaves religion in existence."[8]

By leaving religion in existence, liberal citizenship does little to decrease the divisions among people. Religion is no longer the "essence of community, but the essence of differentiation. It has become what it was at the beginning, an expression of the fact that man is separated from the community, from himself and other men." A real community cannot be built if its members will look upon each other differently, as members of different groups, or if each person sees himself as the bearer of rights, separate from other citizens. The right to choose one's religion, like other liberal political rights, gives the liberal citizen the right to be "separated from the community, withdrawn into himself, wholly preoccupied with his private interest and acting in accordance with his private caprice."⁹ A true community will be built on what unites people, not on what separates them. But liberal rights lead people to see themselves as separate individuals, not as members of a larger community. Religious freedom means that Jews will retain their Jewish identity, preventing them from looking upon non-Jews as members of their community. Only after capitalism and liberalism are destroyed will Judaism give way to real human emancipation. In this new world, the egoism of the Jews will no longer be enshrined in a legal framework, as it is in the liberal state. As this framework disappears, human emancipation will take place. Jews will then willingly work to shed their Jewish identity and become part of the larger community.

Marx contended that contradictions also lie within liberal citizenship. By allowing Jews to have citizenship but remain separate, liberalism creates a contradiction between the universal public sphere and the particular, egoistic private sphere. Citizenship is universal; all members of the state receive citizenship. Yet these very same citizens have their private interests and obligations in civil society, which may contradict their obligations as citizens: "The contradiction in which the adherent of a particular religion finds himself in relation to his citizenship is only one aspect of the universal secular contradiction between the political state and civil society." The split between public and private, between the state and civil society, means that the liberal citizen lives a double life. The citizen "lives in the political community, where he regards himself as a communal being and in civil society where he acts simply as a private individual." How can people see themselves as separate, liberal bearers of rights or as members of different groups *and* as members of the state, of the larger community? According to Marx, one cannot coherently be both: "In other words, [the Jew] is and remains a Jew, even though he is a citizen and as such lives in a universal human condition; his restricted Jewish nature always finally triumphs over his human and political obligations."¹⁰ Jews' obligations to the Jewish community will prevent them from fulfilling their obligations to the state; their private interests will prevail over the public interest, revealing the flaws of liberal citizenship.

Marx correctly pointed out that, although liberal institutions may neatly separate the public from the private, people cannot separate themselves out so easily. Marx argued that the private identity of liberal citizens will inhibit the flourishing of the public sphere, but the reverse may be true as well: the demands of the public sphere may very well affect the private identity of citizens like the Jews. The universal nature of citizenship may triumph over, or at least transform, private identities. Liberalism makes far-reaching demands on how ordinary citizens act toward each other in many different settings. The beginning of the theory of liberal citizenship, where these demands arise, is found in liberal toleration. Toleration is not only about establishing a private sphere; it also makes demands on how citizens act in public. Mere toleration of others is not good enough, argues Locke in his *Letter Concerning Toleration*.

> It is not enough that Ecclesiastical men abstain from Violence and Rapine, and all manner of Persecution. He that pretends to be a Successor of the Apostles, and takes upon him the Office of Teaching, is obliged also to admonish his Hearers of the Duties of Peace, and Good-will towards all men; as well towards the Erroneous as the Orthodox; towards those that differ from them in Faith and Worship as well as towards those that agree with them therein.

Locke here chided churchmen about what they ought to teach to their parishioners, but he had the same message when he spoke directly to individuals in the *Letter*. Locke appealed to the gospel to justify his claims about how people ought to treat each other, but he also contended that "Reason directs and [the] natural fellowship that we are born into requires" that "we must not be content ourselves with the narrow Measures of bare Justice: Charity, Bounty, and Liberality must be added to it."[11] Grudgingly admitting the right of others to live despite their erroneous beliefs was not enough for Locke. We should accept others and act toward believers and nonbelievers in the same way: with good will.

When Locke wrote the *Letter*, people were fighting over the religious identity of the state, insisting that for social order to be maintained all of its members had to agree on the state's religion. Locke argued that order was better achieved by making religion a private affair; instead of fighting over the true religion, Locke proposed making it politically irrelevant. Peace is predicated not only on allowing those with different beliefs to live; people also must be treated equally if they are to remain peaceful. If some people are discriminated against because of their beliefs or how they look, they may complain or even revolt. If people feel oppressed, neither peace nor social order will be achieved: "But there is only one thing which gathers People into Seditious Commotions, and that is Oppression."[12]

Smuggled into Locke's division of the public and private spheres is the outline of the concept of equal citizenship. Locke did not say much about citizenship; with fights raging over religion, he was more concerned with peace than with the demands of citizenship. I want here to build upon and move past Locke and to draw out the political implications of citizens treating each other with liberality and good will. I take this to mean that citizens should not discriminate against each other in public settings. The principle of nondiscrimination, which only begins to emerge in Locke's thought, is now central to the idea of equal citizenship in the liberal state.

Civil Society
and Equal Citizenship

In public settings equal citizens are not discriminated against based on their identity. All citizens have the same political rights: to vote, to run for office, to speak freely, to assemble, and so forth. When some people are denied these rights, they are denied part of their citizenship. When Black Americans were denied the right to vote because of their racial identity, they did not have equal citizenship. Just as liberal citizens all have equal political rights, citizens are treated equally in public institutions. In the courtroom, guilt or innocence, not ethnic or racial identity, is the determining factor. All government jobs are open to everyone, not just to members of certain groups. All citizens have equal access to public institutions: schools, parks, streets, and so forth. Equal citizenship means that the government treats its citizens equally.

Equal political rights and equal treatment in the courtroom are not, however, enough for equal citizenship. Citizenship is also about standing. Liberal citizens "are entitled to respect unless they forfeit it by their own unacceptable actions."[13] To have standing, to be an equal citizen, is to be judged on one's actions. It means that others listen to you in public settings; if liberal democracy is (partly) government by discussion and some citizens are routinely ignored, they are not equal citizens. Equal citizenship means being given the opportunities to do what others can and to fail or succeed on one's own merits, not because of one's ethnic or racial group membership. If discrimination against a group of people is rampant, they do not have equal citizenship. Martin Luther King, Jr., explained that you know that discrimination is an obstacle to equality

> when you suddenly find your tongue twisted and your speech stammering as you seek to explain to your six-year-old daughter why she can't go to the public amusement park that has just been advertised on television, and see tears welling up in her little eyes when she is told that Funtown is closed to colored children, and see the depressing clouds of inferiority begin to form in her little mental sky, and see her begin to distort her little personality.[14]

The little girl who can't swim in the same pool as other girls or go to the amusement park attended by others is denied equality. If certain citizens cannot go into a restaurant or hotel, if some businesses won't hire them, if real estate agents will not sell them houses in certain neighborhoods, then members of the group discriminated against will not have equal citizenship; the excluded are set apart as unequal. They will be stigmatized as different and inferior.

People stigmatized by pervasive exclusion from many of society's institutions will not have equal standing as citizens. They will also be denied opportunities—economic, social, and political—that others have. Access to the many institutions that form part of civil society is necessary for equal citizenship. Libertarians generally draw the world into two spheres, the public and the private. Marx also saw two spheres, the state (public) and civil society (private). Many critics of liberalism argue that a major flaw of liberalism is that it rigidly divides the public from the private realm.[15] But this simple dichotomy misses the public nature of many supposedly private institutions in liberal society. The public/private distinction in liberal theory is neither rigid nor simple. Liberals are better off arguing for a tripartite scheme: the public, the private, and civil society.[16] My argument here is not particularly new. The public nature of civil society is already recognized in the practices of many liberal states. Liberal theorists, however, are remiss for not pointing this out more forcefully.

I use the term *civil society* to refer to institutions and associations that are not controlled by the state but that serve the public in many ways, institutions like the media, stores, factories, and corporations. Access to these institutions is necessary to achieve equality, an idea that is in fact widely (although not universally) accepted in the United States. Access to the institutions of civil society is necessary for people to get good jobs and a good education, to buy the clothes they want, and to amuse themselves as they wish; these institutions allow citizens to advance economically and pursue and express their individual talents and abilities. If some stores, factories, or corporations will not hire people or if institutions of higher learning will not accept people because of their ethnic or racial membership, then economic opportunities accorded others are denied the victims of discrimination. They will not receive the education necessary for some jobs; it may be that the only jobs they can have will be unskilled and low-paid. If the liberal value of equal opportunity is to have any meaning, workplaces and institutions of higher learning must be open to all who have the requisite talents and abilities. If members of a certain group cannot use hotels in many cities, for example, then they cannot work at jobs that demand travel or they can do so only at a great disadvantage. If you are to become a doctor, wear certain clothes, see certain plays, visit friends across the country, and spend time at the beach—if you will pursue your plans and projects and develop your individuality—you cannot be barred from stores, concert halls, restaurants, and hotels because of your group membership.

That the institutions of civil society have an important public role is already embedded in some American laws. United States courts and Congress have rightly decided that discrimination in many of the institutions of civil society is illegal. Antidiscriminatory laws passed in response to the discrimination that Black Americans faced in the United States apply to ethnics as well.[17] Institutions that are part of civil society must be open to all citizens for society to realize the goal of equal citizenship. But the principle of nondiscrimination in civil society, widespread as it is, is not neat. Some of the institutions of civil society, such as religious organizations, need to discriminate to retain their identity. It would be strange for the state to accuse the Catholic church of discrimination (and act on this accusation) because it noticed that all of the church's priests and bishops are Catholic. Non-Catholics are discriminated against when the people for these positions are chosen, but to insist otherwise would mean that the Catholic church would become something else altogether. Similarly, a group promoting gay rights may not want to be led by a heterosexual person.

Deciding whether an institution in civil society should be allowed to discriminate depends on the nature of the institution. Two tests can be used to determine whether an institution should adhere to the principle of nondiscrimination. First, is having the option of participation in this institution necessary for full citizenship? Second, can the institution survive the principle of nondiscrimination and still serve its main purpose? Access to a good education and to stores are two of many possible examples where participation in institutions is necessary for equal citizenship. Because non-Catholics need not be part of the Catholic church to be full citizens, discrimination against non-Catholics within the Catholic church is not a violation of equal citizenship. The main purpose of a toy store is to sell toys; such a store can fulfill its purpose by adhering to the principle of nondiscrimination. A kosher butcher may point out that his purpose is to serve the Jewish community, and so he does not want to serve non-Jews in his store. But serving non-Jews does not prevent him from serving the Jewish community as well. These principles are good guidelines to use when the state must decide where to extend the principle of nondiscrimination. Not all cases will be easy to decide. This does not mean that the principles are not useful; it means that there are sometimes hard political decisions to make in liberal democracies.

Libertarians sometimes argue that the nature of business will often force business people to refrain from discrimination.[18] They argue that the market works against discrimination at much less cost than that of government intervention. Libertarians argue that employers or store owners who discriminate will not hire the best possible employees and will reduce their customer base, putting them at a competitive disadvantage. This is a naive view, however, given the history of racism in the United States. In many parts of the country before the civil rights movement, a store that hired Blacks to serve in visible and responsible positions (as opposed to menial jobs) was often not frequented by whites; a restaurant that allowed Blacks to sit next to whites would find itself with a very small white clientele. Since whites made up the majority of the population, it was easier to ignore the needs of the smaller—and poorer—Black population. Angering the richer and larger white population would cause considerable hardship for many store owners. In many places, potential Black entrepreneurs did not have the capital or the suppliers to sell needed goods to the Black community, which meant that Black customers either had no access to certain goods or had to suffer indignities to buy them from whites.

Moreover, many Blacks who tried to open businesses failed because they did not have the proper business training. The argument that everyone can compete equally in the free market ignores the important fact that many Black people have been denied a good education, the sort of education that gives a person the knowledge to run sophisticated businesses. For example, many Black-owned banks in the early twentieth century failed for two main reasons. First, many of the bank managers were poorly trained in management. Second, there were few investment opportunities in the Black community.[19] Unsurprisingly, most of these banks failed, forcing many Black people to use white-owned banks, regardless of the humiliation they faced in doing so.

The market does not magically or automatically work against discrimination. In a society where a minority of the population faces prejudice and discrimination, the market may in fact reinforce its subordinate position. The economic costs of voluntarily following a policy of nondiscrimination in a racist society will be too high for many store owners. If every store, however, had to follow a general policy of nondiscrimination, no one would be penalized for following the liberal principle of equality.

Libertarians also maintain that the public gains when many businesses (and other parts of civil society) are privately controlled. Many of these institutions controlled by citizens better supply the public with goods and services than they would if controlled by a central government. This idea underpinned Adam Smith's argument in *The Wealth of Nations:* he argued that state-sanctioned monopolies provided worse goods and services at higher prices than would a competitive market system. But the market system does not work magically, nor does it necessarily work well for everyone, as Smith well understood.[20] Many businesses in this country have practiced racial discrimination (some still do) and survived; many have thrived. Even a cursory glance at U.S. history shows that the market has not always worked toward reducing discrimination. When businesses discriminate against Blacks or others, they fail their public role. When businesses discriminate, there are no advantages of the market system for Black Americans. When this happens, the justification for the market (that it is . better for the public than other systems) collapses. The government should ensure that this failure is corrected by making sure that the public benefits of civil society apply to the whole public.

Civil society plays an important part in efforts to achieve equal citizenship; it is in civil society that people receive an education, get a job, and amuse themselves. If liberal equality applies only to the public sphere, it will not mean much for many people. Sometimes such a narrowly construed principle of equality is defended in the name of liberty: people ought to have the right to serve whoever they want in their restaurant or hire who they want in their business. But this version of liberty too readily sacrifices equality and the liberty of the victims of discrimination. These victims tend to come from the same groups in most liberal states. It is not as if the victims and perpetrators of discrimination are randomly members of different groups. We know from history that it is often the same group of people who have more liberty than others, that it is often the members of the same groups who face discrimination. Members of the group that faces discrimination usually have less power than others, so that the discrimination they face often harms their plans and projects. When the members of a group routinely face discrimination in many of society's institutions, this discrimination becomes an obstacle to equality.

It's not good enough to say that, if someone can't get hired in one company because he is Black, he can offer his services to another company. Unemployment seems to be a permanent part of most liberal states, which means that there are more workers than jobs. Workers who can't work at some places because of their ascriptive identity will have to work harder to find a job than others; they may find that they will have to offer their services at a lower price because their opportunities are limited. The status (and perhaps education) that degrees from certain elite colleges give to their students is not easily replicated by schools that are not as well known. If some prestigious colleges won't allow Jews into their classrooms regardless of how qualified these students are, these Jews will have to get college degrees that carry less prestige and so obtain jobs that pay less money. If some people in civil society have the "liberty" to discriminate, equality and liberty will be denied others. When this happens, when the liberty of some tramples on the liberty and equality of others, then liberal principles are replaced by principles that justify subordination and oppression.

The principle of nondiscrimination is not only about opportunity; it also supports liberal democratic politics. For a democracy to survive, at least some citizens need to vote and to participate politically; some citizens need to discuss politics and politicians. This participation and these discussions sometimes take place in public and private settings, but they often occur in civil society. In stores, cafés, and restaurants, notices are put up announcing meetings and rallies, and literature on political groups and campaigns is available for those interested.[21] Political events are reported and discussed in newspapers, on television, and on the radio. Call-in shows and letter columns allow people to express their opinions about political and social events. Many political discussions take place on college campuses, both in and outside of classes. If some people are excluded from parts of civil society because of their ascriptive identity, then they are excluded from the discussions and debates that are part of democratic politics. If they are barred from some of the institutions of civil society, they won't have an equal chance to listen to others, nor will they have an equal chance to persuade others of their views. They will have fewer chances to know about political events and rallies. Their opportunities for political involvement will be circumscribed.

Institutions that are part of civil society must be open to all if we are to have equal citizenship. Unfortunately, the Supreme Court does not fully recognize the role of civil society in democratic debate. The decline of public squares in this country—where people used to gather to talk about politics, among other things—means that shopping malls and centers are now, to a large extent, the new public squares. To reach people, political groups must go where the people congregate—at the mall. The Supreme Court used to accept this argument. Owners of shopping centers, bridges, ferries, and so forth profited by opening up their property to the public, the Court argued, and by doing so their property took on a public function and so had to be open to political groups. Unfortunately, the Court has reversed itself on this matter, rejecting the argument that shopping places are the new public squares. Although the Court says that shoppers cannot be barred because of their ascriptive identity, all political groups can be barred from shopping places. Equal citizenship is protected by the Court, but democratic politics is not.[22]

Although citizens cannot discriminate against others in public settings based on their identity, this does not mean that some kinds of discrimination cannot exist in the liberal state. Medical schools need not accept all applicants; corporations need not hire everyone who wants a job; movie studios do not have to let everyone who wants to act in a movie do so. The principle of nondiscrimination, where it applies, means that no one should be discriminated against because of his or her group membership, not that all forms of discrimination cannot exist. Individual talent and ability are supposed to matter in the liberal state. People who are bad at biology or who cannot act probably should not go to medical school or appear in movies. They are discriminated against not because of their ascriptive identity but because of what they can and cannot do. Some kinds of inequality may exist in the liberal state, but these "are not inherently associated with any easily discernible traits, with any class, ethnic, racial or sexual characteristics of persons. Therefore, you cannot justly design political institutions that favor some groups over others."[23]

The list of institutions that should subscribe to the principle of nondiscrimination is long, but it is not infinite. Liberals also treasure the right to associate with whomever they want—this right, however, can be exercised only in the private realm. In homes and some private clubs, liberal citizens can and do discriminate. (If substantial business dealings take place in a private club, the club should not be considered completely private but part of our civil society and so should have to adhere to the principle of nondiscrimination.) The state cannot tell us who to invite for dinner, who to associate with socially, or who to fall in love with. For social purposes, liberal citizens discriminate based on all kinds of reasons, including identity.

The Demands of
Liberal Citizenship

Critics of liberalism often argue that people cannot separate themselves out as easily as the differentiation of the liberal social world demands. It is facile to say, they suggest, that someone can be a devout Christian in one setting but ignore religion in other settings, or that someone can be devoted to his ethnic community on the weekends but ignore his ethnic community at work. Liberals respond that liberalism does not try to separate people but instead tries to draw lines between institutions: liberalism does not "separate individuals; [it] separates institutions, practices, relationships of different sorts."[24] Liberal separation means that, in certain settings, Christians or ethnics do not make decisions based on their religion or their heritage, not that they stop being Christian or ethnic. These identities may matter in church or in the home, but they do not matter in court or at school. These different institutions are blind to certain aspects of people's identity but see others. A person's religion matters a lot in church, but in most cases the court should ignore a person's religion.

When institutions are separated, however, individuals are separated as well, the denial of some liberals notwithstanding. My quarrel is not with the liberal theory of institutional separation but with the way many of its proponents are blind to how liberal institutions affect identity. One of the consequences of liberal citizenship is that people from different ethnic backgrounds come into contact with each other in a variety of settings where the norm or law of nondiscrimination applies. Jews must publicly recognize others as Americans, not as Italian Americans or Sikh Americans. A Jewish person who owns a store must hire employees based on their qualifications, not on their identity. A person with Italian heritage who hires people to work in a government office must also ignore ethnic identity when screening job applicants. An Irish American must serve everybody who walks into her restaurant, regardless of her feelings about them. In these ordinary, everyday settings we can see the demands of liberal citizenship.

Lisa's Jewish identity may matter a lot in her personal life; she may have mostly Jewish friends and make sure that her lovers are Jewish. From the liberal state's point of view, these are private choices that can be ignored. But in other places where public norms apply, the state can demand that citizens don't make choices based on their ethnic identity. Lisa cannot believe—or rather, she cannot *act* on the belief—that because she is Jewish she is better than others and can treat others as inferior or different. Liberal citizens should not be treated differently in public settings because of their ethnic identity. Richard Rorty describes what happens when very different people meet: "All you need is the ability to control your feelings when people who strike you as irredeemably different show up at City Hall, or the greengrocers, or the bazaar. When this happens, you smile a lot, make the best deals you can, and, after a hard day's haggling, retreat to your club."[25]

"All you need is the ability to control your feelings"—Rorty makes it sound easy, but it is not. Liberal citizenship is far more robust than is usually acknowledged; it demands that liberal citizens act toward their fellow citizens in a certain way, even if they want to act otherwise. Rorty even suggests that citizens must pretend to like each other—"you smile a lot" in his bazaar (though liberalism does not prescribe this). Citizenship in the liberal state is not only about occasional voting or working in a community organization; liberal citizenship makes demands on people almost every day, when citizens are in a store, on the streets, and in the classroom. Citizenship is about how citizens see and treat others—and how they are viewed and treated by others.

Citizenship, however, is traditionally conceived of in terms of participation. Aristotle defined citizens as those who rule and are ruled in turn. Contemporary critics of liberalism often contend that the problem with liberalism is that it constructs a public sphere that makes rather weak demands on citizens. Echoing Marx, critics of liberalism complain that liberal citizenship allows people to be politically apathetic, purely private people, interested only in economic gain. Liberalism's foundations cannot lead to a

"firm theory of citizenship, participation, public goods or civic virtue."
One may be a liberal citizen and "yet do absolutely nothing after having
obtained" citizenship. Supporters of liberalism have a similar view of citizenship. Michael Walzer says that citizenship "is today a mostly passive
role: citizens are spectators who vote." Richard Flathman argues that "citizenship [is] one of the roles that we play." We are also parents, plumbers,
professors, and so forth.[26]

But the demands of liberal citizenship show up in many of these seemingly passive roles. Liberalism is not only about the arrangement of institutions; it is not just refraining from telling people how to live the good life.
Nor is liberal citizenship simply about voting or political participation.
Liberalism is also a prescription for how people ought to act when they
meet their fellow citizens in civil society and in the public square. In many
different settings liberal citizens may see others whom they dislike, but liberalism calls on them to control their feelings. Liberal citizens must put
away their hate and prejudices in public. The large demands of liberal citizenship can be seen in the fact that many white citizens in the United
States have been unable to follow them in their dealings with Black Americans. If it were so easy for people to control their feelings about others, if
the demands of liberal citizenship were as feeble as many suggest, there
would be a lot less racism and prejudice than there is today.[27]

The demands of liberal citizenship mean that there are virtues of liberal
citizenship. Liberalism cannot only be a theory of pluralism; it can't be
neutral on the good life and allow an infinite variety of ways of life to
flourish. Mediating the important liberal commitment to pluralism is liberalism's commitment to equal rights for citizens. The liberal commitment
to pluralism should not allow a store owner to discriminate, even if his
version of the good life means that he does not want to serve Black or
Jewish customers.

A merchant may hate Irish Americans or Jews or want to give preferen-
tial treatment to Italian Americans, but liberalism demands that he or she
do otherwise. While this demand is often ignored, it is also often followed,
sometimes because of the threat of legal penalties and sometimes because
of the profit that can be gained by refraining from discrimination. Although the state can teach the idea of mutual respect in the schools, the
liberal state cannot control its citizens' thoughts. The liberal state cannot
demand that people think of everyone as equal; it can merely demand that
citizens treat each other equally in public institutions. This is not, however,
a distinct dichotomy: our actions may affect our thoughts. It may not be
easy to treat others equally in public and then retreat to your club or home
to discriminate against these very same people. Aristotle noted this when
he discussed the character of individuals. "It is activities exercised on par-

ticular objects that make the corresponding character. This is plain from the case of people training for any contest or action; they practice the activity the whole time. Now not to know that it is from the exercise of activities on particular objects that states of character are produced is the mark of a thoroughly senseless person."[28]

People cannot just decide to change themselves and then be changed. Who we are depends not only on who we want to be. We must work to change who we are. To change one's character one must change one's actions. To become just, Aristotle said, one must perform just acts. People can habituate themselves to act justly; after some time, acting justly may become instinctual.

It is possible that the demands of liberal citizenship may have a similar effect on people's character. Habituated to treat others equally or at least civilly, liberal citizens may begin to look upon others equally or civilly. The demands that liberalism makes on citizens, the demands entailed by the quest for equal citizenship, mean that liberalism is not and cannot be "morally agnostic" on the character of its citizens, as Ronald Beiner contends. Beiner argues that in every society "moral life is based on ethos, that is, character formation according to socially bred customs and habit." Liberal society has an ethos as well, he claims—lack of ethos. Liberal citizens are not, Beiner complains, habituated to anything.[29] This argument has been encouraged by the liberals who insist that neutrality on the good life is at the core of liberalism. But the preconditions needed to allow people to pursue their version of the good life mean that liberal citizens are habituated to act in certain ways and not others. Liberal citizens must respect each other in public and treat each other accordingly. This seemingly minimal restraint can have far-reaching effects on the identity of liberal citizens. The ethos of liberal society is not an empty shell but has substance; the ethos of equal citizenship in the liberal state is not something that liberal citizens can ignore all the time. Critics of liberalism may still find liberal citizenship to be weak or morally defective in some way; they also may argue that not enough citizens live up to the demands of liberal citizenship. But these arguments need to be made. There is a substance to liberal citizenship that can be criticized but should not be ignored.[30]

These criticisms, however, need to take into account the diversity of most contemporary liberal societies. Many nonliberal theories of citizenship assume that citizens are homogeneous, or they bemoan the fact that citizens in liberal societies are akin to strangers.[31] In a society that is characterized by ethnic and racial diversity, many citizens are in fact strangers to each other. Embedded in liberal citizenship are the principles that lay the groundwork for citizens to listen to one another and treat one another as equals. These are precisely the principles needed to arbitrate relations among citizens who are not friends. This may not be a problem in a homogeneous state where discrimination is not an issue (although women and the poor may face discrimination), but discrimination is clearly a problem in a diverse place like the United States. The liberal character allows strangers to get along; it also allows them to become friends if they want.

The Transformation of
Ethnic Identity

Aristotle discussed how people can change their character if they so choose. The chances of people's actions affecting their beliefs are not quite as good if they are forced to act a certain way against their desires. Contact with others may confirm our worst suspicions about them. For some people, however, treating others equally on a routine basis may change how they think of others.[32] Liberal institutions encourage a belief in equality among liberal citizens; although this encouragement will sometimes be successful, it won't always be. The possibility that the constraints of liberal equality will lead to a change in people's attitudes can also result from what John Murray Cuddihy calls the *religion of civility*. Liberal citizens are, he contends, nice to each other so they can get along; this is the result of the "tyranny of democratic manners."[33] If people believe that they are equal, then it will be hard to maintain that they are somehow special or different from others. Some Jews, however, do not believe they are equal. They believe that they are better than others or, at the least, different because they think they are the "chosen people" or for some other reason. Yet they cannot discriminate in public settings because someone belongs to an ethnic or religious group that they dislike or because they think they are better than others. In public Jews have to get along with others. Citizens have to negotiate, discuss, and debate with each other. To do this, to get along in public, citizens are civil to each other. In public, ethnics say they are all equal—that, for political purposes at least, everyone is the same. When fighting for equal citizenship, Jews argued that they had the abilities to be citizens; they had the requisite rationality or the same capacity for loyalty to the state as others. The result of this doctrine, Cuddihy argues, is that "Judaism and Jews must pretend in public that they are like the [non-Jews]."[34] Jews can pretend they are equal for only so long before they—or their children—believe it. In other words, ethnics may actually believe what they say.

Habituated to argue for equality and habituated to act toward others as if they are equals, ethnics may find it difficult not to believe in equality. And the liberal idea of equality makes it harder for ethnics to retain a distinct identity. Ethnics can remain different in the private realm, but the division between public and private makes this hard. Ethnic identity is only one part of a person's life in the liberal state. In many public places, Lisa cannot discriminate against others in public. If Lisa cannot hire, fire, or serve people based on their identity, how can she distinguish between members of her group and others? Lisa may find that in many settings there are few distinguishing characteristics between Jewish Americans and others. Over time, she may see her fellow ethnics and other ethnics in a similar light. If this happens, however, her ethnic identity will weaken. If members of an ethnic group cannot distinguish between members of their group and others, then it may be hard to maintain a distinct ethnic identity.

Liberal citizenship means that citizens bracket off their ethnic identity to take on many of their roles. Lisa may not identify strongly with some of these roles; she may work in a store every day but hate her job and the people with whom she works. She may forget about work as soon as she arrives home. At home, she may partake in ethnic rituals and play an important role in her ethnic community. Before emancipation, of course, Lisa would have little choice about her identity; it would be intertwined with the Jewish community. In the liberal state, however, this is only one possibility for Lisa. She has choices about how she wants to identify. Because Lisa takes on roles that have little to do with her ethnicity, she can make connections with others based on shared interests that have nothing to do with ethnicity. Once she takes on a role, she can identify closely with it. Lisa may identify strongly with the Jewish community but go to a secular school. In the classroom she may find others who are not Jewish but who share her passion for twentieth-century literature, or she may find others with whom she likes to play basketball, or she may fall in love with someone who is not Jewish. She may make strong connections with those at work who are not Jewish. She may find herself increasingly identifying with some of the non-Jewish roles she takes on. Lisa may find that ethnicity is only one of many parts of her life and that it is far from the most important part. If this happens, Lisa's ethnic identity will change and probably weaken. In fact, this route has actually been traveled by many ethnics in the United States. The demands of liberal citizenship have already transformed the ethnic identities of many people.[35]

The possibility that nonethnic roles may become important to our identity is recognized by the Amish. The Amish are pacifists, so during wartime in the United States they either receive farm deferments or perform alternative service. During the Vietnam War, alternative service for Amish men of draft age meant serving in public hospitals. Amish leaders became unhappy with this arrangement; too many of the young Amish men "were led astray." After completing their alternative service, many Amish men did not want to return to the Amish community or could not, having married a non-Amish woman. Having taken on non-Amish roles, these Amish men began to identify with them, which weakened their Amish identity. Because of this threat to their community, the Amish leadership worked out an alternative arrangement to service in public hospitals for Amish men of draft age.[36]

Freely interacting with others does not inevitably lead to the weakening of ethnic identity, yet the Amish understand that this is a strong possibility. Some people's ethnic identity may be strengthened by interaction with others (by seeing how degenerate others are), but the ethnic identity of some will weaken. The forces bearing down on ethnicity will be too strong for some ethnics. For ethnic identity the paradox embedded in liberal citizenship is this: just as Lisa cannot discriminate against others because of their identity, she cannot be discriminated against because she is Jewish. When ethnics gain liberal citizenship, the distinctions between them and others can rather easily become murky. Lisa's interactions with non-Jews are not strictly regulated by the state and the Jewish community. This reveals an advantage of liberalism over preemancipation Europe: ethnics can interpret their identity as they wish in the liberal state. Their identity is no longer imposed upon them from above. Lisa need not dress the way her community wants her to, in a way that identifies her as Jewish. She can dress like non-Jews if she so chooses; she can live near non-Jews if she wants; she may live like them as well. She can eat nonkosher food with impunity. There is no reason to assume, with Marx, that the Jew's identity as a Jew will always triumph over his or her identity as a citizen. Of course, Lisa can also celebrate her Jewish identity if she chooses. In preemancipation times, the Jewish and Christian worlds were starkly divided, but with liberal citizenship Jews can and do live in both worlds. Jews can now interpret their own identity; they can decide for themselves what it means to be Jewish. Jews can ignore the dictates of the rabbis and remain Jewish. Liberal citizenship does not mean the inevitable end of Jewish identity, but it does mean that Jews can drop, add, and combine cultural practices in ways that will transform Jewish identity.

In her interactions with others, Lisa may find that members of other ethnic groups have admirable qualities and practices. She may find that she wants to copy some of their practices. When ethnics become accepted as citizens, when they are not discriminated against, their cultural practices are no longer exclusively theirs but can be copied by other members of the political community. Similarly, once ethnics are accepted by others, they can borrow the cultural practices of others. To make their life bearable here, immigrants bring their recipes and houses of worship with them. The wide variety of religions, cuisines, and forms of music in the United States has been bequeathed by ethnics. One of the markers of citizenship for ethnics is the acceptance and incorporation in American culture of elements of ethnic cultures. When St. Patrick's Day became a holiday recognized by many Americans and public officials, three things happened. First, Irish Americans were accepted as Americans. Second, the celebration of St. Patrick's Day no longer marked one as an Irish American. Third, the meaning of St. Patrick's Day was no longer defined by Irish Americans themselves but was open to debate by the entire political community. David Dinkins, the former mayor of New York, could insist that gays and lesbians be allowed to take part in the St. Patrick's Day celebrations. As the culture of the old country becomes further removed from ethnics and their descendants, the opportunity to partake in the ethnic rituals and customs of others increases. Consider this recent announcement in the *Albany Times Union:* "The German-American Club of Albany will observe St. Patrick's Day with a dinner-dance on March 19."[37]

Food is probably the most prominent marker of ethnicity in the United States today. Although food can be a barrier between cultures, more often in the United States ethnic foods are routinely enjoyed by members of different ethnic groups. After all, you need not have an Italian ancestor to enjoy pasta. Irish Americans, along with German Americans, can celebrate St. Patrick's Day by eating corned beef and sauerkraut.[38] Indeed, part of American culture includes a steady diet of ethnic foods; American cuisine is no longer restricted to hamburgers and hot dogs. Having access to a good Chinese restaurant, for example, is for many an important part of the American eating experience.[39] Other ethnic institutions have spread from their ethnic bases as well. Many ethnics established their own churches (and synagogues and mosques) soon after arriving here; the myriad of denominations that exist in the United States now is the result. Yet people with no German heritage can join the Lutheran church; many non–Christians celebrate Christmas. Some Americans with no Asian ancestry have become enthralled with Eastern religions over the past three decades. Americans of all sorts enjoy Irish folk music.[40]

The implications of the ability of people to share in the cultural practices of others are often lost on those who want to respect diversity. bell hooks argues that respecting diversity should be an important part of the feminist movement. To illustrate her argument, she discusses a Japanese-American student of hers who was reluctant to participate in feminist organizations because of the tendency of many feminists to speak aggressively and quickly; this student was raised to think before speaking and to consider the effects on others of what she wanted to say. hooks says that in class "we learned to allow pauses and appreciate them" and that, "by learning one another's cultural codes," she and her students learned to respect their differences. "Respecting diversity," she announces, "does not mean uniformity or sameness." hooks rightly included pauses in class, yet she misinterprets her own story, for all the people in the classroom learned to pause: "*By sharing this cultural code,* we created an atmosphere in the classroom that allowed for different communication patterns."[41] Everyone in the class—white, Black, and Latino students alike—learned about and shared the cultural practice of pausing before speaking. This does not mean that all of the students in the class became the same, of course, but hooks's story nicely shows the irony of respecting the cultural practices of others. To respect the cultures of others, it helps to learn about them, and, as we learn about the practices of others, we may decide to take them on as our own.

Political Participation and Identity

Because Marx did not realize the demands of liberal citizenship, he exaggerated the divisiveness of ethnic group identity in the liberal state. The demands of liberal citizenship make it hard to keep up vigorous and distinctive ethnic identities. These demands affect all citizens, but they may be even more poignant for the politically active. Liberal citizens who are at all politically engaged think about issues that affect the entire political community; they debate these issues and expect their elected representatives to debate and vote on them. Although there are many issues that affect certain communities more than others, public officials must debate and vote on many issues, not just those that affect certain communities. Political participation, J. S. Mill noted, entails the ability to think past oneself and about others. Mill argued that political participation would cause people to leave their narrow self-interest behind.

In response to those who argued against extending suffrage to the working class because the working class was not politically astute, Mill responded that the working class would never become politically informed until it had the vote: "It is by political discussion that the manual laborer, whose employment is routine . . . is taught that remote causes, and events which take place far off, have a most sensible effect even on his personal interests." But, Mill argued, laborers will not partake in political discussions if they do not have any political influence, for "political discussions fly over the heads of those who have no votes." Because few would become interested in politics without political influence, Mill argued for the extension of citizenship in nineteenth-century Britain: "The maximum of the invigorating effect of freedom upon the character is only obtained when the person acted on either is, or is looking forward to becoming, a citizen as fully privileged as any other."[42]

Give people the right to participate, Mill said, and they will become politically informed. Becoming politically active, Mill argued, would engage people's minds and make them think differently; politics was a sort of education. Participation, he argued, would transform the way a citizen thought: "He is called upon, while so engaged, to weigh interests not his own; to be guided, in case of conflicting claims, by another rule than his private partialities; to apply, at every turn, principles and maxims which have for their reason of existence the common good. . . . He is made to feel himself one of the public, and whatever is for their benefit to be his benefit."[43] Participation may lead citizens to confront and consider the views and arguments of others; it may also lead citizens to reconsider and reformulate their own views. Citizens may not be able to vote simply in their self-interest, for their self-interest may not be so simple. This may force citizens to think more deeply about a policy and its effects. When citizens participate politically, they may begin to think of who is affected by politics; they may see that political decisions affect many people, not just themselves. And citizens may begin to think about others and their needs.

Mill's view may be too optimistic; participation will not always have the transforming affect on people that he thought it would. Consider Thomas Hobbes's view of democracy. Ridiculing democracy and discussion, Hobbes argued that discussion allows us "to have our wisdom undervalued before our own faces, . . . to hate and to be hated, by reason of the disagreement of opinions, . . . [and to] lay open our secret councils and advices to all, to no purpose and without any benefit; to neglect the affairs of our own family."[44] The only transformation that participation leads to, Hobbes said, is to increase our hate for those with whom we disagree. Ethnics may learn to hate other ethnics when they participate; they may find that their political participation leads them to neglect their community. They may decide that they are better off staying home than participating. Or they may decide to participate in politics only to further their ethnic communities' interests.

But this may not be so easy to do. Engaging in public debate may change how citizens view the political community. Although Mill may be too optimistic about participation's effects, participation does constrain the way people can talk about politics. The demands of liberal citizenship mean that citizens cannot simply announce that they desire something, even if that is what they want to say. Hanna Pitkin explained the effects of participation on citizens: "We are forced, as Joseph Tussman has put it, to transform 'I want' into 'I am entitled to,' a claim that becomes negotiable by public standards." Citizens must explain why they think a certain policy should be implemented, and to do so they need to appeal to public standards in a public language. "We are forced to find or create a common language of purposes and aspirations, not merely clothe our private outlook in public disguise, but to become aware ourselves of its public meaning." Citizens need to try to make the larger political community understand their reasons and needs if they are to convince others that they should support a specific policy. Citizens have to think about what sort of appeals to the larger community will work; this makes citizens think about the larger community, its problems, and its needs. As citizens change the way they think, their identity may change. Citizens become part of the larger community even as they battle parts of it. Engaging in politics, citizens make allies in their political battles and so learn about others and the things they care about. As citizens participate, they "learn to think about the standards themselves, about our stake in the existence of standards, of justice, of our community, even of our opponents and enemies in the community: *so that afterwards we are changed.*" Citizens "discover connections to others and learn to care about these connections."[45] As citizens learn to counter the arguments of others they may even find themselves persuaded by these arguments.

To be sure, American political life is filled with "special interest" groups, but even these groups couch their claims in terms of the common good. They may try to mask their selfish desires with an appeal to the common good, but they almost always make this appeal. They rarely say that they want a bill passed because it is good for them, regardless of its other consequences. They instead argue that, although they may benefit from this bill, so too will many others; that, overall, this bill is better for the community than it is harmful. By making public appeals these groups open themselves up to unmasking; as Hobbes said, participation means that you open up your "secret councils and advices to all." Special interest groups are often criticized when they are perceived to look out only for their own interests, as surely some of them do. Having exposed their interests to others, they try to defend their interests, which they must do in a common language, a language that other citizens can understand.

Participation will not necessarily lead people to a concern with the common good as Mill argued; the common good is not always so obvious or may be of little interest to some. People involved in community organizations, however, may have to build coalitions with others, forcing them to consider the interests and views of others. When people lobby a legislature, mount a letter-writing campaign, stage a protest, or campaign for a candidate, they must try to figure out ways to convince others to side with them. By forcing people to think of others, participation may change ethnic identity. Ethnics may become convinced that they should no longer be concerned about only their ethnic community, but also other ethnic or nonethnic groups or the larger political community. This may lead to devaluation of their ethnic identity. (The term *people of color* is, for example, an attempt to get Blacks, Latinos, and Asians Americans to think of themselves as part of the same group so they can together address common problems. If members of these groups think of themselves as people of color instead of Blacks, Latinos, or Asians, their identity has changed.) Elected officials find that they must work with others to get bills passed; coalitions with people from different groups and with different constituencies must be built. Even if politicians are largely concerned with their ethnic constituents, they still must make coalitions with other politicians, which entails learning about issues that affect others.[46]

It is not surprising that weak ethnics participate in politics more than do strong ethnics. Strong ethnics, like the Amish, interpret policies and issues only through the eyes of their particular community; most do not take part in public life. There are Amish leaders, but they are interested only in leading their communities. It is no accident that Amish people do not run for public office. To get elected they could not always portray themselves as Amish. They would have non-Amish constituents in their charge. They would have to think about the needs and wants of others; they would routinely have to make political allies with non-Amish people. Doing this would almost certainly mean that they would have to reconceive themselves—after participating they would be changed. They would have to think beyond their small communities, which could lead to making strong connections to others. The Amish rarely join community organizations that include others because this may alter their identity.

Community and Diversity

The demands of liberal citizenship make it hard to keep a distinctive ethnic identity, but this difficulty does not translate into inevitability. The range of ethnic identification in the United States is quite diverse, but, with each passing generation, ethnic identity often fades. Because most ethnics strive for inclusion in civil society, because they want to be seen as equals by the state and other citizens, because of the demands of liberal citizenship, Marx's fear that liberal citizenship allows group identity to become divisive is mostly unfounded. Marx cannot be blamed for not anticipating twentieth-century American Supreme Court decisions that outlawed discrimination in civil society, but he did not understand the impetus behind these decisions and similar laws passed by Congress—the desire of most ethnics to be treated equally in the public sphere and in civil society. Most ethnics in liberal societies clamor for laws outlawing discrimination, since discrimination in civil society often harms their plans and projects.

Many ethnics want more than formal equality; they want to know that they can be an important part of American society. Many ethnics celebrate when "one of their own" becomes a prominent American. For example, many people of Greek heritage were proud when Michael Dukakis ran for president in 1988. Dukakis did not do anything quintessentially Greek; rather, he promised to act as an American for all Americans if elected. Still, for many Greek Americans, his running for president had considerable symbolic value; Greek Americans were accepted and successful in the United States. This is a typical story in ethnic lore. Ethnic heroes are people who have "made it" in the United States. The influence of ethnicity has made the United States diverse, as the practices and institutions of different ethnic groups have become diffuse, spreading out across the country, and as people with different heritages have combined elements from different cultures into their lives.

Yet some ethnics may shut themselves off from others. Marx did not point to a phantom tension in the liberal split between the public and private. This tension exists, even if the problems it causes are not nearly as severe as Marx thought. By allowing ethnicity to continue, even in circumscribed form, liberalism allows some citizens to stay away from public life and civil society to retain their identity. Ethnics must establish walls between themselves and others to maintain their identity as ethnics. (It is no accident that many of the Jewish ghettoes in medieval Europe were built voluntarily by Jews.) Some ethnics may live near their fellow ethnics and work in their ethnic community; they may devote much of their free time to ethnic organizations. They may shy away from participation in and not identify with the larger community. This is not easy to do; it probably means forgoing many of the opportunities offered by many universities, cities, and jobs in the United States. Some ethnics, though, are willing to make this choice.

The tension in liberal citizenship may also play itself out in the lives of some ethnics. Some ethnics may be torn between their concern and loyalty to their ethnic community and the attachments they may make to others in their nonethnic roles or their loyalty to the larger political community. These different roles and attachments will not always conflict, but sometimes they will, forcing ethnics to sometimes make painful choices.

The tension in liberal theory between the public and private spheres is not, however, cause in itself to abolish these two spheres, along with civil society. We need to know the alternative to this tension before we disparage the public/private/civil society distinction. One alternative, the one Marx wanted, is not an improvement over accepting this tension. There's little reason to believe with Marx that separate identities would fade away after the revolution of the proletariat. The revolution, if it is to come, will happen after the influence of ethnicity in the United States has already pervaded American life. It is hard to imagine how the revolution would obliterate the different manners, religions, foods, and customs of Americans. Indeed, my argument that ethnicity is transformed by liberal citizenship should not be construed as implying that ethnic practices evaporate. Many people who do not identify as ethnic nonetheless inherit ethnic practices. Some people want to touch people when they talk to them; others use their hands a lot when they talk; still others like some distance between them and their conversation partner. These same people may not identify as ethnics, but their hand gestures and way of talking may be inherited from ethnic ancestors; so too might be their religion, some of the foods they eat, and so forth. Many people are unaware of how they are influenced by ethnic cultures, but they are influenced just the same. Even when ethnic cultures fade, the practices of these cultures may live on. Indeed, so many different peoples have come to live in the United States that the mark of ethnics is indelibly stamped on the country, even if this stamp is a hodgepodge of different cultural practices. A program to force people to give up their different practices can only be accomplished by restricting people's lives in rather painful, draconian ways.

Moreover, ethnicity (and nationality) is simply more resilient than Marx thought; it is not simply a product of the material conditions of a society. Judaism is not the same as capitalism, as Marx asserted. Jews have survived several thousand years and in many different economic systems and places. They have fought tenaciously to hold onto their identity, sometimes at the cost of their lives. Just as the Jews have survived the collapse of other economic systems and empires, the Jews will probably survive the demise of welfare state capitalism, if that happens. Other ethnics have also survived many tumultuous events, even if these same events have transformed them; some ethnics will undoubtedly outlive the revolution as ethnics. Many people who feel attached to their ethnic identity will not give up this identity very readily.

People interested in constructing a larger sense of community among liberal citizens would do well to allow ethnicity to endure within the confines of liberal citizenship. If you insist that ethnics drop their identity, you immediately divide the political community, defeating the very purpose of the attempt to force people to shed their ethnicity. Diversity, Locke argued, cannot be avoided. Refusal to accept this diversity is the cause of conflict, he said, not the diversity itself.[47] When you demand that people give up their ethnic identities, you demand that they change who they are, that they abruptly alter their conceptions of themselves, something that is not done easily or willingly. Liberal citizenship will transform ethnic identity gradually. This transformation does not necessarily mean the end of ethnic identity; some ethnic practices will survive, perhaps even thrive, in liberal society. Some practices will be noticeably ethnic; other ethnic practices will survive even if they are not identifiable with a specific ethnic group.

Liberalism is partly founded on the realization that the quest for uniformity in some areas will lead to more divisiveness, not more harmony. There is no reason to believe this is less true for religious groups than for ethnic groups, especially since religion and ethnicity often intertwine. Ethnicity will cause some division in the liberal political community, although not as much as Marx seemed to fear, but attempts to eradicate ethnicity will probably cause even more divisions. When ethnic groups become accepted in the United States, their practices become part of the larger community. Accept ethnics and they can be incorporated into the political community; accept them and the community can be built on liberal citizenship. Indeed, the liberal community in the United States is constituted by its diversity. Acceptance of this diversity strengthens the community. Reject ethnic identity and the political community may very well explode, as it did in Locke's time.

In a large, advanced industrial society, ethnicity may be a compelling connection between people, a shared bond on which other bonds can be built. Ethnic identity may be a way for some to make a large, anonymous world a little more intimate. When two people who share an ethnic identity meet, they may feel a strong connection. This connection may fade with time (they may not like one another), but it also may be the beginning of a meaningful relationship. Ethnicity may be a great source of comfort. Some may feel that their fellow ethnics understand them better and know their cultural practices better than do others. They may feel more comfortable in their ethnic communities. Some liberal citizens, perhaps most, will not find much comfort and meaning in their ethnicity. But attempts to destroy ethnic identity will take away an important source of meaning for some people, making a large, anonymous world larger and more anonymous for them. Marx wanted to create some kind of universal community, but the details of this community were quite sketchy; it is unclear how this community can be constructed in a large, modern state. To destroy ethnic communities in the name of a larger, vague community may very well leave people in the liberal state even more separated from each other than they currently are.

CHAPTER 4

PLURALISTIC INTEGRATION

IN THE EARLY PART of this century, immigration and ethnicity were important issues in the United States, a result of the massive immigration that had begun in the early 1880s. The debates were often between assimilationists and nativists: the former argued that the new immigrants could become "American," while the latter contended that the new immigrants threatened America's "Anglo-Saxon stock." But this debate did not satisfy everyone. In 1915 Horace Kallen, a philosophy professor, argued for a culturally plural America. Kallen decried the pressures to assimilate faced by immigrants. The assimilationists tried to change members of different ethnic groups into people similar in background, tradition, outlook, and spirit to the descendants of the Anglo-Saxons, he charged. Attempts at assimilation, however, would never quite succeed, according to Kallen. People are simply not that malleable. Kallen argued that ethnic identity is a part of each person that cannot be forgotten or ignored. It is the strongest tie between people, even stronger than class.

> The poor of two different peoples tend to be less like-minded than the poor and rich of the same peoples. At his core, no human being, even in a "state of nature," is a mere mathematical unit like the "economic man." Behind him in time and tremendously in him in quality are his ancestors, around him in space are his relatives and kin, carrying in common with him the inherited organic set from a remote common ancestry.

A person can change his clothes, his values, and his philosophy, but "whatever else he changes he can't change his grandfather."[1] The idea that everyone is a rational calculator, looking out only for his economic interests, is flawed, Kallen argued. We all are, he said, part of our ethnic or national group, as it is part of us, regardless of what we do or what is done to us.

What troubled the nativists, Kallen contended, was difference. To form America into one nationality as the nativists wanted would be to deny different groups the liberty to preserve their own institutions and cultures. Furthermore, the idea that an American identity could be created, Kallen maintained, was misguided: "In historic times so far as known no new ethnic types have originated." There is no reason to believe, Kallen argued, that the old ethnic identities would disappear in favor of a new, American one. Kallen wanted to redefine what Americanization meant; to be "Americanized" should be the opportunity for immigrants to be free "from the stigma of 'foreigner' [as] they develop group self-respect." As groups gain self-respect, they learn or recall "the spiritual heritage of their nationality." Soon after, infused with cultural pride, "the public schools, the libraries and the clubs become beset with demands [from ethnics] for texts in the national language and literature." To preserve liberty, Kallen contended, America must allow different nationalities to flourish. He called for a federal republic, with its substance being a "democracy of nationalities."[2]

Although Kallen's argument for cultural pluralism had little effect when it appeared, it has recently been heard anew, particularly (but not exclusively) by educational theorists. The authors of a book on multicultural education, for example, praise Kallen's ideas on cultural pluralism. They resurrect his argument for cultural pluralism, which, they argue, means that "all cultural, racial and ethnic groups in American society have the right to mutually coexist and have the freedom to maintain their own identities and lifestyles." Another book on education approvingly states that different cultural groups can now contribute to "the national culture while maintaining their distinct identity." Though they do not mention Kallen, L. S. Lustgarten's arguments are uncannily reminiscent of Kallen's. Lustgarten contends that ethnic minorities should "be recognized as independent legal entities" and should be permitted "unrestricted freedom to follow their own customs and religious practices."[3]

Iris Marion Young does not invoke Kallen either, but her arguments are similar in some respects. Although Young says "that individuals should be free to pursue life plans," she argues that "it is foolish to deny the reality of groups." Young maintains that it is a mistake to give only individuals political standing. A better alternative, she says, is to affirm group identity in politics: "Radical democratic pluralism acknowledges and affirms the public and political significance of social group differences as a means of ensuring the participation and inclusion of everyone in social and political institutions." She calls for institutional mechanisms and public resources supporting self-organization of group members so groups can analyze and propose policy proposals that affect group members; she also calls for group veto power over policies that directly affect the group. Young is particularly concerned with oppressed groups, which for her means members of racial groups as well as the elderly, gays, and the disabled. But her definition of cultural imperialism means that many ethnics, particularly new immigrants, are oppressed as well and so deserve some kind of public recognition as a group.[4]

Unfortunately, the variety of ways in which people identify with their ethnic group make the vision of the cultural pluralists misguided. Cultural pluralists do not take into account the way cultures change, particularly after the effects of immigration and industrialization are accounted for. The liberal approach to cultural groups recognizes that the boundaries between cultures are quite fluid. Limits to cultural pluralism are intrinsic to liberalism itself. Liberalism emphasizes the protection of cultural practices that are compatible with liberalism, but it either forbids or discourages practices that are illiberal. This emphasis on particular practices may transform certain cultures, but a culture should not be considered sacrosanct simply because it is a culture. Some cultural practices, often because they are anti-egalitarian, should not be protected by liberals. This emphasis on practices distinguishes the liberal approach to culture from the approach of cultural pluralists, who blindly celebrate all ethnic cultures, regardless of their practices. Yet, as Kallen noted, group self-respect is important for ethnics. Cultural pluralists are right to point out that the onus of change is too often on the shoulders of only immigrants and ethnics and not on those of citizens already settled. The demands of liberal citizenship mean that liberal citizens must learn to accept ethnic practices that are compatible with liberalism. Instead of trying to become a culturally plural society, American society should strive for "pluralistic integration," where, within liberal limits, ethnic groups can preserve their differences.[5]

The Limits to
Cultural Pluralism

Kallen noted that ethnic groups tended to congregate in the same geographic area. Scandinavians lived in Minnesota and Wisconsin; the Irish lived in the Northeast; Jews lived in New York. Although ethnic groups tend to congregate in the same areas, few areas in the United States are ethnically homogeneous. Kallen himself was Jewish but spent some time early in his career teaching in Wisconsin.

Kallen did not say what the political structures of each ethnic group would look like or what would happen to minorities within each area. (Although Kallen recognized racism against Blacks, he did not distinguish between ethnic and racial groups. Perhaps this was because of the rampant racism faced by many immigrants when Kallen wrote about cultural pluralism.) Because ethnic groups were and are geographically dispersed, it is hard to imagine what Kallen's federation of nationalities would look like. Kallen's modern day followers do not improve upon him in this regard. Lustgarten and the other cultural pluralists do not address these problems, nor do they say how the political community is to decide which ethnic groups should be politically recognized.

Kallen argued that ethnic group members tended to congregate into the same occupations; this would, he thought, preserve ethnic differences. Kallen was right to note that much of ethnic culture here was rooted in economic conditions, but ethnic group congregation in the same jobs is hardly something to celebrate, nor does it tell us anything immutable about culture. Many ethnics took undesirable, low-paying jobs when they first arrived in the United States. Jews were garment workers in sweatshops, Italian Americans were construction workers, and Polish Americans worked in steel factories.[6] The available jobs at the time of their immigration to the United States, along with the skills they brought with them, determined the jobs ethnics took. Unsurprisingly, these jobs did not please many immigrants. Many ethnics (or their children) successfully fled the horrid economic conditions that greeted them in the United States as soon as they could.

To be sure, economic domination and oppression is one of the surest routes to cultural pluralism. Prevent members of certain groups from having access to the dominant institutions of a society, and they will almost surely retain their different culture or construct an alternative one. The denial of citizenship to Turkish "guest workers" in Germany illustrates this point. During the 1950s and 1960s, the German government invited Turkish citizens to work in Germany. Although Germany encouraged the Turks to return to Turkey in the 1970s, most stayed in Germany. The Turks work at mostly low-paying, low-skilled jobs, usually living near their fellow Turks. Until the 1980s, the Turks had few rights and could easily be expelled from Germany. German citizenship is difficult for the guest workers or their children to obtain. Unsurprisingly, the culture of the Turks is different from (and subordinate to) German culture. The Turks are marked out as unequal: they are not German. Their access to many jobs and to higher education is restricted by both formal and informal means. These Turkish Germans do not share in Turkish culture, however; many have been born in Germany and know little about Turkey. They created a

Turkish-German culture; their subordination ensures that their way of life will remain distinct from that of other Germans.[7]

Ethnics would probably have constructed and maintained distinct cultures in the United States if they too had been forced to remain in low-paying jobs. (Indeed, many of the cultural practices of Black Americans spring from their subordinate status in the United States.) Deny ethnics liberal citizenship, and the effects of liberal citizenship on ethnic identity will not take place. The challenge is to give immigrants (or, at the least, their children) the chance to get good jobs. The social mobility in an industrial economy provides the groundwork for people to mix with others of different backgrounds, working together and living near each other.[8]

The examples of Black Americans and Turkish Germans show that cultural and racial hierarchies can exist in modern economies. Liberal citizenship, in combination with the conditions of a modern economic system, reduces the importance of ethnicity. When liberal citizenship is successfully granted to ethnics, they are no longer restricted to certain occupations. Their members can choose, like other equal citizens, the occupations they want. With many different occupations available to people in a modern economy, ethnics with liberal citizenship will find themselves working alongside many who do not share their ethnic background. With the money they make, these ethnics can (and do) move into neighborhoods with people from other groups.

Kallen did not recognize the possibility that ethnic cultures might be transformed, nor did he see the creation of a new, American identity, because he mistakenly thought that cultures were somehow biologically part of people. Cultural differences are identifiable "to the end of generations," he said. Not even intermarriage changes this. "Intermarriage or no intermarriage, racial quality persists and is identifiable. . . . Different races responding to the same stimuli are still different, and no environmental influence . . . can ever remold them into an indifferent sameness."[9]

It's true that people must have some culture, but this does not mean they are biologically attached to a specific culture. Cultures are not independent, free-floating forces. They are rooted in economic, political, and social structures; climate; land; food; and so forth. What food is eaten by people depends on what food is available, which in turns depends on climate and soil (and wealth). Unsurprisingly, people in Scandinavia eat different foods than do people in India. Architecture can also depend on climate. The amount of precipitation in an area will determine how roofs are constructed; heat or cold will influence other building decisions. Climate and the crops and animals that inhabit a piece of land will help determine the clothing of the land's inhabitants. The landscape, too, can be connected to a person's cultural identity. An immigrant from Laos who felt quite dislocated in the United States explained how the landscape affected him. "In Laos we believed there were spirits in the mountains. Here maybe the American Indians believe in spirits, but those (pointing in the direction of a nearby mountain range) are *their* mountains, not ours."[10] Clearly, religion and class affect culture, but the shape of their influence is tied to the location of the cultural group.

Although some Italian Americans may feel a connection to Italy that other Americans lack, this does not mean that Italian Americans and Italians share a culture. When immigrants come to the United States, their culture is wrenched from its roots and will inevitably change as they and their children make America their home. The weather, the soil, and the economic, political, and social structures of the United States will be different from those of their former country. This means that Italian Americans are not the same as Italians; members of these two groups have (at least) two different cultures. After Italians immigrate to America, they help create and become part of a new culture. They make up a new ethnic group, Kallen's proclamation that no new ethnic groups have formed notwithstanding.

Cultures change as new ideas, inventions, and political structures take root. Although cultures change all the time, the pace of change for immigrants is usually accelerated. When immigrants come to the United States, they enter an industrial society with a mobile population that at least pays lip service to the idea of equality, that has an extensive educational system, and that gives citizens the right to vote and voice their opinions about politics. These values and institutions will affect the changes in the culture of immigrants. This does not mean that all of the cultural values of immigrants immediately change when they arrive on the shores of the United States. Immigrants bring their values and practices with them, and some of these are incorporated into American culture. Surely, the old cultural values and practices will have some effect on immigrants and their children. But, just as surely, these values and practices will change.

Undoubtedly, many in the first generation will have trouble accepting the changes wrought by their move—they grew up in and know best another culture. Our identity is tied up with our memories; who we are depends on who we were. We may sometimes want to change our identity, but this means reflecting on who we were; it means we react to our memories. Immigrants have memories of the old country, of the customs and traditions of their native land. With these memories, they often stand between two cultures. They often fondly remember (part of) their past, but they are in a place where that past can no longer continue on the path it was taking. Cultures always change; they are always moving along a path. Just as the culture of Italian Americans changes, so does Italian culture change. But the ways in which they change are different. The path of change for immigrants has been radically altered; they have moved, in a sense, onto a path that is different from the one they were on in the old country. The memories of the old path are an important part of the identities of most immigrants, but these memories will be lost or, at least, transformed. Their children and grandchildren will have very different memories; born in a different land, these generations will have memories rooted in a different place. The cultural influence of our grandparents will probably not disappear; it has influenced our parents, who have influenced us. But the other influences on our lives may mean that the influence of our grandparents is rather small. A biological connection to our grandparents does not translate into a cultural connection.

Young, perhaps reacting to the misguided Americanization programs in our history, argues against the assimilation of immigrants. "Self-annihilation is an unreasonable and unjust requirement of citizenship. The fiction, poetry, and songs of American cultural minorities brim over with the pain and loss such demands inflict, documenting how thoroughly assimilationist values violate basic respect for persons."[11] Evidence of pain, however, is not an argument that a policy should be changed. There *has* been too much pressure to assimilate in this country, but Young's argument is too simple; it ignores the ways in which cultures are shaped and formed and the small chance that ethnics really have of keeping intact their culture from the old country. Much of this pain is surely caused by generational differences, differences between people who grew up in the old country and those who don't know this other culture very well, having grown up in the United States. A common cause for this pain is intermarriage; ethnics often want their children to marry within their ethnic group, but the children often fall in love with people from a different group. Pain, in this situation, is inevitable. If the children follow their parents' wishes, they will hurt; if they do not, their parents will.

Fights over intermarriage are often fights over which memories—and their attendant identities—will survive. When the offspring of ethnics feel more attachment to the United States than to the old country, the possibility of intermarriage and of the transformation of identity increases dramatically. What is the identity of the offspring of an Italian-American man and an Irish-American woman? What happens when their child marries someone with a different ethnic ancestry? What ethnic memories will their children have? Under these sorts of circumstances, it is difficult to see how ethnic identity can have a strong hold on those who intermarry or on their children. The immigrant generation can try to pass on their memories and their identity, but, without roots in a specific place, only a portion will be passed on successfully. This is why Stephen Steinberg doubts that even robust ethnic cultures can last long in the United States: "As transplanted minorities, ripped from their cultural moorings and lacking a territorial base, [their] cultural survival would have been problematic under the best of circumstances."[12]

Indeed, intermarriage between ethnics by the third generation is so common that I doubt it can be called intermarriage anymore.[13] Liberal citizenship, as I've argued, allows people to have many different attachments and interests, many of which will have little to do with ethnicity. For many, ethnic identity will merely be one among many attachments. The sociological evidence on ethnicity is unsurprisingly clear and convincing; by the third generation, there is not much left to ethnic cultures in the United States. Along several dimensions, ethnicity fades for many white ethnics: food, language, living arrangements in neighborhoods, friendships, and so forth.[14] While some ethnic differences can be detected among whites, these differences are small.

Many ethnics by the third generation have weak ethnic attachments. They have what Herbert Gans calls symbolic ethnicity, an ethnicity "of the last resort." Third or fourth generation ethnics hold onto symbols of their ethnicity, going to an occasional parade celebrating an ancestral saint or identifying with the country of origin, but these symbols have little to do with the way people live their lives. Many people want to express their ethnicity, but this ethnicity does not play an instrumental role in their lives as it did for the first and perhaps second generations. "The old ethnic cultures serve no useful function for third generation ethnics who lack direct and indirect ties to the old country and neither need nor have much knowledge of it."[15]

As ethnicity becomes increasingly symbolic and intermarriage with other ethnics climbs, there are more and more people of mixed ethnic background in the United States. They often choose the part of their heritage with which they want to identity. For those who want to celebrate their ethnicity, the celebration can take place with few constraints imposed upon them by others. Some people, however, do not want to express any part of their ethnicity, and there are an increasing number of whites here who do not adhere to an ethnic group at all. Many white Americans simply think of themselves as Americans.[16]

The fading of ethnicity for some Americans and the high rate of intermarriage pose a huge challenge for cultural pluralists. To what ethnic groups do the offspring of interethnic marriages belong? If ethnic groups are to have political standing, presumably everyone has to be assigned to an ethnic group. This is not a minor problem that can be easily dismissed, not with massive intermarriage and tens of millions of Americans with a weak ethnic identity. What should be done with those Americans who do not identify with any ethnic group? or who identify with two? Should they be forced to choose one? And what about those ethnics who have borrowed the cultural practices of other ethnics? Without good answers to these questions—and I do not think that good answers are available—neither ethnic group representation nor a federation of nationalities is a good idea.[17]

Illiberal Cultural Practices

Empty, rootless lives do not await those who choose to forgo an ethnic identity or the many who identify only in symbolic ways. Many people, in fact, want to flee their cultural attachments.[18] They may find the ways of their parents constraining; they may want to explore the other cultures and kinds of people in the United States. Many people tend to romanticize the past, but in doing so they often forget about suffering. When people remember past pain and suffering, however, they may realize that the changes in ethnic culture are not only cause for regret. Irving Howe explained that "some time ago I attended a pageant in an eastern city recreating the Lower East Side: pushcarts, onion rolls, flexibly-priced suits, etc. Someone asked me whether anything was missing and I answered . . . that a touch of reality might have been added by a tubercular garment worker spitting blood from his years of exhaustion in a sweat shop."[19] Nostalgia for the old ethnic cultures is often misplaced. The loss of seventy- or eighty-hour work weeks, tubercular garment workers, and child labor is hardly something to mourn. Although changes in society may mean that something is lost—perhaps families are not as tight-knit as they once were—the gains for most people have outweighed the losses. Families who lived together in the same room may have been close, but they were also overworked and malnourished and, so, extremely prone to sickness.

Moreover, people who eschew ethnic cultures are not rootless; rather, it is the ethnic cultures that often lack connectedness to their surroundings. Italian culture can flourish easily in Italy, but it is no surprise that it will be impossible for it to flourish in the United States. An attempt to keep the culture of Italy or Poland alive in the United States is actually an attempt to keep the culture's adherents rootless. The complicated structure of cultures cannot simply be transported from place to place. You cannot take a few thousand people from one land, plunk them in another, and expect their culture to survive intact. Even an ethnic culture that thrives in the United States is different from the culture of the "home country"; ethnic cultures are a mix of the old and new cultures. Symbolic ethnics are no longer rooted in cultures that are torn from their foundations. Instead, they interpret their cultural heritage in the context of a new country; their heritage is mostly rooted in the United States, not elsewhere. The real question about the culture of immigrants is not if they will change; undoubtedly, they will. A better question is to ask *how* these cultures will and should change.

Some ethnic practices will survive in the United States, although not all ethnic cultural practices can be accepted here. This is perhaps the biggest blind spot in the theories of cultural pluralism; some ethnic practices violate important liberal values and so ought to be discouraged or forbidden. Practices that pose a physical threat to others should be forbidden. Practices that do not pose a direct physical threat to anyone but that nonetheless violate liberal principles should be discouraged by the liberal state. The liberal political values of equality and nondiscrimination ought to be taught in the schools and realized in institutions in the public sphere and in civil society. Liberals should not, however, charge into people's homes to make sure that parents teach their children the liberal value of equality. The private realm is not open to any intrusion the state wants to make. The liberal state should foster the principles of equality and nondiscrimination, but it should not try to impose these values on people at all costs. The state can, however, prevent physical harm with force—it can and should enter the homes of citizens who physically abuse their children.

Attitudes toward women and their role in society are often at the center of cultural clashes in the United States. Although American society is far from achieving equality between men and women, many immigrants from traditional societies find the freedom that women do have in the United States antithetical to their cultural values. They often do not want their daughters to go to college, choose their mates, or live independent lives of any kind, regardless of their age.[20] The example of gender is not random. The control over the boundaries of an ethnic group often centers around control of women's bodies. Since women give birth, they are often seen as the ones who will continue the ethnic group; consequently, the leaders of ethnic groups—often men—try to control women's bodies. The liberal state, however, should insist that all girls attend school and that they ought to be able to attend college if they want. If ethnic women want to leave their ethnic communities because they find these communities oppressive, they should be able to do so. The political community should not, in the name of cultural pluralism, support the attempts of ethnic communities to prevent their daughters from leaving. This is demanded by the liberal principles of nondiscrimination and equality.[21]

Indeed, as middle class white ethnic women enter the work force in greater numbers, the chances for ethnic transformation probably increase considerably. When women stayed home to take care of their families, they could be the caretakers of ethnic identity. Unlike their husbands, they would not necessarily study and work with many people from other ethnic groups. Instead, women would often marry young, with their communities typically consisting of church (or synagogue), neighborhood, and family. As women enter the work force, they are more able to meet and fall in love with men with different backgrounds. Those women who do marry often do so at a later age than in the days before the modern feminist movement; this increases their opportunity to meet and marry someone who is not from their neighborhood or church or even from their college.[22] The push for gender equality will probably weaken ethnic ties. (As the opportunity to support themselves increases, some women decline to marry men at all, sometimes for reasons of sexuality. This will change ethnic identity as well.)

Liberal citizens should welcome immigrants into the United States; citizens should try to learn from immigrants and make their transition here as easy as possible. But this does not mean that liberal citizens have to accept all of the practices and values of ethnics. Even practices that some ethnic communities may see as central to their identity may be ruled out by the liberal state. When Sikh school children wear daggers to school—daggers are an important part of Sikh dress and identity—the state can and should demand that the daggers be left at home (or that they have rubber blades). The state should demand this not out of antipathy to the Sikhs, but out of concern for the school children who might be injured or killed by the daggers. In a violent society, prudence dictates outlawing weapons in schools, regardless of their importance to some communities.

Minimal values and rules that constitute the liberal community need to be followed for the community to function. Young, given her political commitment to helping the oppressed, would not support the oppression of women in the name of cultural pluralism. In fact, Young says that culture should be politicized; she wants people to revise cultural norms that contribute to the oppression of others.[23] Those practices that contribute to oppression, argues Young, ought to change. I agree, but it is not only dominant groups that have oppressive practices. Unfortunately, few cultural pluralists consider the possibility that the liberal state may be right to reject some cultural practices, probably because their celebration of all ethnic cultures is quite vague. Cultural pluralists argue that all cultures should be supported. They fail to say how one state can coherently support many different and conflicting values. If a federation of nationalities is a bad idea, as I've argued, how are ethnic cultural values translated into political practices? Does the state say that employers cannot discriminate against women, except if they belong to a specific ethnic group? How is ethnic group membership determined? What happens if many people suddenly claim membership in an ethnic group that is exempt from the principle of nondiscrimination?

Furthermore, ethnic claims are often masks for discrimination. Placing a premium on the importance of nondiscrimination might mean dismissing some genuine ethnic claims, but many ethnic cries for community control over housing are motivated by racism. In Canarsie, a Brooklyn neighborhood, the Italian and (to a lesser extent) Jewish residents raised the cry of community control over their neighborhood when the issue of integration with Blacks arose.[24] This poses another problem for Young's argument. She says that participatory democrats should "promote the ideal of a heterogeneous public, in which persons stand forth with their differences acknowledged and respected, though perhaps not completely understood by others."[25] Surely, racist residents can claim that outsiders do not understand their cultural practices and so should not intrude on the way they run their neighborhoods. Yet this claim violates the important liberal principle of nondiscrimination. Still, Young raises an important epistemological point here. Not everyone sees the world in the same way. The experiences of some people, the cultures of some, will give them a point of view that is different from that of other members of the mainstream community. Sometimes, because of differences between communities, the views and values of some ethnics will not be understood by others.

Imagine an immigrant whose culture and religion (for this immigrant, culture and religion aren't separate) lead him to believe that the good of the family is more important than an individual's desires. He believes that his daughters simply must accept the mates he chooses for them. By obeying their father, the daughters support their cultural values and act for the good of the family. Other liberal citizens, disturbed by this, try to convince the daughters to disobey their father; they try to convince the daughters to choose their own husbands or not marry at all. The angered immigrant accuses these citizens of trying to change his culture and life; they don't understand, he charges, why his daughters must obey him. Too caught up in liberal individuality, these nosy citizens fail to see how his actions support his culture, a culture that is as worthy of support as their culture.

These liberal citizens in fact do not completely understand the immigrant's culture; they probably cannot, given the cultural gap between them and the immigrant. The immigrant is not completely helpless, however; he can use the liberal language of nondiscrimination and tolerance to help protect his way of life, even if this language does not help others understand his culture. Liberal citizens can tolerate the actions of others without understanding them. But this will probably not be enough to convince the prying citizens to go away. The immigrant's liberal language is employed to break down discrimination; it is stacked against a culture where nondiscrimination is not valued. The immigrant's argument that he faces discrimination because some people try to convince his daughters to disobey him will be countered by an argument that these citizens are trying to free his daughters from the discrimination they suffer because of their gender.

Even if the nosy citizens can't understand the cultural values they attack, they can realize that these values are antithetical to liberal principles and so should be criticized. This does not mean that liberal citizens and the state should avoid understanding the practices of ethnics. The political community should try to understand what they see as mysterious practices to determine whether they violate liberal principles. An unfamiliar practice that does not violate liberal ideals should not be discouraged. Religious practices that appear strange but harm no one should be respected (although this does not mean that they must be liked) by the political community. If these practices are understood by others, it is more likely that they will be accepted. Still, liberal citizens can accept a practice without understanding it; they simply have to understand that it does not violate liberal principles. Young is probably right to say that all members of a large political community cannot completely understand each other. Yet liberal citizens cannot hide behind a wall of epistemological misunderstanding and refuse to judge the cultural practices that surround them. Practices that violate liberal principles should be either discouraged or forbidden, even if they are not completely understood by the larger political community. A liberal society should not accept all cultural values in its midst simply because they are somebody's cultural values. Respecting all cultural practices and values means accepting racism and sexism; it means giving up on the liberal value of equality and becoming a nonliberal state.

David Dinkins understood this when in 1991, as mayor of New York City, he criticized the mainstream Irish-American community in New York for refusing to allow gays and lesbians to take part in the St. Patrick's Day parade. For him to march at the head of the parade would be to sanction this exclusion. Many Irish Americans complained that Dinkins was trying to change one of their cultural traditions; part of their identity was at stake in the way St. Patrick's Day was celebrated. Dinkins may not have completely understood why some Irish Americans wanted to exclude gays and lesbians, but this does not matter. The parade was not a private affair; it did not take place in a private home or a private hall. It went through the public streets of New York, designed so that many residents of New York City could see the parade; it was a parade for and by members of civil society. Such a parade should not be able to hide behind the mask of privacy to protect its discriminatory practices. Dinkins rightly held his ground; liberal principles, while flexible enough to incorporate many eth-

nic practices, are not infinitely malleable. Sometimes they will clash with cultural practices in public and in civil society, and, when this happens, these practices need to change.

Toward Pluralistic Integration

Ethnicity has not completely faded away from life in the United States. Some memories and attachments to ethnic cultures are passed down and remain part of the lives of some ethnics. Ethnicity will continue to matter in American life, but it will always be in flux. Many people here identify as ethnics in only symbolic ways; others do not identify as ethnics at all. Yet some succeed in reweaving their ethnic identity so it remains a vibrant force in their lives. Moreover, some people's character will be influenced by their ethnic heritage, even if they do not know this.

Ensuring the persistence of ethnicity in American life is the continuation of immigration. Immigration infuses old ethnic communities with new life and brings into the country altogether new ethnics, who establish new ethnic communities. In cities with many immigrants, ethnicity may seem to be a dominant social and political factor. Even if the descendants of these immigrants become symbolic ethnics, this process usually takes two or three generations, which means that ethnicity will matter for many years after each immigration wave. Furthermore, equal citizenship is not automatically conferred on immigrants. The arrival of new ethnics means that new forms of discrimination may arise and have to be fought. Even as differences among ethnics here fade, new immigrants bring new differences with them, differences that liberal citizens have to learn about, respect, and incorporate in their culture. This means that the political community should be suspicious of arguments that ignore ethnicity or try to reduce its importance. Yet the political community must also be wary of arguments for constructing a new vision of American life based on ethnicity—ethnicity matters but for most people it is not all-encompassing.

What I am sketching here is akin to what the historian John Higham calls *pluralistic integration*.[26] Although a common citizenship binds ethnics together (integration), this bond need not obliterate all ethnic ties (pluralism). To achieve pluralistic integration, citizens must accept new ethnics much more quickly than they have in the United States. Citizens need to bestow upon ethnic immigrants full citizenship and to teach them the values of nondiscrimination and equality. In turn, new ethnics will teach citizens the full meaning of these values as citizens learn to accept new practices. When citizens here face new practices they dislike, the real meaning of nondiscrimination comes to light; when liberal principles are tested, citizens come to understand their real meaning. In this way, new ethnics teach citizens already here the meaning of many liberal ideas. Ethnic cultures will be transformed to fit American culture, but American culture will also be transformed as it accepts ethnic cultures.

Transforming ethnic cultures into a part of the American landscape is a process that may take two or three generations. Part of this process takes place behind closed doors; the fights between immigrants and their children about the rules of their home, about the lovers of the children, and about their religious practices are mostly private fights. As the memories and identities of the children are shaped in the United States, many will find themselves in conflict with their (immigrant) parents, whose memories and identities were shaped elsewhere. The transformation of ethnic cultures is also a public matter that will have to involve public discussions and negotiations. Deciding how ethnic cultures will change to fit in with liberalism and how American culture will change to accept the new ethnics will take time. It is a matter of public negotiation between the newcomers and the citizens already here. This negotiation should take place at schools and in the workplace.

When ethnics arrive in the liberal state, liberal citizens need to expand their notion of who qualifies as a citizen; members of the dominant culture may have to revamp their conception of society, of their culture, to accept new ethnics. Citizens have to learn to accept or ignore the practices of others if they do not violate liberal values. As the cultures of immigrants change, they will not automatically mirror the dominant culture. Too often citizens demand complete conformity from immigrants; at other times, citizens grant that they will merely tolerate others. Both of these attitudes enable citizens to escape the hard work that should be done in liberal society in accepting immigrants. The view of tolerance held by then prime minister of Britain, Margaret Thatcher, is instructive. She announced in a speech to the General Assembly of the Church of Scotland that "the Christian religion—which, of course, embodies many of the great spiritual and moral truths of Judaism—is a fundamental part of our national heritage." Thatcher reported that people with "other faiths and cultures" are welcome in Britain and will be treated equally, with respect and with open friendship. "There is absolutely nothing incompatible between this and our desire to maintain the essence of our own identity. There is no place for racial or religious intolerance in our creed."[27]

Perhaps Jews can aspire to full citizenship in Britain, but what about the many Muslims or nonbelievers in Britain? Notice the language Thatcher used: *other* faiths will be tolerated; *we* desire to maintain *our* identity. Muslims, then, are not part of Britain's heritage but are somewhat akin to guests in Thatcher's Britain. This speech would have been less exclusive if Thatcher had been speaking as a Christian asking other Christians to be tolerant. But Thatcher was speaking as the leader of Britain. She allowed that non-Christians have a place in Britain, but she did not want them to challenge the fundamental identity of Britain as a Christian state. As long as this attitude prevails, non-Christians will not have full citizenship in Britain. If the state backs certain religious or ethnic celebrations but not others, it is making a statement about its identity, intentionally or not. As the membership of the state changes, these celebrations should be scrutinized. The idea of the public culture should change as its membership changes. By public culture, I mean the standards of acceptable behavior and appearance in public, public celebrations, the pronouncements made by public officials about the identity of the country, and the history and values taught to its children by the political community. If society's celebrations exclude some members, they ought to be changed. This does not mean that the state can have no celebrations and no holidays; there can be many holidays that celebrate state heroes or that commemorate groups of people (including ethnic groups) that have contributed to the state in important ways.

Announcements like Thatcher's are illiberal because they exclude members of certain groups from full citizenship. Group membership is not cause in itself for exclusion. Liberal citizenship is not predicated on Christianity, or white skin, or European ancestry. If the ideals of liberal citizenship will actually be granted to the state's citizens, people like Thatcher must rethink their conception of the state's identity. Once again, demands of liberal citizenship arise. If the principle of nondiscrimination is to be upheld, liberal citizens must learn to accept others as equal citizens, even if they find them weird or distasteful. This demand is constantly evolving. British Americans had to learn to accept German Americans in the eighteenth century; both had to learn to accept Irish Americans in the middle of the nineteenth century; members of all three groups had to accept those from Eastern and Southern Europe in the nineteenth century; Black Americans, Asian Americans, and Latinos all still have to be fully accepted by white Americans. Just when a citizen may think he or she has accepted others as equals, another ethnic group may come along with its own distinctive practices. And so the stylized vision of a citizen held by this person must be revamped. Liberalism calls upon citizens to revamp their image of the citizens of their state as the state gains new members or as old members take on new practices. Liberalism constantly makes new demands on citizens; it calls upon citizens to consider and accept new practices as they arise and as long as they are not illiberal.

The pressure to drop practices that do not violate liberal values is not confined to Britain. Margaret Gibson reports that many Sikh-American children in California feel considerable pressure to leave their turbans at home when they go to school. This pressure comes from both their fellow classmates *and* their teachers.[28] The Sikhs are expected to "act American." But there is no reason for Sikhs to shed their turbans if they do not want to. It may be that, without any pressure to do so, the effects of liberal citizenship in an industrial state will mean that more and more Sikhs in the United States (and especially their children and grandchildren) will take their turbans off. Or non-Sikhs may think turbans are attractive or "cool" and begin to wear them. But liberal theory does not demand that Sikhs take them off. Instead, this is exactly the sort of practice—a practice that differs from the norm but harms no one—that liberal theory supports. It may help if it is explained to the teachers and students of this high school why Sikhs wear turbans, but this practice should be respected whether it is understood or not.

Within liberal limits, ethnic cultural practices ought to be able to flourish in the liberal state. There is no reason why Sikhs need to become like (white) Christians to be equal citizens. As long as Sikhs do not violate the tenets of liberalism, citizens already here should accept them and their cultural practices. As long as new ethnics arrive and bring their different cultural practices with them, a clash between liberal citizens here and the newly arriving citizens will occur. Both new ethnics and old citizens must work through these tensions so new ethnics receive full citizenship. Old citizens will have to learn to accept new practices, just as new ethnics may have to take on new values in the liberal state. This process will not be quick or painless; a country as diverse as the United States is bound to be home to many ethnic tensions, to tensions within ethnic groups and those between ethnic groups. Sometimes, efforts to gain acceptance for particular ethnic practices will be an uphill struggle. If enough people are committed to liberal principles, however, many ethnic tensions will be eased over time.

Once members of an ethnic group are accepted by others and their practices are refitted to the United States, they will no longer seem strange or eccentric. Instead, their practices may become part of the dominant culture. This points to an important difference between cultural pluralism and pluralistic integration. Cultural pluralism emphasizes the *protection of different cultures;* by doing so, it does not distinguish between the good and bad aspects of cultures. Pluralistic integration, however, emphasizes the *protection of cultural practices that are compatible with liberalism.* It also discourages or forbids illiberal practices. By emphasizing specific practices and not cultures, pluralistic integration rejects the idea that cultures are somehow sacrosanct and need to be protected at all costs. Pluralistic integration readily accepts the fact that there are parts of many cultures that should not be protected. To reject a cultural practice will often change a culture. Making it harder to see cultures as distinct and organic wholes is the borrowing of cultural practices that occurs between cultures. Cultures change considerably; some disappear, some combine with others, and some are transformed. There is no reason to prevent these processes, although liberals need to try to ensure that these processes take place within liberal principles. As the different cultural practices of ethnics are accepted in the liberal state, the dominant culture will often be reinterpreted as it incorporates different practices, and ethnics will often take on the practices of mainstream culture as their own.

It is not, however, just liberal citizenship that makes it hard to maintain distinctive ethnic cultures; modern institutions also play a part. J. S. Mill argued that industrial society leads to assimilation.

> Every extension of education promotes it [assimilation], because education brings people under common influences, and gives them access to the general stock of facts and sentiments. Improvement in the means of communication promotes it, by bringing the inhabitants of distant places into personal contact, and keeping up a rapid flow of changes in residence between one place and another.[29]

In an advanced industrial society, people learn many of the same skills in schools: math, science, grammar, history, literature, and so forth. Even as the community debates what exactly should be taught, the decisions on what to teach often affect many schools. If attempts to make the curriculum more inclusive are successful, all or most students in the United States will read about marginalized groups. The curriculum may change, but education will still bring people under "common influences." Moreover, math, science, and grammar are similarly taught in schools across the country. They must be, for people to know the basic skills needed for either a college education (where they can specialize in certain fields) or many jobs. People who lack this education often wallow in poverty, unable to get well-paying jobs.

Besides a similar education, modern modes of communication (and transportation) may decrease differences among people. People who live miles away can easily communicate through telephones, computers, and fax machines (if they have the money). People from different backgrounds move from place to place, enabling people to share their cultural practices with many others. Instead of each locality existing in isolation and developing its own distinct culture, people who live hundreds of miles apart easily influence each other. Millions of people in advanced industrial societies read the same magazines, go to the same movies, see the same television shows, and are subjected to the same advertisements. Distinct cultural practices are hard to maintain in the face of this onslaught, particularly when liberal citizenship means that certain ethnics are not channeled by the government into certain occupations or cities.

Pluralism, Power, and Standards

Even if there are no laws forbidding unconventional ways of life, there is pressure on those who act and look differently to conform to the prevailing conventions and norms, which are set by the dominant group in society. This pressure need not always be overt and obvious; ethnics are not always told to stop being "different." Mill recognized that power need not be enshrined in law: "There needs protection also against the . . . tendency of society to impose, by other means than civil penalties, its own ideas and practices as rules of conduct on those who dissent from them; to fetter the development and, if possible, prevent the formation of any individuality not in harmony with its own ways."[30] Power and pressure are manifested not only through the blunt instrument of law but also in subtle ways. There need not be a formal rule forbidding turbans for Sikhs to feel uncomfortable wearing them. When ethnics are a minority in a school or in the workplace, they may feel different; they may be given strange looks by others when they act differently; they may feel (and actually be) penalized because they do not conform to the norms of the dominant culture. When a certain group of people controls many of the dominant institutions in civil society, it can set the norms and cultural tone of these institutions. Made to feel weird, penalized because they are different, ethnic minorities may take on the norms of the dominant culture. They do this to fit in socially and advance economically.

Mill noted that the norms of standard behavior in the United States are set by the "whole white population." Black Americans, along with immigrants who are not viewed as white, may be seen as threatening, inferior, or eccentric by the ascendant white class. Mill wanted white Americans to accept the practices of others. Some may worry about the problem of maintaining social order in a liberal society; they may argue that, if the different practices of ethnic and racial groups are supported, even liberal ones, chaos will somehow result. But the real problem of liberal society, Mill rightly pointed out, is not too much diversity, too many different cultures, but the lack of diversity and distinct cultural practices. A wide range of diverse lifestyles is hard to maintain in an industrial, liberal state. The conforming forces and pressures on people, although not overwhelming, are strong. Mill contended that there should be "different experiments of living"; short of injury to others, "free scope should be given to varieties of character; and that the worth of different modes of life should be proved practically, when anyone thinks fit to try them."[31] The majority can benefit by supporting different ways of living because different ethnic practices in the liberal state will enable many citizens to see and consider alternative forms of living. Liberal citizens may decide to take on the practices of others and make them their own. Accepting others may mean gaining new restaurants and different kinds of music, something that many citizens can enjoy. Furthermore, a state with a diverse range of lifestyles will satisfy more of its citizens, since different people will find satisfaction in different kinds of living.

Demands for diversity, like Mill's argument in *On Liberty*, have often fallen on deaf ears. For some, this reveals a pernicious flaw in liberal theory. Catherine Mackinnon argues: "Liberalism defines equality as sameness. It is comparative. To know if you are equal, you have to be equal to somebody who sets the standard you compare yourself with." Mackinnon's claim is far-reaching; she claims that liberal equality means that women must think and act like men to be equal. In the context of ethnicity, Mackinnon's argument means that ethnics must think and act like members of the dominant culture to achieve equality. Similar arguments are made about liberal neutrality. Liberals place great importance on neutral rules, critics say, but this misses the way that power works. Young, for example, argues that the fiction of impartial standards really means that the most powerful group will define the standards of a society's institutions; other groups who come "into the game after it is already begun" have to adhere to these standards. In other words, the most powerful group will set the standards by which all are measured.[32]

This is a powerful critique. I agree that liberals cannot merely pay attention to neutral procedures. (Mill is one liberal who understood that power could work without the official sanction of law.)[33] Yet some of the standards established by Anglo-American Protestants should not be disparaged just because they were established by one particular group and not others. It is possible that American culture is deeply permeated by Protestant values in ways that few citizens really recognize. Max Weber famously argued that capitalism is grounded in the Protestant ethic (although his argument has been criticized by many). Let us pretend that Weber is right and say that industrial society, too, is based in Protestantism. Surely, there is a connection between the Reformation, Protestantism, and liberalism. Liberalism is, in large part, a response to the religious differences produced by the Reformation. It is no accident that liberalism did not arise in a world permeated by medieval Catholic values. Both liberalism and Protestantism are more egalitarian than the more hierarchical Catholic Church. Even civility, simply being nice to each other in civil society, has been called a Protestant value.[34] It's possible, in other words, that much of the modern, liberal state is based on Protestant values.

If this is right, then my insistence that immigrants take on liberal values may be understood as insisting that they become like Protestants. This is not in itself cause for alarm. It's difficult to disentangle what is Protestant from what is liberal in the United States. If industrialization is a result of Protestant values, it is hard to imagine how society could reject these values; it would mean beginning society anew. Attacking the Protestant influence on American values simply because they are Protestant is as wrong as attacking the values of ethnics simply because they are ethnic. Even though Protestantism and liberalism may be entangled, they are not the same. Liberals can and should reject certain Protestant values in the name of liberalism. The attempt by some fundamentalists, for example, to make the United States a Christian country and to enshrine this in a variety of laws is clearly illiberal. Mill was partly attacking Protestant norms in *On Liberty*, but he didn't attack them because they were Protestant; rather, they deserved criticism because they were stifling the human creativity that he wanted to release. Each cultural value and practice should be judged on its own merits—if it violates liberal principles, it should be rejected; if not, it should be accepted. Values and practices should not be accepted or rejected simply because they are Protestant or Jewish or African American or Polish American.

Like Mill, I do not think that it is possible to eliminate through legal reform the social pressures to conform. It is not possible to make a list of ethnic practices that accord with liberalism and should be upheld by the state. There are too many ethnics here and too many different practices for such a plan to work. But this does not mean that there is nothing to be done; ethnicity and cultural identity should not simply be dismissed as a private affair. As long as ethnics feel pressure to drop their distinctive though liberal practices, ethnicity is a public matter. This does not mean that the state should tout certain ethnic practices as particularly good ones or that the state should give money to some ethnic groups; rather, public institutions should work to make ethnic practices that accord with liberal principles acceptable to all citizens. Once particular ethnics and their practices are accepted, then their ethnicity need not be a public concern. Until this happens, however, the social pressures on ethnics to conform must be fought.

The criticism that liberalism has a hard time counteracting the effects of power is not a problem endemic to liberalism. It is easy to imagine groups in nonliberal societies establishing institutions and then demanding that others conform to the standards of these institutions (or simply ignoring members of other groups). In the former Soviet Union, many non-Russians complained that Russians set the standards for many Soviet institutions. In preemancipation times, when Jews left their community Christian society hardly changed its standards to accommodate its new members. And in early modern England power worked in overt ways; members of certain social classes were unable to wear certain types of clothes, and many laws publicly favored the nobility. The problem of power exists in most and perhaps all societies.

Liberalism, however, can give people the conceptual space to criticize those in power. The concepts of rights and equality can be powerful; when people are told that they have rights, they have the language to decry the abuse of their rights and they can mobilize around the idea that their rights are violated. Surely, many do this in the United States. They can point out how those in power abuse their authority. To be sure, the powerful may continue to abuse their power, but pointing to the failures of liberalism's ideals is the first step toward correcting these problems. Liberalism also gives the space to politicize culture; as Young notes, cultural change cannot occur by edict. She calls for providing means "for fostering politicized cultural discussion"; she wants people to ask "what practices, habits, attitudes, comportments, images, symbols and so on contribute to social domination and group oppression."[35] In the liberal state groups can organize to point out the ways in which they face discrimination. Toward this end, ethnic and racial organizations are needed to fight the discrimination faced by their members. Unsurprisingly, many organizations in the United States do just this.

Kallen rightly argued that, when ethnic groups were ridiculed, the groups' members were mocked as well. Members of a newly arrived ethnic group, feeling vulnerable, are bound to lose some of their self-respect when the group to which they belong is ridiculed. When people identify with a group, their self-image is often tied up with the group. When Irish Americans are stereotyped as drunks, it is not only alcoholic Irish Americans who are belittled, but all Irish Americans. Ethnic organizations can help ethnics gain the self-respect that is important to liberal citizens. First, even if ethnics are ridiculed by others, in the safety of their ethnic organization they can realize that it is not they who are failing the demands of liberal citizenship, but others. Second, ethnic organizations can alert the state when ethnic citizens face discrimination. Citizens should not trust the government to always fight discrimination; the state itself can and has discriminated against members of ethnic and racial groups. Ethnic organizations are needed to fight the state in these times, to point out how the state is abusing its power and violating its own liberal tenets. Ethnic organizations are also needed to explain their practices, describing their meaning and importance to the public and the media. They are needed to begin the process of negotiation between new ethnics and citizens here about the inclusion of these new ethnics. Ethnic organizations give a voice to citizens who might otherwise be silent. Without ethnic organizations and without anyone paying attention to them, there will be little negotiation. Citizens may demand conformity from the newcomers; ethnics may be hard-pressed to resist these demands. Under the umbrella of organizations that collectively pool resources and talent, ethnics are not completely powerless. They can demand to be heard.

Ethnic organizations are not enough, however, for ethnics to receive full citizenship. Even if the official doctrine of the state is to encourage a plurality of lifestyles and cultural practices, minority ethnics may have a hard time resisting the pressure to conform to the larger community's norms, particularly if they live apart from each other. People living away from others with similar practices and values will have difficulty maintaining them and passing them on to their children. It is harder to keep kosher, to think of Saturday as the day of rest, or to wear turbans if few nearby do the same. Children may wonder why they are the only ones wearing certain clothing or eating certain foods. Living near each other helps people maintain a community. This is not only a matter of psychological support; ethnic institutions must have a community to be supported. Kosher butchers will not exist where there are few Jews; synagogues will have a hard time surviving with a small constituency; Jewish Community Centers will not be established unless there is a substantial Jewish community.

Although Jews and Sikhs may be tiny minorities in the context of the United States, they may be more noticeable in particular cities. Living near group members, they will feel less pressure to conform to majority standards. With a community of people, they will feel less strange and less isolated. To achieve full citizenship, some people need to live near other members of their group. An ethnic community can also help change the norms and expectations of a community. Where Jews are plentiful, few will think it strange when they want to take off from work on important Jewish holidays. If enough Sikhs live in a particular place, wearing turbans may seem not weird but acceptable. If ethnics congregate in some areas, they will also be in a better position to explain and protect their practices by forming ethnic organizations; people scattered across the United States are unlikely to form effective organizations. Ethnics who live near each other will have some power; those scattered will have less power to demand that their practices be noticed and accepted.

Hundreds of different ethnic groups are represented in the United

States; every citizen cannot be expected to know a lot about all of these groups. This knowledge must be local. Not everyone needs to know why turbans are an important part of Sikh identity or that some Jews and Muslims do not eat certain foods. In the California city where Gibson reports that turbans are ridiculed, however, knowledge about turbans is needed. An ethnic community can demand that this knowledge be taught in the schools; it can demand that the local political leadership recognize the community and its needs. The public negotiations about ethnic practices necessary for the acceptance of these practices should go on between ethnic organizations and school officials, elected officials, civil servants, and business associations. When teachers and principals notice that members of a new ethnic group are attending their school, they should not act as if nothing in their school has changed. They need to learn about the new ethnic community and its practices from the community's members. They should work to make sure that other students and teachers do not ridicule those practices that are compatible with liberalism. For practices that are not compatible, it must be explained to the ethnics why this practice cannot be accepted; the ethnic community must be given the chance to alter the practice so it is acceptable. A similar process should go on in the workplace. Business leaders need to learn about the particular practices of different ethnic communities; it is not only in schools that Sikhs may feel uncomfortable wearing turbans. Although it may not be possible to pass laws recognizing specific ethnic practices as legitimate, political leaders should speak about these practices in their communities. Elected officials can help set either a hostile or a welcoming tone for new ethnics; these officials should meet with ethnics who face problems, learn about their communities, and defend their practices in public.

Pluralistic integration means that some neighborhoods and cities will have concentrations of people from the same ethnic group. In between two cultures and with only tentative standing in ours, immigrant ethnics often feel most comfortable with others who are in between the same two cultures. More-established ethnics who want to retain some of their practices will also live near each other. The state usually does not have to do much about these ethnic living arrangements; ethnics who want to live near each other typically do so. The state should not discourage ethnics from living near each other, as the United States briefly did with its policy of dispersement in the early 1980s. This policy aimed to disperse immigrants from the same country all over the United States. But this policy is sure to cause havoc in the lives of immigrants. It will make it harder for them to maintain their ethnic practices and enter mainstream society. There may be good reason to steer some immigrants away from New York or Los Angeles, for those cities can comfortably absorb only so many immigrants each year. When this is done, however, immigration policy should allow substantial numbers of the same ethnic group to go to another city or two, instead of directing the immigrants to many different places.

Refusing to discourage ethnics from living near each other does not mean the balkanization of American society. Jews do not necessarily want to live in a community with all Jews, but some Jews will want to live where there are many Jews. It should be no surprise, then, that Jews tend to congregate in large cities. In these cities they will find many other Jews, but also many non-Jews. Clusters of Jews live near each other but with permeable boundaries; they live in the midst of other communities. Jews can live next to non-Jews, go to school with them, but still socialize with other Jews as long as enough live nearby. Pluralistic integration will not mean that, in avoiding the problem of complete assimilation, the United States will be turned into a country of distinct cultures. The demands of liberal citizenship make this unlikely.

Every city, state, or neighborhood should not replicate the racial and ethnic composition of the United States. Attempts to mirror diversity everywhere will condemn many ethnics to being a tiny minority in many places, making it much harder for them to maintain their ethnic community. Instead, pluralistic integration means having clusters of ethnic communities scattered across the United States, communities that can support ethnic practices and institutions. Pluralistic integration is equally applicable to other, smaller settings. Educators should not try to ensure, in the name of diversity, that each class has one or two ethnic or racial members. That's not diversity; it condemns minorities to a sort of psychological isolation, increasing the pressure on them to conform to others. It makes individual ethnics powerless. Pluralistic integration means that different clusters of ethnic and racial groups will exist in different places, in neighborhoods, in social and civic organizations, in dorms, and in schools. Clusters of ethnic and racial groups will give their members a chance to maintain their cultural practices while also being full and equal citizens.

Pluralistic integration will make it easier for ethnics to fight pressures to conform; sometimes, though, this pressure is manifested in the rules of institutions under the guise of neutrality. Neutrality is important to liberal equality; laws and rules are supposed to apply to everyone equally (except under special circumstances). When the wealthy do not have to obey laws that the poor do, liberal equality does not exist. John Locke argued that the government should "govern by promulgated established Laws, not to be varied in particular Cases, but to have one Rule for Rich and Poor, for the Favourite at Court and the Country Man at Plough."[36] But rules that are apparently neutral may discriminate against members of some groups.

Some rules may have to revamped when they are seen to be discriminatory. A neutral school dress code that forbids students from wearing anything on their heads, for example, discriminates against Sikhs. In a school without any Sikhs, this rule may pose no problems but, where there are Sikhs, it must be shown that there is a compelling pedagogical reason for this rule. As different ethnic groups arrive in different parts of the United States, different institutions here need to review their rules to make sure they do not wrongly discriminate against ethnics; this is part of the negotiations between ethnics and established institutions. Of course, not all rules need to be changed because they discriminate; a rule that no weapons be brought to schools should not be changed, regardless of the Sikhs' cultural practices.

Ethnic Failures, Ethnic Successes

Pluralistic integration is, at best, an imperfect solution. It is also a goal that may not be reached in the foreseeable future, although it should be pursued nonetheless. To give up trying to reach this goal would probably mean that liberal states would become more inhospitable to ethnics than they currently are. Ethnics will frequently have a hard time getting their practices and values accepted by members of mainstream culture. It is easy to say that schools should be more supportive of ethnics, but some teachers and students will look with scorn upon the way some ethnic students dress and act. The state may officially try to be responsive to the practices of different ethnics, but not all of the state's employees will follow the state's dictates very well. Moreover, the culture of the United States is heavily influenced by Christianity. Even if Thatcher's ideas about the identity of Britain are illiberal, her ideas are shared by many in both Britain and the United States, including many elected officials, bureaucrats, and judges. Many institutions in civil society and the public sphere celebrate Christian holidays. Liberalism can open up some space for ethnics to fight these norms. These fights will often lead to increased tensions between different groups, as some will resent and resist the efforts of others to change the norms of society. This is simply part of the price of having a diverse society.

Sometimes misunderstandings and tensions will arise from clashing cultural practices. For example, immigrants from some cultures tend out of respect not to look people in the eye when they talk; many Americans, however, think that averting one's eyes in a conversation is rather shady. Getting each community to understand the practices of the other is necessary to decrease the tensions that may result when members of these groups interact. It takes time, however, to reach this understanding. Ethnics themselves will often have to struggle to be understood and to have their practices accepted. Ethnics who engage in these fights will have some successes, but it would be foolhardy to say that ethnics will always win these battles. Liberalism may give the tools for ethnics to fight for acceptance of their practices, but this does not guarantee that these battles will be successful. Successful fights in some places will be followed by failures in other places.

These battles will be even harder to fight where there are only a few ethnics or Black Americans, and, although Jews and Sikhs may be plentiful in one city, this same city may have a tiny community of Mexican Americans who may feel culturally beleaguered. It is certainly possible for scattered minorities to maintain their cultural practices. The neighbors, teachers, and colleagues of ethnics should do what they can to avoid ridicule of the few ethnics in their midst or pressure for them to drop their distinctive practices. Because ethnics live all across the United States, liberal citizens should teach their children that people's different ways of living ought to be respected. It would be misleading, however, to suggest that isolated ethnics will have little trouble maintaining their identity. Abstract teaching about respecting others will help, but it will not end all pressure on ethnics to conform. I do not know any way to ensure that ethnics will not feel pressure to conform, especially isolated ethnics who may have a hard time maintaining their ethnic identity.

CHAPTER 5

THE ETHNIC REJECTION OF
LIBERAL CITIZENSHIP

IN 1968 THREE AMISH MEN were arrested in Wisconsin because they had not enrolled their fourteen- and fifteen-year-old children in high school, thereby violating Wisconsin law, which mandated compulsory school attendance through the age of sixteen. The Amish parents did not object to sending their children to elementary and junior high schools, as they wanted their children to learn basic language, math, and science skills. However, these Amish parents (like most Amish parents) did not want their children to attend public high school because they worried that the "worldly" influences of public high schools on their children would lead the children away from the traditional, "otherworldly" Amish lifestyle. The Wisconsin arrests were not a new event in Amish history; in the few decades before the Wisconsin arrests, many Amish men had been arrested in other states for not sending their children to public schools. In these circumstances, however, the Amish community and local school officials had usually worked out some arrangement, which often meant that Amish children received vocational training in high school by working on an Amish farm or in an Amish house. But Wisconsin school officials and the Amish could not reach a similar agreement. The state arrested the Amish parents because, it argued, it had an interest in ensuring that each child would receive an adequate education to succeed in the modern world. The education the Amish children received from their community, the state argued, did not prepare them for much except to live an Amish way of life. Amish children who wanted to pursue modern life plans—to become pianists, astronauts, or oceanographers—were not prepared to do so by their education. The state's argument, however, failed to persuade the U.S. Supreme Court, which sided with the Amish in *Wisconsin v. Yoder*.[1]

The Amish argued that sending their children to public high schools would transform their children's identity so radically that they would no longer be Amish. Amish identity is affected by the liberal state, but the Amish take explicit measures to ensure that their identity remains unquestionably distinctive. The effects of liberal citizenship on the identity of weak ethnics are not replicated when it comes to the Amish. The Amish remain a community apart from the mainstream community, a community with a different set of values, loyalties, and aspirations. Many of their values and practices, however, are illiberal. The Amish live in patriarchal communities that cherish unthinking obedience to the community's rules. At the heart of the issues brought up by insular ethnic communities in the liberal state is the question of tolerance: to what extent can the liberal state tolerate illiberal communities? The liberal state encourages its citizens to be self-reflective and promotes the political ideals of autonomy and equality.[2] Liberals who argue that the state need not concern itself with the self-reflective capacities of people fail to take note of the requirements of liberal citizenship.[3] Although the liberal state can encourage its citizens to be self-reflective and to act autonomously, it cannot force them to do so. Paradoxically, liberal toleration means that, within certain limits in the liberal state, people can reject liberalism. The Amish have considerable latitude to try, as they do, to withstand the encouragement to become self-reflective citizens.

The Amish Community

The Amish are descendants of the Anabaptists of sixteenth-century Europe.[4] The Anabaptists rejected a close alliance between church and state; for them being a Christian meant voluntarily yielding oneself to a committed community, a spiritual brotherhood of believers. Like other nonconformists, the Anabaptists challenged many of the dominant religious beliefs of their day; what distinguished the Anabaptists was their rejection of infant baptism. The Anabaptists also believed in social separation from the evil world and the exclusion of errant members from communion; they rejected violence and refused to swear oaths. The Amish, led by Joseph Ammann, split from the Swiss Anabaptists in the 1690s over three issues. Ammann proposed holding communion twice a year instead of annually, he argued that foot washing (where members of the church wash each other's feet) should be practiced as a religious rite in the communion service, and he maintained that expelled members should be not only banned from communion but also shunned in routine social relations as well. Ammann actually excommunicated the senior Swiss Anabaptist bishop for refusing to accept Ammann's interpretation of shunning. The followers of Ammann became known as the Amish; other well-known descendants of the Anabaptists in this country are the Mennonites.

Like other nonconformists, the Anabaptists were persecuted by the state. Fleeing persecution, the Amish began to emigrate to the United States in the early eighteenth century. Most of the Amish settled in Lancaster County, Pennsylvania, although the Amish today reside in many states (mostly in the Midwest) and in Ontario, Canada. There are several different Amish sects, but the largest is the Old Order Amish. (When I speak of the Amish in this chapter, I refer only to the Old Order Amish, except where I explicitly indicate otherwise.) The other, smaller sects split off from the Old Order Amish because of disputes over rules, with the breakaway sects usually interpreting rules more liberally than the Old Order, although some sects are more strict than the Old Order.

Central to Amish belief is the idea of *Gelassenheit*—roughly, submission to a higher authority. For the Amish, Gelassenheit means "self-surrender, resignation to God's will, yielding to God and to others, self-denial, contentment and a calm spirit." Children of the Amish learn at an early age that their self-will must be given up if they want to become children of God. The Amish do not cherish individuality; rather, they try to "lose themselves" in their community. This can be seen in their dress; all Amish men wear the same black jackets, vests, and pants. The type of hats they wear, the number of suspenders they use (the Amish do not wear belts), and the absence of buttons on their clothes are all regulated by their community. Women are allowed to wear more colorful clothing, but the colors must be solid and without pattern. The women wear one-piece dresses; over their bodices they wear a *Halsduch,* which is like a cape. Amish people do not try to distinguish themselves, they are not competitive, and they are not interested in intellectual achievement. Devotion to God and to their community is central to their lives. Amish people who are perceived as trying to stand out are censured. Religion for the Amish permeates their lives: "the Old Order Amish religion pervades and determines virtually their entire way of life, regulating it with the detail of the Talmudic diet through the strictly enforced rules of the church community." Amish behavior is regulated by the *Ordnung,* which is an unwritten code of conduct. It is not a set of rules but "is the understood behavior by which the

Amish are expected to live."[5] The Ordnung evolves over time, as new challenges posed by modernity must be met and settled. The Ordnung is similar in all Amish communities, although some of the details may differ. The bishop in charge of each community is the final arbitrator of the community's rules.

Negotiating the terrain between modernity and the Amish desire to live traditional, simple, and humble lives is not always easy. The rules about which modern inventions can be accepted by the Amish are established almost haphazardly.[6] Once these rules are made, however, they must be followed or the transgressor will be punished. The Amish do not own cars (although they can ride in them as passengers), they do not use electricity from conventional 110-volt sources (although gas- or hydraulic-powered generators are permissible), nor do they own televisions or radios. Some of the rules of Amish society may seem incomprehensible to the outsider, but their rejection of parts of modern technology serves a crucial function: it sets them apart from mainstream society. It makes them live lives that are starkly different from the lives of the members of mainstream society. The rules identify the Amish; the rules show to the Amish and to mainstream culture that the Amish are different. There is little confusion about identity in the Amish community; no one straddles the line between the English and Amish worlds. For the Amish, one is in either one world or the other.

People who break the rules of the Amish community are punished and sometimes even expelled. The distinction between public and private in the liberal state is not replicated in Amish society. Amish people can be punished by their community for actions in their own homes. The Amish do not argue that what they do in private is no one else's business; indeed, gossip is one of the methods used to regulate behavior. If a bishop gets word that a member has a radio, that member is punished. Punishment can mean anything from gentle admonishment to a six-week ban to expulsion. Using rubber tires on a tractor, wearing jewelry, joining a public baseball team, or participating in a Bible study group are all examples of behavior that would result in some sort of punishment by the community. As long as there is repentance, most infractions do not result in expulsion; unrepentant people are shunned from social relations until they repent. Stubborn members who refuse to repent their transgressions will eventually be excommunicated. Social relations with the excommunicated are minimal. The excommunicated cannot eat at the same table with other Amish; other Amish cannot accept favors, goods, or services from the excommunicated. Those who seem to be permanently excommunicated typically leave the Amish community and begin their lives anew elsewhere. A few actions, like buying a car or cheating in a business deal, are cause for immediate expulsion.

The Amish family is traditional and patriarchal. The ideas of equality or individual rights are not part of the Amish community. A wife is "her husband's helper but not his equal." Women cannot take on any church leadership positions; their role in religious services is taken from the teaching of the Apostle Paul: "Let the women learn in silence with all subjection." At home, the wife takes care of the children, cooks, cleans, makes clothes for the family, preserves food, shops, and gardens. She helps harvest the crops when needed. The men take care of the fields and animals, with the help of their sons. (Most Amish men are farmers.) Children are taught the Amish ways; after age two, "restrictions and exacting disciplines are continuously imposed upon the child until adolescence."[7] Although children attend school, where they learn how to communicate with the "English" world, they work from an early age, helping in the fields and at home. (Except for new settlements, most Amish communities run their own elementary schools.) Amish families are usually large, with an average of over six children.

Amish life is carefully regulated, but the Amish exert no force over wayward members. Anyone can leave the Amish community at any time. A person who violates the Ordnung cannot be forced to follow it. The Amish stress the voluntary nature of their community. Indeed, there really are no Amish children, though there are children of the Amish. No one is baptized until adulthood, usually around the age of eighteen. At that time, each person must decide if he or she will become a part of the Amish community. Although most children of the Amish join the church, not all do. The author of one of the few scholarly books on the Amish reported his decision about baptism: "I did not want to take a vow I could not keep, nor take a vow that implied social avoidance in case I could not live by Amish standards. Consequently, on the day my chums began their instruction for baptism, I drove my horse and buggy to the nearby Mennonite church."[8]

The Amish way of life is admired by many, who see them (rightly) as hard-working people who maintain "traditional values." Chief Justice Warren Burger maintained that the Amish are a "highly successful social unit within our society. . . . Its members are productive and very law-abiding members of society; they reject public welfare in any of its usual modern forms."[9] Burger implied that the Amish are admirable citizens, but in many ways they are not. The Amish are uninterested in many issues that are important to the larger community. Their world view, their identity, prevents them from seeing themselves as part of the larger political community. If they don't help others, they hardly harm others either. Yet they don't want to try to make the United States a better country; they are not interested in the problems about which other citizens and politicians worry. The

Amish do not run for public office. Although the Amish are a gentle people, their rejection of liberal values should be worrisome for liberals. A celebration of Amish values is, at least in part, a celebration of patriarchal and hierarchical values—values that are not liberal.

Liberal Changes

Liberal and Amish values did not always conflict. In the *Letter Concerning Toleration,* Locke argued that good Christians are characterized by charity, meekness, love, and good will toward others. No church, Locke said, should use force to keep its members; instead, Locke proclaimed the church a voluntary society. And, though each church could kick out any member, Locke insisted that it also must tolerate others, regardless of their religious beliefs.[10] Locke's version of good Christians fits the Amish fairly well. Locke would have little difficulty with the Amish practice of excommunication. The Amish are meek and treat others with good will (even as they avoid too much contact with others). They never force anyone to conform to their beliefs or use force to try to control the state. The Amish want only to work, trade with their neighbors, and worship without interference from the government. Good Christians like the Amish have the makings to be good citizens in a Lockean state. Civil peace—a major goal of Locke's *Letter*—is easily achieved with Amish citizens.[11]

If the Amish are good Lockean citizens, why aren't they now good liberal, democratic citizens? The answer lies in the ways that liberalism has changed since Locke's time, one of which is the change in the demands that liberalism makes on citizens. The main duty of government, Locke argued, was to "guard the peace, safety, and public good of the people," which for Locke meant protecting the property and liberty of people (for people have property in their person, according to Locke). Locke charged the government with establishing settled and known laws, administered by impartial judges. The demands on people in a Lockean state are quite few; someone need only judge the government by how well it is protecting him and his property. Locke did say that the government should protect the common good; presumably, people are to judge the government based on how well it does this. But Locke also argued that "great mistakes" made by rulers would probably be accepted by the people. Only "a long train of abuses, prevarications and artifices" would result in the people taking action against the government. Furthermore, Locke was fairly certain that few would oppose the government unless it threatened their own property. If only a few people were oppressed by the government, Locke said there was little they effectively could do; they could not expect their fellow citizens to come to their aid.[12]

Some liberals today continue to follow the Lockean justification of toleration as the basis of the liberal state, arguing that neutrality on the good life is a central aspect of liberalism. These liberals would still find the Amish to be good liberal citizens, arguing that the liberal state should not "take sides in the dispute about individualism and tradition."[13] According to neutrality theorists, liberalism ought to be about forging a peaceful society among groups with different conceptions of the good life. Neutrality theorists, however, are woefully inattentive to the *political* considerations of liberal citizenship. Arguments that imply or state that liberals should be pleased with the Amish ignore the requirements that citizens need to meet to uphold the liberal state. For Locke, liberalism is a protective device, the best way to ensure that the government does not overstep its bounds. Since Locke's time, however, the job of liberal government has moved beyond the protection of property. The role of citizenship has expanded, in liberal theory and practice.

Much of the expansion in the demands of liberal citizenship has to do with the coupling of democracy to liberalism. Liberal democracies do not run automatically but demand participation by their citizens. Citizens in a liberal democracy must be schooled in the virtues of citizenship for two reasons: first, so they can learn the principles of liberal democracy; second, so they can intelligently participate in government. For a liberal democratic government to work tolerably well, at least a good portion of the citizens must be able to evaluate the work of their political representatives, tell their representatives what they think government ought to do (and not to do), and vote their representatives out of office when they are doing a bad job. Moreover, modern citizens become politically involved in a variety of ways: besides voting, they work for campaigns, petition their representatives, participate in protests, run for office, and so forth. Locke did say that people vote for the members of the legislature, but, in a telling use of language in the *Second Treatise,* Locke spoke of people, not citizens. Locke said little about the character of democratic citizens or the importance of debate in a liberal democratic government.

The intellectual capacities of liberal citizens must be developed; they should be given the tools necessary to make intelligent decisions about government and politics. Without the development of these capacities, citizens will not be able to watch over government very well; they won't be able to participate intelligently in politics. The two goals of having citizens capable of making intelligent political decisions and having citizens able to make reflective decisions about their own lives are closely connected; critical citizens and autonomous people use the same reflective capacities to judge government policies and to evaluate their own lives. Modern liberals, recognizing this connection, often argue that democratic participation is one of the best ways to help people develop their reflective capacities. Benjamin Constant argued that "it is not to happiness alone, it is to self-development that our destiny calls us; and political liberty is the most powerful, the most effective means of self-development that heaven has given us."[14] Through interaction with others, liberal citizens develop their individuality, and political participation is one of the more important ways in which citizens interact with others. Since the capacity to think critically is linked to the virtues of liberal citizenship, the modern liberal emphasis on choice cannot be divorced from the demands of liberal citizenship. Charles Larmore may contend that the "ideals of autonomy and individuality effectively blind us to the real merits of many ways of life" and that a life ruled by custom is no worse than a life of self-development, but the political demands of liberal citizenship favor the latter way of life over the former.[15]

Liberals highlight choice not only to promote individuality, but also to ensure that liberal democracies work well. Good liberal citizens who have "broad sympathies, self-critical reflectiveness, a willingness to experiment, to try and to accept new things, self-control, and active [and] autonomous self-development" not only will be good citizens, but also will increase their own self-development.[16]

The Amish frown upon the human abilities to be self-critical and reflective; they are not interested in debate and discussion; they are not eager to experiment or sculpt their own identities. The Amish shy away from cultivating intellectual skills. They escape the political demands of liberal citizenship. And this escape poses problems for liberal democrats who want to avoid favoring one kind of life over another, but who also argue that liberalism makes political demands on citizens. John Rawls contends that a plurality of religious, moral, and philosophical doctrines is a permanent feature of modern democracies. Liberalism, he argues, must accommodate this plurality of "comprehensive doctrines." He argues that political liberalism does not favor one citizen's doctrine over another, as long as each doctrine is "reasonable," which means that citizens desire a social world in which they, "as free and equal, can cooperate with others on terms all can accept." Rawls rejects the comprehensive liberalisms of Kant and Mill because these liberalisms encourage one particular kind of life, one marked by the "ethical values of autonomy and individuality." Yet while Rawls says that political liberalism tries not to favor one kind of life over another, he also says that it asks that "children's education [include] such things as knowledge of their constitutional and civic rights. . . . Moreover, their education should also prepare them to be fully cooperating members of society and enable them to be self-supporting; it should also encourage the political virtues."[17] The political virtues include toleration, mutual respect, and a sense of fairness and civility.[18] Rawls's list of political virtues is quite close to the liberal virtues I've discussed. Indeed, educating children to be good liberal, democratic citizens may, Rawls admits, sometimes "educate them to a comprehensive liberal conception." This consequence, he says, must simply be accepted, although with regret. Regardless of how this consequence is accepted, however, Rawls's conception of political liberalism is not very far from the liberalisms of Mill and other "comprehensive liberals."[19]

Partial Citizenship

Although some citizens will not become self-reflective despite liberal encouragement, the possibility that liberal institutions might succeed in encouraging citizens to think critically leads the Amish to shy away from these institutions. The Amish argue that, if their children attend public high schools, they will leave the Amish community, and their community will eventually die out. Chief Justice Burger explained why: "During this period [high school], the children must acquire Amish attitudes favoring manual work and self-reliance and the specific skills needed to perform the adult role of an Amish farmer or housewife. They must learn to enjoy physical labor." Attending high school is dangerous for Amish children because of the "pressure to conform to the styles, manners and ways of the peer group" and also "because it takes them away from their community, physically and emotionally."[20] The high school years are the years when Amish teen-agers must begin to think about whether they are prepared to accept baptism into the Amish community. Spending time in a public high school during this period may very well lead many Amish children to reject this baptism.

The possibility that liberalism will eradicate cultures worries Will Kymlicka, who argues that destroying cultures harms the members of the destroyed culture. Kymlicka is not directly concerned with the Amish, but he does talk about the importance of culture, arguing that it should be a central liberal value. Culture, Kymlicka argues, gives meaning to how we live our lives; it supplies the context that makes sense of what we do. "We decide how to lead our lives by situating ourselves in these cultural narratives." Liberals need to be concerned with culture, Kymlicka contends, because it is only through a secure cultural structure that people can live meaningful lives: "it's only through having a rich and secure cultural structure that people can become aware, in a vivid way, of the options available to them, and intelligently examine their value." Kymlicka notes that cultures change, so he emphasizes the importance of maintaining cultural structure and cultural membership, not the maintenance of particular cultural practices. People need to have secure membership in a culture, although the practices of that culture may change considerably. Kymlicka's main example of a cultural structure is Canadian Indians. Canadian Indians need to be secure as members of particular Indian tribes, even as Indian cultures change. If people's cultural structures are insecure, they will be insecure. When a culture is denigrated by others, the people who are part of that culture also are denigrated.[21]

Liberals must explicitly support minority cultures, Kymlicka argues, because, if they do not, they are implicated in the denigration of these cultures and their members. A secure cultural context is necessary for self-respect, a value Kymlicka argues is central to liberalism.[22] But Kymlicka allows his liberalism to run amuck, destroying the very cultures he wants to protect. Kymlicka emphasizes cultural structure, not the content of cultures. This is a crucial distinction for Kymlicka. In his view, "the cultural community continues to exist even when its members are free to modify the character of the culture, should they find its traditional ways of life no longer worthwhile." Kymlicka argues that liberal rights transcend cultures. He defends, for example, the right of some Pueblos to become Protestants while enjoying equal rights in the Pueblo community, even though some "American Indian bands are essentially theocracies. . . . Were the theocracy ended, each majority member of the Pueblo would have as much ability to use and interpret their own cultural experiences as the dissident minority. . . . Supporting the intolerant character of a cultural community undermines the very reason we had to support cultural membership—that it allows for meaningful individual choice."[23] But insisting that all Pueblos have liberal rights in their community may very well mean destroying the Pueblo way of life. The liberal emphasis on choice is anathema to political communities that may treasure other values (devotion to God or to the community). Liberalism and theocratic government are incompatible.[24]

According to Kymlicka, diversity should be allowed to flourish in all communities. All communities should allow meaningful individual choices, even if this means radically altering the culture of the community. In other words, the liberal state should protect minority cultures in its midst—as long as they are liberal! I doubt that some cultures would find this idea all that comforting.[25] The structure of Indian culture must be protected—the context in which Indian culture exists—but particular Indian cultural practices may have to be given up in the liberal state. Kymlicka would be happy if we could point to an Indian society that replicated liberal society. Kymlicka triumphantly announces that his theory "supports, rather than compromises, the rights of individuals within the minority culture."[26] But his argument compromises, rather than supports, minority cultures. To be sure, liberalism does not insist upon only one set of cultural practices, but it does restrict the kind of cultural options available. Kymlicka's formula would radically alter Amish society to the point where it would no longer be recognizably Amish. Like other contemporary liberals, Kymlicka rests much of his argument on the meaning of choice. Kymlicka wants individuals to be able to choose their plans and projects, even if they are part of an illiberal culture, but this emphasis will hurt the cultures that Kymlicka wants to protect.

I partly agree with Kymlicka when it comes to weak ethnic groups. Members of those cultures should be able to choose the kind of life they want to live, even if this means changing or forgoing some of the cultural practices of their ethnic group—and even if this means that some people will not have a secure cultural context because they live between two different worlds. Indeed, there's no need to give weak ethnics any special recognition as a distinct culture, precisely because their culture is not distinct.[27] Yet I think the argument that the liberal state ought to try to ensure that liberal citizens choose their way of life is limited in an important way. The liberal virtues should be encouraged among those who have (or aspire to) full liberal citizenship but not among those who live in a liberal state but who are not, and do not want to be, full members. Native Americans who live on reservations, for example, have citizenship in their own political communities. The U.S. government has done enough damage to Native American communities as it is; to now force these communities to take on American political values and principles is the height of misplaced arrogance.[28] The liberal state should facilitate the liberal virtues only among full citizens, not among people who are citizens of other sovereign communities.

Similarly, it is a mistake to think of the Amish as liberal citizens. Although most ethnics want full citizenship, the Amish opt out of mainstream society; they choose to forgo liberal citizenship. I suggest that we should think of the Amish as a community apart from the political community in the United States, a community that wants to stay apart. The Amish are *in* the United States, but not *of* the United States. They came here so they could live in their church community unharmed, not because they believed in some kind of liberal ideal, although they benefit from liberal values. This shows a paradox of liberal theory; liberalism allows people to reject liberal values. The liberal state cannot insist that its citizens embrace liberalism. Liberalism allows people to think for themselves, to make their own decisions—or even to decide not to think for themselves. The liberal state can (and should) fight against this tendency, but it cannot forbid it. With the Amish, however, the liberal state should not fight this tendency. The Amish do not embrace liberalism; they are partial citizens, and as such the state should intervene in their community only when they harm their members or when they harm the mainstream community.[29]

To explain partial citizenship, I recall the distinction among public, private, and civil society that I discussed in chapter 3. These spheres are animated by different liberal virtues, virtues that build upon each other. In the private sphere, the avoidance of harm to others is the dominant liberal virtue. Although state interference in the private sphere ought to be minimal, private actions are limited if they harm others. Child and spouse abuse, for example, are actions that take place in private but demand state involvement. The avoidance of harm continues in civil society, but in this sphere the principle of nondiscrimination is also supposed to be followed. The public sphere, along with the institutions of civil society that play a part in democratic debate, cultivates the liberal virtues of self-reflectiveness, equality, and autonomy. The Amish have minimal involvement in the public sphere and in civil society; consequently, the liberal state should be mostly concerned that in Amish society the prohibition against harm is followed.

That the Amish are not part of the public sphere can readily be seen in their actions. The Amish do not care if their history is taught in public schools. They are not marginalized citizens who want to be accorded the respect and dignity that comes with full citizenship. They want to be respected, of course, but the respect they want is a respect of distance; they want to live their lives apart from, but in the midst of, mainstream society. The Amish rarely become involved in the political process. They infrequently vote; they never serve in political positions. When they do become politically active, it is almost always to protect their way of life. Because the Amish do not aspire to be part of the public, the liberal state need not encourage the Amish to cultivate the liberal virtues that are important in the public sphere.

The Amish also shy away from involvement in civil society. The Amish do not rely on the institutions of civil society for jobs, education, or amusement. They use the institutions of civil society occasionally, but this involvement is minimal. Amish people can and easily do live from cradle to grave in their communities, contributing to their community and, in turn, being taken care of by their community. The Amish do not own large factories on which many non-Amish people rely for their jobs; they do not run prestigious universities, whose degrees confer important status on their recipients. They do not run businesses, like gasoline stations or hotels, to which others need access to live fulfilling lives. Most Amish men run family farms. The Amish primarily live in the private sphere. Because their involvement in civil society is minimal, the Amish rarely find themselves in a position where they must follow the principle of nondiscrimination.

The liberal virtues of the private sphere do apply to the Amish. The Amish cannot harm others—just as the liberal state is tolerant of the Amish, so the Amish must be tolerant of others—nor can the Amish harm their own members or force them to be Amish. If children of the Amish are physically abused by their parents, then liberalism calls for state involvement. (For the same reason, the state should not allow Christian Scientists to withhold medical treatment from a child whose life is endangered without the treatment.) Furthermore, the liberal state can ensure that the children who choose to stay in their community actually make this choice. The liberal state cannot force people to have liberal values, but it can try to ensure that the people who reject liberalism actually do so by choice.

Choosing to Be Amish

How can the state know that people actually choose to join the Amish when their children live their entire lives in the Amish community and do not attend public schools? The retort that liberal citizens, including the Amish, can raise their children as they want to—except for abusing them—is not an argument that falls under the rubric of liberalism. Though liberalism generally has alarmingly little to say about children, liberal theory does not allow parents to treat their children as if they were their property. Ridiculing this argument, Mill said that "one would almost think that a man's children were supposed to be literally, and not metaphorically, a part of himself, so jealous is opinion of the smallest interference of law with his absolute and exclusive control over them." Children grow up to become adults; how they grow up will affect how they live as adults. Consequently, parents should prepare their children for adulthood. The state is interested in children as future citizens; it also should watch how children are educated, for the sake of the children. The state should act as the advocate of children if their parents do not raise them to live ably in society. Mill maintained that the state "should require and compel the education, up to a certain standard, of every human being who is born its citizen." Indeed, Mill recognized that how people are raised in private will affect their attitudes and behavior in public. Relations between parents, he said, should be a "school of sympathy of equality, of living together in love, without power on one side or obedience on the other." This would, Mill believed, teach the liberal virtue of equality to children.[30]

Mill did not suggest that the state reach into the home to ensure that husbands and wives treat each other equally; rather, he tried to persuade people to change the relations between men and women from hierarchical to equal. But Mill made it clear that the state has a role in the education of children, even if that means interfering with the family. One of the purposes of this education is to ensure that the children are able to choose the sort of life they wish to live when they become adults. Every liberal citizen ought to be able to choose the sort of life she or he wants to lead, even a life of partial citizenship. The question of how to determine whether people actually choose to be Amish, however, does not lend itself to an easy answer. What does it mean to choose to be Amish, to live a life that frowns upon independent thought? What does it mean to choose any way of life, for that matter?

No citizen has a full menu of life choices from which to choose. Choice means being aware that you can pursue different life plans and that you can interpret your identity to fit these plans. Choice need not mean experiencing many different roles; it means being aware that other roles exist and that you can take them on if you so choose. (Choice does not mean much if the options before you are not significantly different; the choice between working in two different automated pin factories, for example, is not meaningful.) One way to ensure that the Amish choose their way of life would be to force their children to go to high school to see other ways of living. However, the state does not argue that non-Amish people should be made to live with the Amish for two or three years so they can know the Amish way of life and make an informed decision about whether they want to join Amish society or not. Everyone is raised by certain people, with certain values, and in certain communities. People's choices are influenced by how they are raised. This is true for the Amish and non-Amish alike. People cannot sample all the different ways of life in their society and then choose to follow the one they like best. People cannot try on values like they try on clothes.

Surely the manner in which people are raised will heavily influence the way they want to live their lives. Although most citizens influence their children, they also expose their children to other ways of life and values through schools and other institutions like sports leagues, camps, and clubs. Exposed to a variety of influences, children can then form their own values, preferences, and principles. Amish children, however, are not members of a variety of institutions that have diverse memberships. Many parents, Amish and non-Amish alike, may not encourage their children to be self-critical, but at least non-Amish children may learn this skill in schools or in other institutions. Amish children, because the scope of influences on their life is so narrow, are less likely to learn to be self-critical.

Members of small cultures, like the Amish, will almost always know that they have a choice about their ethnic membership. As long as the Amish are not brainwashed, it is safe to assume that the Amish choose to be Amish. As a small minority culture, the Amish cannot help but see mainstream culture; it is all around them. The Amish live in their own world, but their world is not completely separate from mainstream society. The interaction between the two worlds means that the Amish must accommodate themselves to the modern world; the Amish constantly address issues raised by new technology. Many of the Amish who leave their community do so because they want to use a modern device that is forbidden by the Ordnung. The Amish can see that other people own cars and telephones, that they ride on airplanes and go to college. Amish girls can see that non-Amish women are not always subordinate to men. Amish men can see that many others manage to make a good living but are not farmers; they see doctors, lawyers, merchants, and so forth. The Amish are fully aware that there is another world out there, a world that will accept them if they want to join it.

It is also a world that some Amish teen-agers experiment with. Because they are not baptized, Amish teen-agers cannot be expelled for violating the rules of the Ordnung. They have been known to buy cars, see movies, attend horse races, and drink alcohol. A recent problem for Amish teen-agers is preventing thieves from stealing their stereos from their buggies. Amish teen-agers often have semisecret parties on Sundays, where they drink, dance, and listen to music, just like other teen-agers. Each year there is a "Florida Reunion," where Amish teen-agers who spent time in Florida during the previous winter have a rather large party in one of the northern states. Attended by hundreds of Amish teen-agers, the reunions take place at a large country club or a campground and cost thousands of dollars. Live music and liquor are provided, paid for by the money collected from the individuals who buy admission tickets. On occasion the police have had to talk to the parents of Amish teen-agers about their children's rowdy behavior. Amish teen-agers know that they can live a non–Amish life if that is what they want. When the time for baptism comes, they can climb into their buggy and drive away. With 20 percent of the Amish community leaving, the choice to leave is obviously recognized and acted upon regularly. (Because of their high birth rate, however, Amish society steadily grows.)

It is not surprising that most of the Amish who do leave their communities do not become nuclear engineers. They are most likely to join the more liberal Anabaptist communities, particularly the Mennonites. They take up a new identity, but one that is not completely new; many of the rules of the community and the way of life of its members are familiar to the newcomers. They interpret their religious identity differently than the way it is interpreted by the Amish church. Those who leave Amish society do not simply choose another identity; rather, they reinterpret their identity in a way that better fits their plans and projects.

Knowing that other ways of life exist is not the same as having the confidence and ability to take them on as one's own. Amish children may see the outside world, they may know that they have the formal choice to join it, but they may not have much confidence in their ability to make their way in this strange world. The Amish children probably do not have as many choices in their lives as do other children, but they do have a modicum of choice. The steady number of Amish that leave the Amish community shows that many believe that they have the ability to survive outside the Amish community. Furthermore, the Amish do not raise their children ill-equipped to live meaningful lives. The Amish prepare their children to live in the Amish community, just as other parents prepare their children to live in their communities. With most Amish children choosing to live in either Amish or Mennonite communities, their upbringing does in fact prepare them for their life plans and projects.

If many Amish left their communities to join mainstream society, the liberal state's commitment to helping people pursue their plans and projects would mean that it ought to help these people adjust to their new surroundings. Under these circumstances the state should teach the former Amish the ways of mainstream culture. Indeed, if it became apparent that the Amish were not preparing their children for the lives they wanted to pursue—if the number of young adults leaving the community for mainstream society increased from a trickle to a stream—then the *Yoder* decision would have to be revisited. Mandatory attendance at public schools might very well be one of the measures the state should take to prepare the children of the Amish for their adult lives.

Although I am defending *Yoder,* I do not want to deny the hardships involved in leaving the Amish community; it is not always as easy as climbing into your buggy. Balancing the need to ensure that the Amish have some choice about their lives with the need to give the Amish the autonomy they need to survive is not easy. Although the state does not need to worry about the political education of Amish children, it does need to ensure that these same children have the choice to leave their community and become full democratic citizens. This is hardly a neat solution to the problem that the Amish pose for liberal democratic theory. However, unless the political community is willing to destroy Amish culture, the Amish must have some autonomy to establish the rules governing their community. As long as there is evidence that the Amish do choose their way of life, the liberal state can tolerate them; for some problems, tidy solutions are hard to find.

The tensions between liberalism's concern for children and its respect for the family are not fatal to liberalism or to the Amish. Toleration of the Amish, however, does not mean celebration; liberal democrats (and others who support democracy and equality) should not glorify the Amish. A celebration of Amish values is, at least in part, a celebration of patriarchal and hierarchical values. Institutions in the liberal state should not romanticize the Amish, as often happens in textbooks, movies, and displays in schools and libraries.[31] A grudging tolerance of the Amish is different from a celebration of their culture and the pronouncement that it is equal to liberal cultures, which is what advocates of cultural pluralism must do if they are to remain cultural pluralists. In a culturally plural state, where all cultures are protected regardless of their practices, there may be many cultures with values similar to those of the Amish. Cultural pluralists must explain why societies permeated by traditional, patriarchal values should be celebrated, cultures where women wash, clean, cook, and obey their husbands, where all members learn to be obedient and to accept the community's rule without much thought, where discussion and debate are frowned upon. Even if the liberal state cannot stamp these values out, it can actively discourage them. Although the liberal state should not actively work to dismantle the Amish community, it would not be a terrible loss if it were to disappear. Certainly, if the Amish brainwashed their children so it was impossible for them even to contemplate leaving their community, then stronger state involvement would be appropriate. Cults that·brainwash their members cannot claim that they give their members any choice about their way of life. A claim to partial citizenship does not shield the Amish from the state's purview.

Partial citizenship, though, does allow the Amish to establish the rules governing their community unless they break liberal democratic strictures. Although Amish people can interpret their identities as they wish, the Amish community in which they live may reject their interpretation. A member of the Old Order Amish who reinterprets what it means to be Amish to include owning a telephone, radio, and car is moving past the boundaries of what it means to be Old Order Amish. Kymlicka, however, wants to encourage this sort of reinterpretation; he wants to combine people's cultural structures with individual choice, which means that he would allow Amish people to violate the rules of the Amish community and yet remain in the community. If the Old Order were forced to accept all reinterpretations of what it means to be Amish, even those that do not accord with the community's vision of itself, then the Old Order would probably not exist for very long. The Amish would become like a weak ethnic group, with perhaps a kernel of a distinctive culture.

Kymlicka thinks that, by imposing liberal values on each culture, he increases people's choices, but, if the liberal state follows Kymlicka and refuses to allow communities the ability to insist that their members share certain beliefs, these communities will probably disappear. This will mean that the reinterpreters will live in a non–Amish community anyway but that those who wanted to live in an Amish community will not be able to do so. Kymlicka's argument, because it destroys distinctive cultures, actually allows less choice in the liberal state. Instead of forcing the Old Order Amish to accept the diversity of liberal society, the state should simply insist that the reinterpreters be allowed to leave their communities without interference. This allows each individual to interpret her or his own identity as Kymlicka wants but also allows Amish society to endure.

Beyond ensuring that the Amish do not harm their members, state intervention is also needed if the Amish harm others. Although it is difficult to imagine the Amish hurting others, issues of public safety surrounding their horses and buggies have arisen. Most states insist, in the name of public safety, that the Amish put colorful slow-moving vehicle (SMV) emblems on the backs of their black buggies. Most Amish have reluctantly agreed to use the emblems, but some have refused because they view the bright emblems as too ostentatious. In Minnesota, the Swartzentruber Amish (who are more conservative than Old Order Amish) were routinely fined for not putting orange emblems on their buggies. They proposed using silver reflective tape instead, but the state did not accept this proposal. Eventually, the Minnesota SMV law was struck down by the Minnesota Supreme Court, which said that silver tape would be enough to protect public safety.[32] The Amish need some emblem on their buggies that will protect public safety. If silver will suffice and it is the Amish's preferred alternative, then there's no reason to insist upon orange. However, if orange is needed, then the state must simply insist that Amish beliefs take a back seat to the public safety. The Amish do not have a right to endanger others so they can maintain their practices, regardless of the importance of these practices to their culture.

Cultural pluralists need to take note of the Amish; the Amish understand how to remain culturally distinctive in the modern world. They understand what it takes to maintain a separate culture in the midst of a liberal society. The demands of liberal citizenship bear heavily on those who integrate into the larger community; by eschewing this integration, the Amish escape the full demands of liberal citizenship. Cultural pluralists need to explain how members of different cultures can integrate, have some measure of economic equality with others, *and* remain culturally distinctive. Ethnic groups that, unlike the Amish, do not strive for separation will be faced with the probability that liberal citizenship will transform their identity. Cultural pluralists, who want to maintain a rich variety of definable cultural differences among groups, must argue against the integration for which most ethnic groups strive. Unsurprisingly, few other ethnic groups have followed the Amish model. It's not, after all, easy to do.

Justifying *Yoder*

Chief Justice Burger justified the *Yoder* decision by arguing that freedom of religion meant that the Amish did not have to send their children to high school, for this would interfere with their religion. Yet freedom of religion is not an absolute freedom, as Burger noted; civil interests override religious interests when the two clash.[33]

Clearly, teaching liberal values to children is an important civil interest. Indeed, if my argument that the Amish are partial citizens fails, then the state must try to inculcate liberal values in the children of the Amish. If the Amish are partial citizens, however, the state need not make this same demand. For partial citizens, the demands of citizenship are weaker; the state need only ensure that partial citizens are aware that they can leave their community, that they have choices about the kind of life they want to lead, and that they are not physically abused. Partial citizens do not have to be encouraged to think critically about politics. Partial citizenship need not be a legal category; the Amish, through their actions, show that they are partial citizens. This does not make partial citizenship an empty category; it can be used to help the government get along with the Amish.

Many misunderstandings can be avoided if local and state officials recognize that the Amish are a different kind of citizen and that government expectations of the Amish should be changed accordingly. When the Amish move to a new area, which is relatively common, government officials ought to recognize that the Amish are unlike other citizens; these officials should strive to discuss issues of mutual concern with the leaders of the Amish. To handle the problems that arise between the Amish and the state, as a matter of convenience government officials should recognize the Amish as a group and handle matters of concern with the recognized leaders of the Amish community. Doing so will help avoid costly and painful litigation, as occurred in Wisconsin.

Partial citizenship should not be a privileged category of citizenship.[34] Although my suggestions here may be construed as allowing the Amish to opt out of the obligation to provide a liberal education for their children, this is predicated on their forgoing many of the privileges and advantages of modern liberal society. Because of their devout avoidance of many of the institutions of modern life, the state should be less concerned about their fulfilling responsibilities to the state, as long as their children choose to be Amish. The Amish, though, should follow the formal requirements of citizenship; they should pay taxes and provide service to the country in time of war (even if this is alternative service to fighting). The Amish do, after all, benefit from the protection of the state and use some of its services.[35]

Another objection to the category of partial citizenship is its political apathy. The Amish are hardly the only ones in contemporary society to shy away from politics. Some citizens see political matters as a bother; other citizens do not want to develop their critical capacities. Because encouraging the liberal virtues is different from coercion, many citizens will simply withstand any pressures to increase their autonomy, just as the Amish do. There's danger, however, if the state decides not to encourage citizens to be reflective. Certainly, the problem in the United States today is that there are too few citizens with the liberal virtues, not too many. Teaching liberal democratic values does not ensure that the lessons will be learned well, but it presents the possibility that some future citizens will learn these lessons. Decreasing the number of citizens who are taught the liberal virtues will mean a probable reduction in the number of good democratic citizens. Because it is not possible to know in advance who will embrace the values of liberal democracy, all future (full) citizens should be taught about democracy.

To avoid the possibility of other citizens claiming that they deserve exemption from the liberal virtues, we need narrow principles upon which to decide who can withdraw from full liberal citizenship. Partial citizenship fits this bill; if someone dislikes the education her child receives in a public school, she cannot simply announce that she is a partial citizen and exempt her children from the state's educational demands. This is not a fanciful possibility. Some citizens actually clamor for exemptions of this sort.

In one court case, *Mozert v. Hawkins*, Christian fundamentalists objected to their children's exposure to books that encouraged the use of the imagination beyond what Scripture teaches, for this was supposedly an "occult practice."[36] Biographical material about women who were recognized for their achievement outside the home was also objectionable (as "role reversal"). The parents objected to exposing their children to other religions and to beliefs that contradicted the parents' religious views unless the children were also told that these other religions and beliefs were wrong. However, the Tennessee schools sued by these parents did not impose a particular belief on the children. The students were not taught that their religious views were wrong. The teachers did, however, expose the students to different beliefs. Part of the mission of the teachers was to teach more than reading; they also wanted to teach students the cognitive skills necessary for critical evaluation of the material they read, certainly a laudable goal in a liberal democracy. The children were taught about different ways of life and about different beliefs; in this process they were taught to be tolerant of different political and religious views. In other words, they were taught the liberal virtues.

These students were not raised to be partial citizens. In *Mozert,* their parents said they wanted their children to acquire all of the skills necessary to live in modern society. Unlike the Amish, the fundamentalists did not, the Court noted, "separate themselves from the world and avoid assimilation into society."[37] The parents wanted their children to be part of mainstream society, but they also wanted their children to be taught Biblical Truth, as they understood it.[38] If the teachers could not or would not do this, then the parents wanted their children exempt from the lessons that were contrary to their interpretation of the Bible. However, the liberal state has an obligation to teach its future citizens the liberal virtues, even if they violate someone's religious beliefs. Parents do not have the right to control the education of their children completely. The liberal virtues are demanding not only because they can be difficult to achieve, but also because they open up the possibility that children will choose to differ from their parents in their religious, political, and social beliefs. Liberals should try to "equip children with the intellectual skills necessary to evaluate ways of life different from that of their parents."[39] Seeing their children choose paths different from their own will be, for many parents, difficult to face. The Court recognized the demands of liberal citizenship and rightly argued in *Mozert* that the children could not be exempted from the reading classes.

Few will follow the Amish and radically separate themselves from civil society and the public sphere as partial citizens. Those who want to be considered partial citizens have to set up another set of rules that will govern their community and find enough people to follow them to have an economically viable community. They need to be able to care for the elderly who are part of their community and no longer work. They must come up with an alternative form of education and prepare their children to live in their community when they are adults. Their children must also learn the basic skills necessary to function in the liberal state (reading and writing English and having basic math skills), so they are at least minimally prepared if they decide to leave the community. The state should recognize people as partial citizens and as members of a group only when they meet this tough standard. It is doubtful that many others will follow the Amish into partial citizenship, since this is rather difficult. Even Hasidic Jews do not meet this standard.[40]

Partial citizenship need not hang on religious belief. I see no reason why communities with a religious basis should be privileged over other kinds of communities. People may think that they have a duty to live a certain way because of their devotion to God, but they may also believe they have a duty to other people, to a philosophical doctrine, or to themselves. Attending public schools—or any school—can conceivably interfere with other lifestyles. If followers of Thoreau decide to establish their own separate community, the state should treat them little differently from the Amish. As long as they do not harm anyone and as long as their children have the option to leave the community, the liberal state should allow partial citizens to live in the midst of, but apart from, mainstream society. Nor does it matter that the Amish are hardworking citizens, as Burger noted. Although this characterization of the Amish is correct, Burger did not say why this fact is important to the *Yoder* decision. Productive citizens who prevent their children from choosing a way of life they find fulfilling, who brainwash their citizens, or who force their members to follow the dictates of their community should not be protected by the Court.[41]

Clermont-Tonnerre would be horrified at this formula; he declared, after all, that it would be repugnant to have a society of noncitizens in France, a nation within a nation. But the Amish do not harm the polity; they remain a small sect, one difficult to emulate, pursuing their vision of the good life as they see it. Even as the Amish community grows, the Amish remain a tiny part of the U.S. population.[42] Clermont-Tonnerre's opponents in the French Assembly argued that, as long as the Jews were a separate nation, they should not receive full citizenship. I've argued here that, in effect, the Amish are not full citizens. They are not quite noncitizens or a nation within a nation; they fit oddly in the liberal state, but they do not threaten anyone. They are quiet partial citizens, content to pursue salvation in their own distinctive, if illiberal, way.

A Liberal Paradox: The Case of the Hasidim

Like the Amish, the Hasidim live starkly different lives from those of people in mainstream society. Hasidic Jews broke from mainstream Jewish traditions in the seventeenth and eighteenth centuries, emphasizing the more mystical parts of Judaism. Originally a rebellious movement, the Hasidim are now often considered to be one of Judaism's more conservative elements. Similar to the Amish in some respects, Hasidic men also wear black clothing that easily distinguishes them from the rest of the population; the Hasidim also live in patriarchal and hierarchical societies and have large families. Their lives are permeated by religious values and religious devotion. The effects of liberal citizenship on most ethnics are, for the most part, not replicated when it comes to the Hasidim; like the Amish, the Hasidim are an insular community. They, too, do not strive for inclusion in school curriculums or want to share their cultural practices with others. Yet there is one important difference between the two communities that makes the Hasidim a more difficult problem for liberal democrats; unlike the Amish, the Hasidim are politically active. The Hasidim vote, sometimes run for local office, and serve on a variety of local political boards and commissions.

The Hasidim in fact have considerable political influence. New York City politicians unashamedly trek to the headquarters of the Hasidic communities to make political deals, hoping that their promises to the Hasidim will translate into a political endorsement by the rebbe. (The Hasidim live all over the United States, but their largest concentration is in New York City. There are several different Hasidic sects. I speak here mostly of the Lubovitch sect, which is the largest and best known.) In New York City, the Lubovitch Hasidim are a solid voting bloc. They vote as the rebbe tells them to vote. This political involvement must trouble any democrat. Thousands of Lubovitchers vote in elections, but they do not think about the best candidate or weigh the issues in a campaign. They are not interested in democratic debate or discussion. The liberal virtues of the public sphere, of self-critical reflectiveness, of weighing the best interests of society against one's own self-interest, Mill's hope that political involvement would be in part an educative process—these do not apply to the Hasidim. For them, voting is simply one more realm in which they follow the rebbe's wisdom without question. One New York political observer commented on the Hasidic vote: "Mayor Daley would be proud of them. They are the last deliverable bloc in the city."[43] A candidate who wins the endorsement of the rebbe is assured of thousands of votes, as his followers almost automatically follow his commands. The Hasidim are really part of a political machine—the rebbe's machine.[44]

The cohesiveness of the Hasidic community has turned it into a political force that few other communities can match. Unsurprisingly, political officials often satisfy the demands of the Hasidim. Only by risking their political future can New York politicians ignore the wishes of a solid voting bloc of tens of thousands. The problem the Hasidim pose for liberal democracy cannot be easily dismissed by classifying them as partial citizens; their political involvement is too extensive not to consider them part of the polity. Consequently, the demands the liberal state makes on its citizens should apply to the Hasidim. As with other ethnics, the liberal state should try to accommodate the particular practices of the Hasidim when possible and within liberal limits, but the state shouldn't exempt the Hasidim from nondiscrimination laws, nor should the state allow them to forgo paying taxes because of their particular beliefs. The liberal state's demands on other ethnics should apply equally to the Hasidim.

Treating the Hasidim on a par with other ethnic groups, however, does not mean that they will ignore their rebbe and think for themselves in the voting booth. In a liberal democracy people can vote for whomever they wish and for whatever reason—good or bad. The Hasidim are bad democratic citizens, yet liberalism supplies only limited resources to try to turn them into good citizens. Liberals want citizens to participate actively in politics, to be self-critical and reflective, and to think for themselves, but liberalism does not have a way to ensure that citizens actually practice these virtues. These virtues are taught in schools and are implicit in the rules that govern the institutions of civil society. To a large degree, however, the Hasidim escape learning about or practicing these virtues by severely restricting their interactions with mainstream society. Hasidic Jews rarely attend secular schools and never go to secular colleges; few, if any, work for large corporations; they hardly ever participate in social or civic activities that include non-Hasidim. A few Hasidim do run for political office, but for most Hasidim an occasional trip to the voting booth, where they follow the rebbe's instructions, is the extent of their political participation. This participation is hardly enough to transform the identity of Hasidim.

The Hasidim do not violate the laws of the liberal state, but they certainly violate the spirit of liberalism. The universalism of liberalism, the idea that everyone is equal, that people should be judged by their individual actions and not by their group membership, is not valued by the Hasidim (not even in some abstract way that is often violated in practice). Discrimination is integral to the Hasidim; they are interested only in their community and restrict their interactions with nonmembers. Group membership, not individual talent or ability, is their primary basis for judgment of others, although they do judge members of their community. Liberalism, however, allows discrimination in the private sphere; the liberal state cannot force the Hasidim to treat others equally. Certainly, this is not a problem unique to the Hasidim; other ethnics, including other Jews, practice social discrimination, often to maintain their group identity. These ethnics argue that too much social integration with others may lead to intermarriage, which will dilute their ethnic identity. Others sometimes look upon these ethnics as clannish and as discriminating against others. To some extent, these charges are true; to maintain ethnic cohesiveness, some amount of discrimination is necessary. This violation of the universalism that underlies liberalism is cause for a sporadic social problem. For the most part, however, the demands of liberal citizenship work to break down the barriers erected by weak ethnic groups. To integrate politically, economically, and educationally but not socially, as many weak ethnics try to do, is not an easy task. A few weak ethnics successfully practice this balancing act, but many fail. The Hasidim succeed at building barriers between themselves and others because they shy away from education and economic integration, while their political integration is quite circumscribed.

The liberal state can make it harder for strong ethnics to maintain their identity by intervening more forcefully in the realm of education. As long as private schools are allowed to exist, however, the Hasidim will teach their own children.[45] The Christian fundamentalists have the option of opening their own private schools as well; of course, money is needed to choose this option, and they may not have enough funds to do this. This is not much cause for concern; the state should not make it easy for antiliberal parents to block their children from learning the liberal virtues. Although the state cannot prevent students from being taught antidemocratic values in private schools, it can insist that liberal democratic values are also taught. The state has a civil interest in teaching liberal democratic values to its future citizens, and the children have an interest in learning how to be self-reflective so they can choose the sort of life they want to lead. The state can insist that each Hasidic student (and all students in private schools, for that matter) take a certain number of courses in American government or democracy as a requirement for graduation; it can also insist that these courses be taught by state-appointed teachers if it suspects that the private school teachers are not doing an adequate job. Hasidic parents cannot exert complete control over their children's education and kick the state out of their children's classrooms, nor can they be exempted from liberal values by claiming partial citizenship. Liberal citizens can choose to disdain liberal values, but this does not give them the right to ensure that their children scorn these values as well.

By learning about democratic values in Hasidic schools, some students may be convinced of the importance of these values; some will choose democracy over blind devotion to the rebbe. There is little assurance, however, that after two or three classes Hasidic children will recognize the antidemocratic nature of their community and become model democratic citizens. It would be naive to think that a couple of classes could make the Hasidim, socialized into thinking a certain way since birth, overturn deep-seated convictions. This might occur sometimes, but surely not all or even most of the time.

This low rate of success does not mean, however, that the state should not try to teach liberal, democratic values to the Hasidim. There are many other people in the United States who hold deeply illiberal values but are full citizens. The state should try to reach all citizens, even if it will sometimes fail in this attempt. Not all students need to learn their lessons well; a democracy can tolerate islands of nondemocratic citizens.

The Hasidim are a problem for the liberal state, but, as long as the Hasidim remain a small sect, this is a problem the state can live with. The difficulties in integrating politically but remaining socially separate mean that the chances of many groups emulating the Hasidim are quite small. Still, liberal democrats can hardly be comfortable with the Hasidim. As long as liberalism gives the family some autonomy, however, and allows ethnic identity to exist, groups like the Hasidim may exist. They are the outcome of efforts to preserve diversity in the liberal state.

The fact that liberalism can survive this sort of tension is small solace for the non-Hasidim who watch politicians trek to the rebbe's door. One answer for those who dislike Hasidic political power is to organize themselves, to look to the Hasidim as a model.[46] But, just as the Amish should not be replicated, neither should the Hasidim. Unthinking voters who automatically follow the commands of a leader, who worship their leader and look upon him as a mystical, almost God-like figure, are not good democratic citizens. As long as other communities are not organized as tightly as the Hasidim, however—and few groups can even aspire to their organization—battling the political influence of the Hasidim will be an uphill struggle. Surely, arguments that the Hasidim receive too many favors from politicians, if they ring true, will resound within the larger community. The Hasidim are only a small part of the electorate in New York City; other residents may become convinced that the Hasidim have too much political influence and fight against them.[47] This is part of the liberal, democratic process.

Liberals must be honest about the possibility of the success of this process. Although the influence of the Hasidim may be counteracted successfully at times, as long as they are a large enough group to command the attention of politicians they will be politically influential. The liberal state can fight against illiberal values but cannot stamp them out. By allowing ethnic identities to exist, which it does for good reason, the liberal state allows a tension between private identity and the larger community. Often this tension will be minor, but sometimes it will distort the political process. The liberal state, however, must live with this tension. Sometimes liberalism is handcuffed by its own principles.

CHAPTER 6

RACE AND THE FAILURE
OF LIBERAL CITIZENSHIP

LIBERAL CITIZENSHIP has failed Black Americans, not completely, perhaps not irrevocably, but mostly. The principle of nondiscrimination, important to securing equal citizenship, has not been applied by many white Americans to Black Americans. This failure of liberal citizenship means that Black identity has not been transformed by liberalism as has ethnic identity. Black Americans have retained and developed their own distinctive cultural practices, partly out of the need to survive in a hostile world and partly because some Black Americans have rejected mainstream culture, which they see as oppressive. Although Black Americans have made important strides in obtaining formal political equality, this has not been enough to end the discrimination they face.

The subordination and separation of Black people has ensured the development of identity based on race in the United States, posing an acute problem for American liberalism. Despite the principle of nondiscrimination, many citizens in the liberal state look upon Black people as members of a group and treat them badly. For years, laws that specifically treated Blacks as a group were passed. Although most of these laws are no longer in effect, some whites think that Blacks are biologically inferior to whites. Other whites who do not base their prejudices on biology still may group Blacks together. One critic of liberalism argues that the fundamental problem in the liberal state "is that an emancipated and disorganized group does not have any real control over its collective existence—but it does still get treated as a collectivity."[1] Liberal theory says that people should be judged on their individual actions, but many non-Black citizens in the liberal state judge Black people because of their ascriptive identity. Because a few Black people commit crimes, some whites associate all Blacks with crime; although some white people commit crimes, few whites think of all whites as criminals. This means that all Blacks, regardless of behavior, must deal with racism.

The evidence that Blacks still face considerable discrimination at the end of the twentieth century is plentiful. Blacks earn less than whites, even when education levels are the same; Blacks are still victims of real estate redlining; and Blacks of all income levels report that they are victims of undue police harassment and brutality. Perhaps the most persuasive evidence of discrimination is found in the words of Black people themselves, which show that they are victims of discrimination in many everyday settings.[2]

The problem of race is partly about money and jobs, but also about different cultural practices. Black Americans have cultural practices that others do not share, but members of mainstream culture sometimes demand cultural conformity before they give Black people a chance to succeed in many mainstream institutions. Whites often set institutional standards and policies that discriminate against Blacks. These whites may not be racist, and they may really believe in equality, but if they are ignorant of the differences between Blacks and whites, the standards they establish may discriminate anyway.

Blacks mainly re-created their culture apart from the dominant American institutions, even while there was considerable interaction between the dominant culture and African-American culture. In other words, African-American culture is a distinctive American culture.[3] Many slaves, for example, developed a unique form of music that combined African and American elements; music gave slaves hope, pleasure, and inspiration—and it was also a form of communication that whites rarely understood. Slaves also created ways of talking that whites could not understand. And, although many slaves became Christians, they often read the Bible as condemning slavery, while their masters understood the Bible as justifying slavery. When slavery ended, Black-American culture changed considerably, yet the continued oppression of Blacks ensured that Black culture and identity remained distinct from mainstream culture.

As racism has changed, particularly since the 1960s, the cultural differences between some Blacks and some whites have diminished. Some Blacks have jobs in large corporations or government, have a house in the suburbs, and take vacations overseas—in many respects, their lives are similar to those of members of the white middle class. As racism has changed, the connection between race and culture in the United States has loosened. The cultural values of some Blacks are quite similar to the values of many white Americans, and some white Americans have taken on Black cultural practices. If the oppression of Black Americans decreases, the differences between Black culture and mainstream culture will probably fade even more.[4] Although race no longer strictly maps onto culture in the United States, race still matters even for Blacks successful in mainstream America, since racial discrimination persists. Indeed, Black Americans in the public eye report that they feel pressure to do well so their actions reflect well on other Blacks. There are few analogous "race men" or "race women" among whites.

While liberals decry the history of racism in the United States, some liberals argue that recognizing Blacks in public policies violates liberal principles. These liberals argue that the state should ensure only that no one faces discrimination in civil society or in the public sphere. However, to think that the effects of the laws that subordinated Black people would magically disappear as soon as they were repealed is, at best, wishful thinking. Even if all white people in the United States had no racial prejudice, the legacy of past racism would persist. Despite the rise of a Black middle class, many Blacks are concentrated in urban areas where low-skilled manufacturing jobs used to exist. The end of racist views would do little to stop the decline in the number of manufacturing plants in many cities.[5] If racist attitudes were suddenly to vanish, the percentage of Black Americans who are impoverished would still be three times the percentage of impoverished white Americans. Continued racism contributes to these problems, but the problems faced by many Black Americans will not simply disappear if all white people no longer hold racist views.

Some liberals recognize that the social ills afflicting Black Americans show that race matters in this country and that it matters in ways more harmful to Blacks than to whites. This, however, leads to a liberal dilemma: liberals do not want to enshrine a specific Black identity, yet they want to rectify the legacy of racism. This dilemma is captured in Justice Blackmun's dissent in the infamous *Bakke* case: "In order to get beyond racism, we must first take account of race."[6] A liberal community should try to move past race, but it cannot do so by pretending to ignore race after several hundred years of racial divisions.[7]

Liberalism and Racism

"We were put in the Possession of our Rights of Liberty and Property. But notwithstanding this, we understand a very subtle and daring Attempt is made to dispossess us of a very important Part of our Property."[8] Thus announced a petition signed by hundreds of white Virginians who opposed a gradual emancipation bill introduced in their state legislature in 1784. This petition was couched in the language of Lockean liberalism. Locke had articulated a liberal argument for property rights in the *Second Treatise on Government,* where he provided the justification for an owner to do what he wanted with his property.[9] Because slaves were not persons with rights, these slave owners argued, they were property, and so, they claimed, they could do what they wanted with their slaves. This argument was common; it was also endorsed by the Supreme Court. In the *Dred Scott* decision, Chief Justice Taney declared that "the Constitution recognizes the right of property of the master in a slave, and makes no distinction between that description of property and other property owned by a citizen."[10]

Liberal language helped justify slavery in other ways. Some noted that liberalism grants rights to people with reason; reason, after all, is needed to understand the laws of nature.[11] Only those with reason could be full participants in society and have the right to vote. Blacks supposedly lacked reason and so could not understand the laws of nature. They were fit to live only in the state of tyranny, where they had no rights and could only be slaves. Indeed, slavery helped define liberalism in the United States. By seeing what rights slaves lacked, whites could more clearly define what rights they had. Moreover, by defining themselves in opposition to Blacks, wealthy, slave-owning whites promoted an illusory equality among whites. There were severe class divisions among whites in the antebellum South, but the emphasis on the divisions between Blacks and whites underplayed these rifts. With the end of slavery, the language of property rights could no longer be used as a justification for the submission of Blacks. But other justifications were found. Again, the subordination of Blacks was used as a way to highlight equality among whites; racial divisions were often exploited by industrialists to prevent the unity of the working class. In *Plessy v. Ferguson,* the Supreme Court declared that separate but equal accommodations were legal; of course, separate was rarely equal.

The liberal justification for slavery was uneasy. Slave owners could not kill their slaves with impunity, meaning that slaves had some legal protection; there were court rulings in the South that penalized slave owners for hurting or killing their slaves.[12] This was a theoretical dilemma, however, for how can property have any legal standing? Furthermore, there were some free Blacks and, although their rights were often restricted, they were not slaves. Moreover, the abolitionists used liberal language to attack slavery. All men were created equal, the abolitionists declared, and, since Black men were men, they too were created equal. Rights "were at the very eye of abolitionist rhetoric." The constitutions of many Northern states, modeled after Virginia's Declaration of Rights written by George Mason, proclaimed that men had the right to life, liberty, property, happiness, and safety. But most of the constitutions of the Southern states proclaimed that only free men had rights, and even their rights were reduced from Mason's list. In the South, much of "Mason's rhetoric was snuffed out in quick, barely disguised panic."[13]

Liberalism and its language of rights were used to attack racism extensively in the twentieth century. The National Association for the Advancement of Colored People (NAACP) used the courts to erode the legal structure of racism slowly, with *Brown v. Board of Education* being only the most famous of many decisions. The liberal language of rights and equality permeated the Civil Rights Movement. Blacks and many whites argued that Blacks had the right to legal equality, to get the same education as whites; Black Americans had the right to vote, they argued, and the right to eat and shop where they wanted. Galvanizing many was the large gap between the American promise of liberal equality and individual rights and the reality lived by many Black Americans. Seeing this hypocrisy, many argued that Black Americans be given the rights promised by the Constitution (and subsequent amendments) to all Americans. When Blacks argued that they deserved protection for their constitutional rights, they used the language of rights in which white liberals believed and challenged whites to live up to the demands implicit in that language. The language of rights can be a powerful tool against oppression; it gives the oppressed a language in which to express their claims. Black legal scholar Patricia Williams explains: "Rights feel new in the mouths of most black people. It is still deliciously empowering to say." Williams recognizes that many Blacks are suspicious of rights because Blacks have not enjoyed them. But the worst historical movements in the United States, she notes, "have not been attributable to rights *assertion* but to a failure of rights commitment."[14]

The liberal attack on racism led some racists to abandon liberalism. Although many Southerners persisted in their use of liberalism to justify slavery, some disowned liberalism to find another, better way to justify the subordination of Blacks. John Calhoun argued against majority rule, equality, and the idea of individual rights. Calhoun was concerned about minority rights, but the minority he had in mind was not Blacks, but the South; he worried that the more populous North would eradicate slavery. He argued that each section of society in the country should have veto power over each proposed bill. By giving each section veto power, the South could stop the attempts by some to abolish slavery. George Fitzhugh also repudiated liberalism and the doctrine of rights, arguing that slavery was a natural part of all societies.[15] For many Southerners the subordination of Blacks was more important than liberalism; they were willing to abandon the liberal ideas of rights and equality to retain slavery. Many racists in the nineteenth century firmly believed in hierarchy and the subordination of those who were supposedly racially inferior.

The idea that the American Creed is always essentially liberal and that deviations like racism can be pointed out and attacked by appealing to this liberal American Creed doesn't always work. Racist, hierarchical beliefs are the core beliefs of some Americans; if liberalism reveals an inconsistency in their ideas, then it is liberalism that will go.[16] American racism didn't die with the Civil War. Quite the contrary; many of the steps toward equality taken during Reconstruction were reversed by the end of the nineteenth century, and many in the twentieth century are nonliberal racists. Most notorious are the Nazis, racists who had little use for liberal values. Some of their descendants are still around today, both in the United States and in Europe.

Racism can survive in a liberal framework—although overt racism often stretches liberalism to the breaking point—yet jettisoning liberalism will not mean the end of racism. This is unfortunate in one sense; if racism depended on liberalism to survive, ridding the United States of liberalism would end racism. The solution to racism might then be simple (assuming a good alternative to liberalism could be found). But it is too easy to point to the racism in our society and blame liberalism. Doing so simply allows one to escape facing the hard question of how to end the effects of racism. The racist tradition in the United States is longstanding; racism is deeply embedded in American society and can easily survive liberalism. Racism is not merely a deviation from central American liberal beliefs, nor is it only a manifestation of liberalism. Rather, racism can and has stood apart from liberalism.[17]

Indeed, it is easy to argue that the racist values and practices in the United States are illiberal. Contemporary liberals routinely argue that liberal rights should be given to Black and white (and Latino- and Asian-American) citizens alike. They point out that invidious discrimination based on race simply has no place in liberalism. Although this argument is right, it is also too quick.

Liberalism has shaped the way racism manifests itself in the liberal state. Racism may be illiberal, but it is not clear that liberalism has the resources to overcome race and racism. The American race problem exposes at least three important flaws in liberalism.

First, most liberals are democrats; the best sort of liberal state, it is often said, is a democratic one. Democratic institutions, however, cannot ensure that power is always used judiciously. A group of people can be oppressed by the government with little recourse if their fellow citizens do not care about them. Although Locke said little about democracy, he recognized that an oppressed minority could do little about its plight.

For if it [tyranny] reach no farther than some private men's cases, though they have a right to defend themselves, and to recover by force, what by unlawful force is taken from them; yet the right to do so, will not easily engage them in a contest, wherein they are sure to perish; it being impossible for one or a few oppressed men to disturb the government, where the body of people do not think themselves concerned in it.[18]

Locke provided little recourse for members of an oppressed group that are ignored by their fellow citizens.[19] Locke's scenario is actually somewhat optimistic; he painted a picture where the majority of citizens are not interested in the problems of the tyrannized minority. Surely the problem worsens when a majority of the people, along with the government, decide to mistreat a minority. Liberals after Locke noticed the problem of protecting minority rights and wanted to secure the rights of all citizens. The idea of a constitutional liberal democracy was born partly from this concern; the Constitution here guarantees rights to all Americans. Yet constitutional safeguards are not self-enforcing; they need the support of a large part of the population. The majority can ignore certain laws if they so choose. Liberal theory may demand that the rights of all citizens be respected, but it is quite easy to ignore theory when you have power.

Madison also recognized this problem of democracy; in response, he developed his theory of factions. If there are many political factions, alliances between them will shift, making it unlikely that a permanent majority will oppress a minority of citizens. By "comprehending in the society so many separate descriptions of citizens [it] will render an unjust combination of a majority of the whole very improbable, if not impracticable."[20] As the shifting political factions make it impossible for several groups to combine to oppress others, they will find that they will be able to unite only to pursue the common good. Unhappily, Madison's theory has not always proven to be true. If all or many issues are defined in racial terms and if members of one race make up a substantially smaller percentage of the population than members of the other race, the majority race can oppress the minority. White Americans often ignore the rights of Black Americans with little penalty.[21]

The second problem lies in the way that some liberals want to realize equality. Formal political equality is relatively easy to obtain—giving everyone the same legal rights can be achieved by passing a few laws. There are now legal penalties for discrimination against Blacks (and others), penalties that have gone a long way to end the effects of racism. Since the 1960s, Black economic progress has come not only from an expanding economy, but also from vigorous enforcement of equal opportunity laws, employment programs, and changes in public norms. There are, however, limits to the effectiveness of legal penalties. Black Americans cannot go to court every time they face discrimination; besides the large costs of doing so, if Blacks sued every time they faced discrimination they'd be in court for much of their lives.²² Although the threat of being sued probably prevents some whites from discriminating, Black people still talk about the discrimination they face.

Because laws cannot ensure that equality is enacted, liberals try to encourage a culture of equality. Liberals want to establish the idea of equality—or, at least, the principle of nondiscrimination—as the norm among citizens. To treat others in a discriminatory way based on ascriptive identity ought to be reason for public censure in the liberal state. The idea of equality is taught in schools, and it is enshrined in public documents like the Constitution, the amendments, and the Declaration of Independence; it is the guiding force behind many American laws.²³ By establishing equality as a public norm, liberals hope that people will treat others equally and live up to the demands of liberal citizenship. Liberals want to habituate people to act toward each other in nondiscriminatory ways. This process began in relation to Blacks in the mid-1960s. There is now less racial subordination than before the Civil Rights Movement; explicit public pronouncements of racism are no longer publicly acceptable. Yet the combination of public pressure and legal penalties has not been enough to give equal citizenship to Blacks.

The attempt to persuade people to believe in equality has not always been effective. Under the guise of liberal rights—freedom of association, of speech, and to privacy—many people have perpetuated racist ideas and practiced discrimination. The liberal virtue animating the private sphere is the avoidance of harm, but private actions that do not directly harm others can have damaging consequences. For example, white people have the right to move when Blacks move into their neighborhood. When a white family moves out of a neighborhood, they are not directly harming another Black family. But if enough white families leave a neighborhood and are replaced by Black families, the goal of many Blacks to live in an integrated neighborhood will not be realized. Property values may drop if white families flee the neighborhood in a panic. If whites have more political influence than Blacks do, the quality of schools and police and fire protection may drop as well.

Not much can be done if some whites are determined to live apart from Blacks; this is one of the costs of allowing people to make some private choices in liberal society. The state can encourage a culture of equality, but it cannot mandate this. A more direct approach to reaching equality can be attempted; the state can encompass a much larger part of people's lives than it does now. The state could force Black and white people to live near each other. State-run businesses could hire Blacks and whites alike. But this is a risky idea. If the power of the state increases drastically, there is no guarantee that this power would be used to decrease racial divisions. A more powerful state could use its power to further racism. The chance to protest and demand change would be radically curtailed in such a state. In a liberal democracy there is at least the language of rights, which can be used to protest the abuse of a minority's rights. In private and in civil society, people can and do organize and protest when their rights are violated. There is no assurance, of course, that these protests will change anything, but the ability to protest assures at least the possibility of change. When the private sphere and the sphere of civil society are abolished, however, this possibility is reduced considerably.

Even if liberal laws could end overt discrimination, Black Americans would not have the same opportunities enjoyed by other Americans. This leads to the third problem that race poses for liberalism: power often works in subtle ways, ways that liberalism sometimes obscures. Liberals often emphasize fair procedures. Little more is needed, some liberals argue, than the establishment of neutral standards that are known to all; the rules of the court, admission standards to schools, and standards for hiring and promotion in businesses ought to be established fairly and openly. People should be judged on their ability or their potential or their guilt or innocence; wealth or poverty, race, and gender should not matter when people are judged. Yet the United States is filled with substantial inequalities that arose out of slavery, discrimination, and exploitation. The legacy of racism means that Black and white Americans are not alike on some sort of neutral playing field; whites have more opportunities than Blacks have. To impose a neutral framework on American society masks this inequality.

This belief in neutrality fuels the common complaint made by many whites about programs, like affirmative action, that are designed to help give Blacks opportunities for education and employment that otherwise might elude them. These programs, the charge runs, give Blacks an unfair advantage over whites. If procedures are neutral, why give Blacks an advantage? Some whites argue that they did not discriminate against Blacks; slavery, they argue, ended years ago and they should not be penalized by this history. Indeed, many of the ancestors of whites faced discrimination as well. This complaint, however, ignores the legacy of racism that persists in this country. The discrimination faced by some whites has mostly ended; more important, it is now rarely an obstacle to economic success. The continued disadvantages faced by Blacks because of past and current discrimination make claims of neutrality suspect. When the slaves were emancipated, they did not receive forty acres and a mule, as some suggested they should. Few Blacks had the property, the income, or the skills to do well economically. Continued racism prevented most Blacks from accumulating economic assets and receiving a good education. The Civil Rights Laws of the 1960s, although important, did little to eradicate the economic impoverishment of the Black community bestowed upon it by racism. To say that people are all now equal and have the same opportunities speciously ignores this past.

Furthermore, even if white citizens purged themselves of conscious racist attitudes, equal opportunity among Blacks and whites would probably still be elusive. W.E.B. DuBois recognized this years ago: "Not simply knowledge, not simply direct repression of evil, will reform the world. In long, indirect pressure and action of various and intricate sorts, the actions of men which are not due to lack of knowledge nor to evil intent, must be changed by influencing folkways, habits, customs, and subconscious deeds."[24] Whites may unconsciously discriminate against Blacks; the legacy of racism may persist in stereotypes and subconscious deeds. Moreover, the standards of many institutions may work to the disadvantage of Blacks. Standards must be established by someone or a group of people; in many institutions in the United States, they have been established by white people. These standards may favor whites over Blacks; the cultural tone of institutions may also work to favor whites. By cultural tone I mean the norms of acceptable behavior: the way people talk, their hand gestures, their dress, and so on. In institutions with a white majority, Blacks may often correctly think they have to conform to the standards set by whites to succeed. Many Black cultural practices do not violate the value of liberalism, however, and so there is no liberal reason why these practices should change. Yet the pressure to change may come from the people in power, who can make these cultural demands if they choose.

Realizing Equal Citizenship

There are several ways to try to solve the liberal dilemma—how to recognize race while moving past racism—which recognize Blacks as citizens yet will not permanently enshrine a Black identity. These suggestions aim at enabling a transformation of Black identity, giving Black Americans more opportunity to interpret themselves. My arguments have two goals. First, they aspire toward a recognition of Black citizenship by other citizens. Black citizenship, I argue, must be made *visible* in a way that induces white citizens to revise their vision of American citizenship so that it includes Blacks. Second, my arguments aim toward allowing Blacks to escape the effects of racism; this means a partial reconfiguration of civil society. To end the effects of racism, Blacks need more than the good will of white liberals and the end of racist laws; Blacks also need "a good job, a good education, a decent house and a share of power."[25]

The franchise is about standing; it is a proclamation of citizenship. The right to vote is the recognition that a person is a citizen, that he or she has the right to influence the government just as much as others; that her or his needs and wishes are as important as the needs and wishes of other citizens. In 1865 Frederick Douglass argued that the franchise is about rights and dignity: "We want it [the vote] because it is our *right*, first of all. No class of men can, without insulting their own nature, be content with any deprivation of their rights." Denying people their rights takes away part of their dignity; it marks them as unequal and unworthy. A person who has the vote is recognized as having the intelligence to make a sound judgment on the state's government. Discussing the deleterious effects of the denial of suffrage, Douglass explained that, "by depriving us of suffrage, you affirm our incapacity to form intelligent judgments respecting public measures." Voting, Douglass said, is also about protection.

> I am for the immediate unconditional and universal enfranchisement of the black man, in every state in the Union. Without this, his liberty is a mockery; without this, you might as well almost retain the old name of slavery for this condition; for in fact, if he is not the slave of the individual master, he is the slave of society, and holds his liberty as a privilege, not as a right.

When people have the vote, they can insist that the government protect their interests. Without the vote, a person is helpless before the tyranny of the state. Indeed, Douglass argued that a person who supports the state should be able to influence it as well; drawing on the American political tradition, Douglass maintained that "taxation and representation should go together."[26] Voting is far from a cure-all; people in a perpetual minority may find that their vote gives them little protection. Still, the franchise is a crucial component of citizenship, as a declaration of citizenship and because it at least gives people the chance to influence government.

Yet all votes are not necessarily equal; even though the Supreme Court affirmed the principle of one person, one vote, the worth of some votes can be diluted. After Blacks won the right to vote, many Southern state legislatures found ways to weaken the voting strength of Blacks. These legislatures often redrew districts so Black voters were spread among many, making up a minority of voters in each instead of constituting the majority in fewer districts. Single-member districts were often abolished in local elections, replaced by at-large voting, diluting the effect of Black votes. In many cities, instead of making up the majority in two or three districts, Blacks found themselves to be a minority of voters in the city or county as a whole. These tactics are not only a Southern phenomenon; legislatures in other parts of the country have also gerrymandered districts to dilute the influence of Black votes.[27]

To counteract these trends, Black voters have often fought to redraw districts so that some have Black majorities; similarly, Blacks have fought to reduce or eliminate at-large voting. Black majority districts would be much harder to construct if there was not so much segregation in American society (although creative gerrymandering efforts do allow race-based districts even in places of limited integration). Since the 1960s many whites have left the inner cities, leaving Blacks to live in mostly segregated neighborhoods. Many Blacks cannot think of moving out of these cities because they are too poor to do so. Furthermore, many Blacks who have moved out to the suburbs still live in segregated neighborhoods. Many Blacks want to live in neighborhoods with whites, but they do not want to be the one token Black family on the block; rather, they want to live in neighborhoods with substantial numbers of Black and white families. White families, however, often flee if more than one or two Black families move into their neighborhood. Too often, whites simply refuse to live near "too many" Blacks.[28] If whites were less racist and did not move once Black families became their neighbors, there would be more districts with large numbers of both Black and white voters.

Liberals ought to support carving out majority Black districts as a partial solution to the political disempowerment of Black voters. Black citizens need a political voice to be able to express their concerns and problems; if they have no voice, then the political community's attempts to solve the problems of racism will be severely handicapped. Furthermore, Black representation is important for symbolic reasons. Black elected officials show that Blacks are equal citizens and that the concerns of Black citizens are as important as the concerns of other citizens.[29] A Black majority does not ensure that the district will vote a Black person into office. Sometimes Blacks elect white candidates (and sometimes majority white districts elect a Black person). And drawing up districts on racial lines does not mean the end of racial cooperation. Black representatives in Congress, who constitute a small minority in that body, must work with white Congress members to get bills passed. Black city council members work side by side with white city council members in many cities.[30] An increase in the number of Black elected officials hardly means that Black people will be able to ignore whites, but it does make it harder (but not impossible) for white politicians and citizens to ignore Black people.

Black majority districts do not permanently enshrine Black identity into the political system. When whites accept Blacks as equal citizens, when whites agree to live in integrated neighborhoods with Blacks, then race-based districts will become impossible to draw. There is a simple answer to those whites concerned that Black majority districts are divisive: don't move out when Blacks move into your neighborhoods, or move into Black neighborhoods yourselves. Doing so will force politicians to listen to your needs and the needs of your Black neighbors. Then the liberal dream of multiracial districts will become a reality.[31] To impose this dream, however, while racism still thrives is simply a way to disempower Blacks and deny them equal citizenship.

Public Recognition of Black Citizenship

Recognizing Black citizenship must go further than granting Blacks the right to vote, however. Standards of institutions may discriminate against Blacks, although those who established these standards had no intention of discrimination. Often, ignorance of Black people is the problem; sometimes a belief that Blacks should become like whites is the cause of this discrimination. To counteract this, Blacks must be recognized as citizens in public ways. Recognition of Black people satisfies another need: it gives Black people recognition as Black people. It says that they are worthwhile as Blacks, that they do not have to become like whites to be appreciated and recognized. The process of recognition has begun in the United States. We have Black history month and celebrate Martin Luther King Jr.'s birthday as a national holiday. But more than this is needed. Too often, white citizens do not revise their notions of citizenship to accept Blacks as citizens. Whites often do not put in the effort necessary to "re-educate themselves out of their racial ignorance. It is an aspect of their sense of superiority that the white people of America believe they have so little to learn."[32]

For many whites, ending racial discrimination means only allowing Blacks to enter formerly white institutions, but this enables white citizens to learn little about Black Americans. Liberal citizenship means that white citizens must revise their vision of citizenship to accept Blacks as citizens. This opposes conventional liberal wisdom, which suggests that matters of culture and identity should be private. When one version of citizenship (a white version) is the norm in society, however, the relegation of Black identity to the private realm denies equal citizenship to Blacks by perpetuating an exclusive version of citizenship. Making Black citizenship a public matter instead of a private concern means making Black culture and institutions legitimate in the public eye. The point of making Black citizenship a public matter is not to suggest that Black culture is superior to mainstream culture (or to suggest the opposite), but to show that there is more than one way to be an American citizen and that there is more than one set of cultural institutions and practices worthy of American citizens.

There are not, however, only two sorts of institutions and cultural practices in the United States, the dominant culture and Black culture. Other racial and ethnic groups have particular cultural practices and institutions. Surely, members of these groups should fight to have their practices and contributions to American life recognized. The contributions of members of these groups to the United States should be discussed in public schools, just as the role of Blacks in the United States should be discussed. Knowledge of many ethnics will have to be local, however, for the large number of ethnics in the United States makes anything else impossible. Because of the legacy of slavery and racism and its integral place in the history of our country, knowledge of Black Americans should be national. The role of Black Americans in this country is not matched by any ethnic group; for most ethnic groups in the United States, the barriers to mainstream society existed for a comparatively short time. Moreover, the recognition of Black Americans can help lead to a more pluralistic society. The recognition of Black Americans as full citizens will help members of mainstream society realize that there is more than one legitimate way to be an American citizen and that there are other American citizens who are not yet completely part of mainstream society. Strategies to help Blacks will also help others.

The strategy often used to end the subordination of Black Americans has been integration. Integration typically means that Blacks can enter institutions once restricted to whites, but this is done at the expense of Black institutions. After integration, many Black schools closed and many Black teachers lost their jobs. Black students had to learn what white students learned in school, often at the expense of their particular knowledge about society. They were often taught by white teachers who knew little about the role of Black people in American history. The aim of integration was an equalization of resources, but citizenship involves more than just resources. After hundreds of years of subordination, many Blacks want to be recognized as Black; they are proud of their identity and want this identity to be publicly acclaimed. The narrow focus on getting Black students into mainstream institutions renders Black institutions and Black life invisible. It allows whites to avoid thinking about the Black community, its history and practices; it means that Blacks have to figure out how they can fit into a predominantly white society. Recognizing Black citizenship means recognizing and supporting Black institutions, particularly historically Black colleges and schools. If the state supports historically Black institutions, they become visible, giving these schools and Black history and culture legitimacy in the eyes of the political community.

Unfortunately, desegregation has already caused many Black schools to close. It would have been better if more white schools had been closed, with their students attending historically Black schools. It is not too late in the case of Black colleges, however. Since desegregation, many Black students have chosen to attend mainstream colleges; many state legislatures give more money to these institutions than to historically Black colleges. This is a vicious cycle; the more Black students attend mainstream institutions, the less support there is for Black colleges. Equivalent state financial support should go to mainstream schools and to historically Black colleges and universities, enabling these schools to have similar facilities. In fact, historically Black schools, with roots in the Black community, ought to be considered "mainstream."

If Black colleges are given adequate financial support, if they can establish quality graduate programs, then both white and Black students will attend them. Integration does not mean, however, that Blacks will become a small part of these institutions. Historically Black institutions that are well supported will undoubtedly attract many Black students, even as the number of white students increases. With pluralistic integration Blacks will not make up 10 percent of the population of every institution in the United States; rather, many Blacks will cluster in some institutions. Whites need not be excluded from these institutions, but Blacks, constituting a majority or a large minority in some institutions, will have power in some integrated institutions. If historically Black institutions are recognized as important and remain intact, even if they eventually become integrated—as they should—they will serve as a reminder of the importance of Black citizenship. Institutions that are closed and bulldozed, however, are not likely to be remembered.

To ensure the visibility of Black citizenship, all schools, whatever their racial composition, should include the history of Black people in their curriculums; it is not acceptable to portray Blacks as slaves, mention the Emancipation Proclamation and the Civil War, proclaim the wounds of our country healed, and leave it at that. White and Black people alike need to learn about the contributions of Blacks to American life; they should know about the struggle for Blacks to achieve equality. History that ignores Black Americans helps to make Blacks invisible, reinforcing the idea that this is a white society where Blacks, to be successful, must become like whites. Teaching a whitewashed history allows whites to avoid confronting the legacy of racism in this country; if white students do not learn about Blacks, they need not revise their notion of American citizenship. Some worry that talking about America's dark past will lead to more divisiveness, but Black (and some white) people know when the history they are taught is distorted. A history that downplays the suffering, achievements, and struggles of Black people will only increase Black resentment.

This does not mean that history should be taught as the history of groups. The history of Black people, or of any group, should not be the focus of all classes. Rather, students should learn about the contributions of different Americans to the United States, regardless of whether the subjects were members of an oppressed or a nonoppressed group.

Reconfiguring Civil Society

Enforcement of the principle of nondiscrimination, both by the state and in the institutions of civil society, is crucial to achieving equal Black citizenship. Government agencies have followed their own nondiscrimination laws comparatively well in hiring, but it has been harder to force businesses to hire Blacks. Consequently, the Black middle class relies more on employment by the state than does the white middle class. The limited power of the state means that some businesses can discriminate without getting caught. More vigorous enforcement of equal employment laws will help considerably, but this will not be enough to end the effects of discrimination. Even if all businesses no longer discriminated based on race, the poverty in which many Black people live and the lack of a decent education for many Blacks would prevent many from attending college or presenting themselves as qualified candidates for many jobs. Liberals must recognize that some forms of racism and its effects will affect U.S. society for a while. The United States should work to end discrimination, but liberals need to figure out ways to bypass discrimination.

Toward this end, the state should encourage an increased diversity of institutions in civil society, supporting the development and growth of Black-owned institutions. A plurality of institutions in civil society—some Black-owned, some owned by ethnics, some by whites, and some by a combination of people—will give Blacks and others more choices about the institutions they want to attend. Liberals want people to be able to pursue their life plans with little interference. If Blacks cannot do this easily in white-dominated institutions, the state should encourage the establishment of Black-dominated institutions. This accepts but does not excuse the fact that the racism faced by Blacks in some white-dominated institutions will continue. A more plural civil society would allow Blacks more opportunities to pursue their life plans and projects and would allow Blacks, in at least some settings, to avoid racism.

In addition to schools and universities, Black-owned businesses should be supported. Black-owned businesses are more likely to hire Black employees and serve the needs of the Black community. Black people are less likely to encounter racial discrimination when they walk into or work at a Black-owned store. Black-owned businesses can sell goods that Blacks want but that whites have little interest in. Black-owned radio and television stations can cater to the cultural needs of the Black community. Perhaps most important, however, more Black-owned businesses in the inner cities could reduce Black unemployment considerably. Much of the racial crisis in the United States is about its inner cities, whose residents are often poor and Black (but sometimes Latino, Asian American, or white) and where hope is scarce and crime is rampant. With legal segregation no longer an obstacle to investment, many Black business people choose to invest away from the inner cities. The high cost of insurance in the inner cities and the high crime rate make doing business there difficult; furthermore, the Black poor do not have much money. It makes business sense to set up shop close to wealthier residents.

Left to the free market alone, it is unlikely that many neighborhoods in the inner cities will prosper. When their residents escape poverty, they leave for safer neighborhoods. To counteract this, the state must support the establishment of jobs in inner cities. Money must be used to train people to operate their own businesses, government must loan money for people to begin their businesses, money for services like police and fire protection is important, and good schools are crucial to any economic development plan. Programs like Head Start, which is, by most accounts, one of the most successful programs stemming from the Great Society days, should be expanded.[33] This may be expensive, but it is naive to think that ending the effects of racism will be cheap. (Funding Head Start, however, is considerably cheaper than sending thousands of poor Black men to prison.) Commenting on desegregation, Martin Luther King, Jr., said that "the practical cost of change for the nation up to this point has been cheap. The limited reforms have been obtained at bargain rates. There are no expenses, and no taxes are required, for Negroes to share lunch counters, libraries, parks, hotels and other facilities with whites." The real cost of racial equality, King noted, would come after legal integration: "Jobs are harder and costlier to create than voting rolls."[34]

The creation of jobs is crucial because the intersection between class and race poses a particular threat to equal citizenship. Citizens in the liberal state supposedly enjoy equal opportunity to construct and pursue their goals, but most poor people have less opportunity. They generally go to schools that are not as good as the schools that serve wealthier citizens; they often lack adequate medical care or enough to eat. The housing of the poor is usually dilapidated. The poor typically receive less police protection and are more likely to live in dangerous neighborhoods than are the wealthy. Furthermore, the poor have fewer resources—time and money—with which to organize to press for political responses to their problems. Unsurprisingly, the poor are usually the most politically alienated citizens. The threat to citizenship posed by poverty holds true for citizens of all racial and ethnic backgrounds, but the added element of race means that a higher percentage of Blacks than whites live in poverty and that it is more difficult for Blacks to leave poverty.

To help solve the problems of many cities, at least some of the businesses established in them should probably not be in the conventional American mold. When unemployment for all citizens increases, the unemployment rate increases faster for Blacks than it does for whites. The deindustrialization of the United States has hurt all working class Americans; because the proportion of unskilled or low-skilled Black workers is higher than for whites, however, the decline of manufacturing has hurt Black people more.[35] When new Black-controlled businesses are established, the workers in these businesses should have substantial control over their work. Worker-controlled businesses have several advantages over conventional businesses. Businesses owned by nonworkers can easily uproot and move to other parts of the country or to other countries, leaving many of their former employees without jobs. Worker-controlled businesses are much less likely to leave, since this would entail uprooting all of the worker-owners as well. Successful conventional Black-owned businesses that begin in the Black community can easily branch out to other non-Black communities. Although this may be a good business decision, it does not do enough to end the problems of cities. In contrast, the profits of worker-controlled businesses are more likely to be reinvested in their community. People who live and work in a particular community have a stake in that community; they have an interest in seeing that their neighborhood has grocery stores, restaurants, and bookstores; they have an interest in good schools so they can be joined by well-trained owner-workers and so others can start up other businesses or community organizations in their neighborhood. People who live and work in a community will work toward improving their community.

Giving people control over their lives is a better route to ending inner-city poverty than figuring out how to entice big businesses, Black or white owned, to enter inner cities. If liberal democracy is about giving people control over their lives, then workplace democracy fits in the liberal tradition. I doubt that many liberals would argue against workplace democracy, but many would probably say that the state has no reason to encourage such institutions. Neutrality on the issue is not enough; some people in inner cities need to be encouraged (and trained and given the resources) to own businesses together. Worker-controlled businesses are not a panacea that will end unemployment or solve all problems created by the market system, nor does every business in cities need to be controlled by the workers. But a substantial number of these businesses will probably give workers more control over their lives and leave them less at the mercy of impersonal forces than they currently are.[36] I see no reason why workplace democracy should be a preserve of inner-city Blacks. Its advantages can benefit other workers, Black and white, in cities and in suburbs. As a matter of practical politics, however, programs that aim to encourage businesses that have many Black worker-owners have a better chance to end inner-city poverty than do other kinds of programs.

Supporting institutions operated by Blacks to serve Blacks in cities is one way to try to reduce Black poverty. This raises the spectacle of separatism once again, which makes many liberals uneasy. But if separatism will allow more Blacks to get good jobs and a good education, if separate institutions will allow Blacks to pursue their plans and projects without fear of discrimination, then the liberal state ought to encourage this process. More to the point, however, is the fact that many inner cities are already segregated. To rail against race-based programs because they recognize race or may increase racial divisions is to ignore the fact that race is recognized by many citizens and that the United States is already a racially divided society. If whites lived in these inner-city areas, there would be no specter of separatism. Whites who enter Black-owned stores ought to be served as Blacks who enter white-owned stores are supposed to be served. If few whites actually enter Black-owned stores in inner cities, the cry of separatism should be aimed at whites, not Blacks. Furthermore, encouraging the establishment of racially based institutions will probably work to decrease racial divisions, not increase them. If the Black poor had more money, they could spend more time in integrated institutions; they could become more active in the political process, where they would have to work with whites. More of their children would attend colleges, many of them integrated, where they would meet and interact with many people who were not Black. If Black poverty in the inner cities decreased, if crime went down, if the schools improved, if more businesses were established, then inner cities would become more attractive places to live and shop. And then more people, Black and white and Jewish, Asian American and Latino, would move into them.

Reducing Black poverty would not eliminate all separatism in this country, but it might lead to more integration. Even if whites continued to leave neighborhoods when Blacks moved in, there would be more integration in universities, the workplace, and other institutions of civil society if there was less Black poverty.

The story of many ethnics in this country begins with separatism but ends with integration. Many ethnic groups had strong ethnic communities with many ethnic-owned institutions, yet this did not lead to their permanent separation from American life. Instead, it gave ethnics the opportunity to build group self-respect, bypass the discrimination they faced in mainstream society, and reduce poverty in their communities. Many Japanese Americans, for example, excluded from numerous occupations early in this century, became self-employed by operating hotels, grocery stores, and other small businesses. Like many other ethnics, Japanese Americans operated grocery stores that primarily served the Japanese-American community.

Whites did not try to serve most immigrant communities because the foods the immigrants ate were unfamiliar to whites. But whites were familiar with many of the basic foods that Blacks ate and so operated stores in Black neighborhoods. Better financed, with easier access to credit, white-owned businesses were more likely to survive than were their Black counterparts. And, when Blacks managed to achieve economic success despite these obstacles, their white competitors often simply forced these Blacks to close their stores (if they didn't lynch the Black business owners).[37]

Ethnics often built institutions that enabled them to enjoy the same things as white Protestants but without facing discrimination. At the end of the nineteenth century, for example, the wealthy Joseph Seligman was barred from the Grand Union Hotel in Saratoga because he was Jewish. In response, Jews bought several of the leading hotels in Saratoga. In another city, the leading hotel turned away Nathan Strauss, "whereupon he promptly built next to it a hotel *twice as large,* for Jews only."[38] After being barred from many country clubs, Jews simply began their own. The moral of these stories is clear: wealth enables members of racial and ethnic groups to bypass some of the effects of discrimination. Furthermore, as the ethnics gain in economic clout, they are able to work toward dismantling the barriers of discrimination. It is true that some members of racial and ethnic groups want to be separate from other members of society, but the bigger threat to the cohesiveness of the United States comes from racism and prejudice. Those who worry about the breakup of America ought to direct their energies toward ending racism and poverty; these are the real threats to the establishment of a cohesive American polity. Attacks on the encouragement of Black-owned institutions and race-based programs only put the burdens of citizenship on Blacks.

My argument here is somewhat paradoxical. Since racism is not about to disappear, society ought to give resources to Black people so they can bypass the effects of discrimination. Why would a racist society, however, give Blacks the resources to do this? This is the problem of what Thomas Nagel calls partiality and equality, the problem of personal interests versus justice: "It is possible for individuals to judge from an impersonal stand-point that a certain form of collective conduct or a certain set of interpersonal relations would be good—or better than what we have now—without being sufficiently motivated to do what would be necessary to play their part in such an arrangement."[39] People can see that a just society would demand certain changes, but they may not favor these changes because they would demand some sacrifice from them or they may not want to work for these changes because they won't benefit them very much.

Nagel points to a rather difficult problem, but I'm hopeful that there is a way out of this paradox. The political community can realize that it has a problem with race, yet also understand that many whites will not do what is necessary on an everyday basis—open up businesses that will create jobs in inner cities, live near Blacks, and alter the standards of the institutions they control—to come to terms with the problem of race. People can recognize that they lack the personal commitment to solve a problem while recognizing that the problem should be faced. They may want the burdens of solving this problem to fall on others; they may be willing to give some money as long as they do not have to spend much time thinking about the problem. Wealthier people may be willing to give resources to poorer Americans to enable struggling Americans to become more comfortable. This won't happen easily; many Americans are not willing to part with much of their money. There have been times, however, when the United States has decided to try to help its poorer citizens. Furthermore, it may be cheaper to try to improve the economic conditions of poor Americans than to try to contain the crime and rioting often bred by poverty.

Yet white people cannot simply give money to Blacks and forget about race. Although the necessary personal commitment to solve our racial problems is not about to be forthcoming from most whites, the absence of a full commitment does not excuse the lack of *any* commitment to address this problem. Even if whites do not immediately agree to live in fully integrated neighborhoods, the behavior of some whites will have to change if racism and its effects are to end. White citizens hurl racial slurs at Black citizens; white police officers harass and beat Black citizens; white store owners discriminate against Blacks. Even if many whites will not become best friends with or live near Black people, whites must learn to treat Black citizens with equal respect. It is white and Black teachers alike who must change what they teach students so these students can learn about the role of race in the United States. Black and white Americans must, for better and for worse, live with each other; racial problems can be solved only with support from members of both races.

Black Power and Black Culture

It is not enough for liberals to point out the ways in which members of the dominant community discriminate against others; this is surely the first step toward changing unequal distributions of power, but pleading for this discrimination to end won't accomplish enough. Persuasion—the recourse on which many liberals rely to produce change—may have some effect, but the continuation of racism shows that persuasion in a context of racial hierarchy will not, by itself, produce enough change. When powerless Blacks ask powerful whites to stop acting in racist ways, many of these whites will ignore the request. The alternative to persuasion, however, need not always be force; a better way is to give Blacks the resources to fight for an equal share of power. King maintained that racism and its effects will not end once the evil nature of racism is pointed out. "Structures of evil do not crumble by passive waiting. If history teaches anything, it is that evil is recalcitrant and determined, and never voluntarily relinquishes its hold short of an almost fanatical resistance. Evil must be attacked by a counteracting persistence, by the day-to-day assault of the battering rams of justice."[40] The battering ram for King was not a gun, but a mass movement of Blacks (and whites) to demand that whites stop their racist practices. Justice is not given to the meek. It is demanded by the oppressed.

The establishment of ethnic- or race-based institutions gives the members of these groups the power necessary to fight for inclusion in civil society, and it gives them a chance to make this fight without giving up all of their cultural practices. Poor people have little time and few resources available to insist on the enforcement of or to push for new antidiscrimination laws. From a position of strength, wealthier members of ethnic and racial groups can try to fight for inclusion in civil society, which many have done; they can organize to press for change through political institutions. They can also choose to retreat to the safety of their cultural communities. Power is necessary for Blacks to have equal citizenship, to fight for inclusion, and to negotiate the terms of this inclusion instead of conforming completely to the values of the dominant culture. If Black people are in charge of institutions recognized as important, institutions that whites want to enter, Blacks will have power. If Blacks have alternatives to white institutions—if they can attend institutions controlled by Blacks— then Blacks will not have to suffer because of the racist actions of whites. Some whites may decide to try to cater to Black people's needs to gain their business; if Blacks have alternatives, white business people will not be able to take their Black customers for granted. Other whites may want to use Black-controlled institutions because they better serve their needs. In any case, Black-owned businesses give Blacks more power over their own lives; they enable more Blacks to ignore racist whites.

Ultimately, my argument is integrationist—I want Black people to use their own institutions as a way of entry into mainstream society. To be sure, some Blacks will want to remain as separate as possible from mainstream America. A mostly separate Black economy, however, will almost surely be a poor cousin to and be dominated by the larger economy. Furthermore, the mainstream economy, being larger and more diverse, offers more economic opportunities for Blacks and whites. Black people cannot wait, however, for philanthropic whites to come to the cities and hire Blacks. Blacks need to take charge of their communities and then negotiate their participation in the mainstream economy.

Unsurprisingly, a major theme in Black political thought is the need for Blacks to gain power. King, for example, argued that "there is nothing essentially wrong with power. The problem is that in America power is unequally distributed."[41] Part of this emphasis on power by Black political theorists is fueled by a fear that a few Blacks will be incorporated into the political and economic system but that most will remain excluded; these few will serve as tokens, as supposed proof that American society is energetically working toward solving its racial problems.

Black power is not only about Black visibility—though this is an important part—but also about giving Black people the opportunity to shape their lives. My emphasis here is also on power and wealth more than it is on culture. In some ways, this is an old theme in liberal theory; recently, "multiculturalists" have emphasized the importance of culture, but this is a dangerous shift. When some say that Black Americans should have "cultural rights" to keep their way of life intact, white Americans can (and some do) say the same thing.[42] If Blacks can argue that the presence of whites threatens their way of life, then some whites will argue that the presence of Blacks threatens their way of life. What is the difference between this and old-fashioned racism? Behind the respectable guise of culture, whites can borrow this multiculturalist argument that Blacks ought to be excluded from "their" institutions. In a way, this argument is right; integration does threaten the white racist way of life, a way of life that should be threatened.

Reifying culture with demands for cultural rights is a mistaken strategy for at least three reasons. First, cultures are always changing; Black culture, too, has changed considerably, even over the past thirty years or so. The differences between mainstream culture and Black culture have narrowed and may narrow even more in the future (and not only because Blacks feel pressure to conform). Second, not all cultural practices should be protected simply because they are someone's cultural practices. Illiberal practices should not be protected. Arguments that aim to protect the practices of Blacks should be couched in terms of liberal rights. Practices that do not harm others should be allowed in the liberal state; no one should face discrimination because of these practices. Third, and most important, talk of culture is equalizing—everyone is part of a culture—but the power and wealth of white and Black Americans are very unequal. The language of culture should not displace the language of power and wealth. The justifications for Black institutions should be couched in terms of income and power disparities. Institutions with Blacks in power give Blacks the opportunity to spend some time without worrying about racism, and they give them the chance to develop economically. These institutions may help to protect Black cultural practices, but that is not their purpose, and the protection of cultural practices should not be given as their justification. In fact, these institutions may actually decrease the distinctiveness of Black culture. They could increase the numbers of the educated Black bourgeoisie, which may be quite similar in its values and practices to its white counterpart.

A society can recognize that it is culturally diverse and still subordinate certain groups. The power of whites allows them to appropriate Black cultural practices as their own. Borrowing cultural practices is not always as benign as I made it out to be in chapter 3. Some white musicians, particularly in the 1940s and 1950s, took on Black forms of music as their own and became famous and wealthy in the process, while many talented Black musicians struggled to earn a living. Without economic and political power and visibility, Black people will not even be able to profit from their own cultural practices. Putting talk of culture at the forefront of discussions of racism will do little to sustain Black culture, will buttress the arguments of white racists, and will help ensure that many Blacks remain impoverished. I am *not* suggesting that the political community avoid talking about cultural practices at all. When Blacks have more power and wealth, they can fight to have their cultural practices accepted. Sometimes Blacks are wrongly excluded from institutions because their cultural practices are different from those of the dominant culture. When this happens, talk of culture and economics ought to go hand in hand. Even if Blacks took on all aspects of the dominant culture as their own, however, the effects of racism would still be present in the United States. More jobs in the inner city will not suddenly appear if Black culture is better understood and accepted by whites. Discussions of culture should not be allowed to obscure the issues of racial economic disparity that pervade society.

Unhappily, Black economic power and Black political representation will not end all of the problems faced by Blacks. White employers have not cornered the market on exploitation; Black employers can exploit workers just as well. Black politicians can become entrenched in the corridors of power, just as white politicians can, and ignore the needs of their constituents. The ability of politicians to accept money and favors from the wealthy at the expense of their poorer constituents knows no racial bounds. Indeed, there is some resentment among the Black poor toward middle and upper class Blacks for ignoring them.[43] The class lines that permeate the United States exist in the Black community as well. This does not lessen the need to push for equal citizenship for Blacks. It does mean, however, that solving racial problems in the United States is not enough to realize the goals of liberalism. The obstacles to equal opportunity and equal citizenship are not only matters of race and culture.

Black Identity in
the Liberal State

The surest route to cultural pluralism is segregation and economic subordination of a group of people. Legal separation lessens the chance for members of groups to share cultural practices; from subordination spring practices that allow people to survive. If racism and its effects in this country decline, Black identity will change even more than it has since the end of slavery. Black cultural practices that arose out of the need to survive in a racist and segregated world may fade. This process has already begun; since the Civil Rights Movement, Black cultural practices have changed substantially and have become increasingly diverse. Although the Black middle class has historically been rooted in the Black community—as lawyers, ministers, and undertakers—now the Black middle class, which has increased in size dramatically since the early 1960s, works in mainstream institutions, for the government, large corporations, universities, and so forth. Members of the Black middle class have considerable contact with whites, as co-workers, students, and teachers. No longer is all contact between Blacks and whites in the form of a hierarchical relationship. Blacks now have jobs that were formerly closed off to them; many Blacks have more money, so they can buy and do things that Blacks previously could rarely afford. Desegregation changed the entertainment life of many Blacks, which before the 1960s centered around the home. Since the end of legal segregation, Blacks have been able to eat at many restaurants, see movies, go to plays, and watch concerts and sports games at places that formerly were closed off to them or had separate and unequal seating arrangements. Unsurprisingly, having more money enables Blacks to do these things more frequently. Consequently, the social life of the Black middle class is centered less around the home than it used to be.[44]

Racism also helped shape a Black viewpoint of the world, one that was (and to large degree, still is) different from the white viewpoint. If racism declines, the conditions from which this particular viewpoint arose will fade, and then it will be increasingly difficult to speak of a "Black perspective."[45] At some point, race may not be as divisive in American society as it is now; the differences in cultural practices between Blacks and whites may diminish. Race and culture are not necessarily connected, but, when racism is rampant, the connection between race and culture is often strong. Since the 1960s the connection between race and culture has weakened. Here lies the irony of many arguments to include Blacks and their cultural practices in the institutions of civil society; these arguments are integrationist arguments that will work to transform Black identity and culture. If institutions become more inclusive of diverse cultural practices, as I think they should, a distinctive Black cultural identity will probably be weakened rather than enhanced. This means that having a "multicultural" faculty or student body or workplace is not necessarily the same thing as having a multiracial institution. People of the same race can have very different cultural practices; an Amish person and an ethnic inner-city factory worker do not share many cultural practices. People of different races can share a culture. As long as racism continues, Black people will share in one important experience, one that few whites face. Race and racism help shape views, but they do not determine them. Most Blacks and whites have some important different views and perspectives, but this does not mean that all Blacks will have the same views or that Black people and white people always see things differently. Indeed, the lives of some Blacks and whites are very similar. Some Blacks live among whites; some attend prestigious colleges and graduate schools. For some Blacks and whites, income and class may have as much influence on values, practices, and viewpoints as does race.

Like many ethnics, some Black Americans strive for inclusion in civil society but do not want to lose their distinctive Black identity. Some Black people think that their cultural practices are better than those of mainstream society; they think that their cultural milieu is fine as it is and do not want to lose it. Some Blacks argue against intermarriage or too much social contact with whites, although they support economic integration. Such a partial separation would be difficult to maintain. Once members of a group are seen as equal members of civil society, the opportunity to make friendships and fall in love with others is available. The rate of intermarriage between Blacks and whites has increased markedly since the Civil Rights Movement, although it is still small.[46] The more successful the

Black struggle for inclusion is, the more interaction there will be between Blacks and whites, and the more diffuse Black cultural practices will become.

The appropriation of Black cultural practices by whites is no longer as common as it once was. Whites no longer need white mediators like Elvis Presley to listen to Black music. White suburban kids listen to rap (and many whites listen to and play jazz and the blues), some phrases begun in the Black community are now used by many non-Blacks, movies and television shows that feature Black families and life are now common, Blacks direct movies and write novels that are watched and read by whites and others. White artists now directly acknowledge their debt to Black artists. As Blacks become more visible to whites, whites know about the lives and practices of Blacks; thus, the cultural practices of Blacks will become available to whites as well.

Despite the increasing murkiness of the boundaries between some aspects of Black and mainstream culture, the distinction between Black and white identity is not about to disappear. Many Blacks will not forget their history of oppression. Although whites can share in the cultural practices of Blacks, not all whites will do so. Some Black cultural practices will be handed down from one generation to the next and will remain distinctively Black. Some parts of Black culture, shaped by racism and segregation, will disappear if racism declines. Yet not all aspects of Black culture will necessarily end if racism evaporates. The role of extended families and the church in Black culture is not replicated in mainstream culture; racism's end will not necessarily mean the end of these aspects of Black culture. Just as ethnics still have their ethnic institutions and practices, so will Blacks— even more so for Blacks, since many of their institutions and practices are deeply rooted in the United States. In any case, racism is not about to disappear. While Black identity has become diverse recently, most Blacks still see themselves tied together by what Michael Dawson calls "linked fate."[47] Blacks understand that racism affects them all, rich and poor alike. Blacks may no longer be tied together as strongly by culture, and the Black community may be ridden by class divisions, but racism will ensure that most Blacks see themselves as part of a group. Only when white citizens live up to the liberal premise of judging people on their individual talents and abilities will this begin to change.

CHAPTER 7

LANGUAGE AND NATIONALITY

ONE OF THE EFFECTS of industrialization in many parts of the world is the dulling of differences between cultures. More and more people in different countries can buy the same goods made by the same multinational corporations, eat at MacDonald's, and work for the same corporations. Clifford Geertz colorfully explained that

> variety is rapidly softening into a paler, and narrower spectrum. We may be faced with a world in which there simply aren't any more headhunters, matrilinealists, or people who predict the weather from the entrails of a pig. Difference will doubtless remain—the French will never eat salted butter. But the good old days of widow burning and cannibalism are gone forever.[1]

Diversity in the Western world is not quite what it was. Geertz flatly stated, "Like nostalgia, diversity is not what it used to be; and the sealing of lives into separate railway carriages to produce cultural renewal or the spacing of them out with contrast effects to free up moral energies are romantical dreams, not undangerous ones."[2] With modern modes of transportation and communication, with industrialization a goal of nearly all states, with the rise of a world economy, with immigration continuing unabated, different cultures have clashed and meshed, and the differences between these cultures, particularly in the Western world, while still existing, have narrowed.

Paradoxically, the onset of industrialization in nineteenth-century Western Europe also saw the emergence of nationalism as a potent political force on the continent. The nation, nationalists contend, is an organic group of people possessing a unique culture. For nations to maintain their distinctive culture, nationalists argue, they must have political control over their boundaries; the nation and the state should be congruent. If differences between cultures are fading, however, why insist on this political control? Indeed, many of the nineteenth-century successors to the Enlightenment—particularly Marxists and liberals—assumed that the softening of cultural differences meant that nationalism would soon fade from the world. Nineteenth-century liberals did not discount nationalism, but many (particularly English liberals) assumed that it was no more than a passing phase. Some liberals saw nationalism as a legitimate political movement, but few saw its staying power. Nationalism was perhaps an outcome of the desire for self-determination, but once this goal was achieved there would be no need for nationalism. Liberals "supposed that the phenomenon of nationalism itself would disappear with its causes."[3]

Predictions of nationalism's decline did not end in the nineteenth century. In the late 1980s, the historian Eric Hobsbawm applauded what he saw as the end of nationalism: "The owl of Minerva which brings wisdom, said Hegel, flies at dusk. It is a good sign that it is now circling round nations and nationalism."[4]

Despite the assumptions of its demise, nationalism is still causing havoc in the world, breaking up old states and establishing new ones. Nationalism is not only a vehicle on which oppressed people climb to demand their liberty, as many nineteenth-century liberals saw it; some nationalist governments and movements have caused the deaths of many, forcibly expelled others out of their homes, and defined many people, who are part of the "wrong" nation, as second class citizens or worse. It can no longer simply be assumed that nationalism, which has been both a movement against oppression and a movement that itself oppresses, will decline soon. Given this jumbled historical record, what should liberals think of nationalism? Why does nationalism seem to be such a powerful political force as cultural differences fade?[5]

The Two Faces of Nationalism

One answer to the question of how nationalism can arise in a world where cultural differences are fading is deceptively simple: most possible nationalisms don't arise. The strength of the few existing nationalisms actually masks the failure of a much greater number of possible nationalisms.[6] It is impossible to know the precise number of actual or potential nationalisms in the works, partly because what constitutes a nation is unclear. Although nationalist theory maintains that each culture should have a state, culture is typically defined rather vaguely. One possible definition of culture is based on language, that each language group corresponds to at least one culture (but possibly more). There are, by some accounts, eight thousand languages in the world—or at least eight thousand potential nationalisms. There are, however, fewer than two hundred states in the world today. An extremely charitable estimate of the number of nationalist movements in the world would be about six hundred. If there was a state for each existing nation in the world, the number of effective nationalisms in the world would be eight hundred—or one-tenth the number of potential nationalisms.

Are there over seven thousand nationalisms waiting in the wings, about to arise at any moment? That seems unlikely. Many of the languages in the world are disappearing, with some already forgotten and others soon to be forgotten. In 1863, for example, French was a foreign language for nearly half of all French schoolchildren.[7] Dozens of different languages and dialects were then spoken in France, but most of these have faded since the nineteenth century. Many languages and dialects in many other countries will almost surely remain of interest mainly to historians and linguists. Although an occasional nationalist movement will arise based on an almost forgotten language, most of the potential nationalisms in France, like most potential nationalisms around the world, will never arise.

Yet some nationalisms do arise as rather powerful political forces. Instead of arguing that nationalism is actually a weak force,[8] it's more accurate to say that, although many possible nationalisms are inert, some are quite powerful, eliciting strong sentiments and inducing many to sacrifice their lives for nationalist ideals. National self-determination is often discussed in stirring language and is considered by some to be a right for every nation, a right that the United Nations endorses.[9]

The right to self-determination is often supported by liberals, but few liberals support nationalism without qualifications. Nationalism, it has been said (by both liberals and nonliberals) has two faces. In this view, nationalism is always "morally, politically, [and] humanly ambiguous."[10] All nationalisms have the potential to be both good and bad, to serve both lofty and base goals. The nationalism of an oppressed people, striving to overthrow their oppressors, is often seen as the good face of nationalism, but this nationalism always has the potential of turning bad. Nationalism is often an exclusionary doctrine; people who are not considered part of the nation, however it is defined, cannot be equal citizens in a nationalist state. Sometimes nationalists try to expel nonnationals from the state; at other times those with the "wrong" national identity are killed. Although the exclusion of some people from a nationalist movement may not have harmful consequences, if the nationalism is successful its exclusionary side may show it to be quite pernicious. Indeed, it is easier for liberals to support nationalist *movements* than to support nationalist states. Nationalist movements often have a romantic side that attracts liberals. A nationalist movement that succeeds in taking over a state, however, will be exclusionary and may also have expansionist designs. Because many places in the world are home to different national groups, different nations often lay claim to the same piece of land. Unsurprisingly, these clashing claims often lead to bloodshed.

This formula—some nationalist movements can be supported by liberals, but nationalist states are suspect—helps explain why many liberals supported the nationalisms that swept Europe during much of the nineteenth century. Most of these movements were seen as movements against social and political oppression. However, the success of these movements showed the other side of nationalism. When the Hungarians gained control of over half of the Austro-Hungarian empire in 1848 (Hungarian nationalism was supported by liberals), they tried to force everyone in their midst, including Slovaks, Croats, Germans, and Romanians, to speak Hungarian. When the Italian nationalists conquered Rome in 1870, many thought that Italian unity was accomplished, an accomplishment applauded by many liberals. Some Italian nationalists, however, had their eyes on Trieste, Nice, and Ticino, among other places. These areas had large numbers of Italians living in them, but Trieste was home to many Slavs, Nice to many French, and Ticino to many Swiss. These groups were not very keen about the prospect of joining the new Italian state.

The German nationalist movement in the first half of the nineteenth century was seen by many of its liberal supporters as an opponent to the petty tyrants of the many German states that existed before German unification. In 1848 the German liberals who established the Frankfort Parliament invited to its proceedings not only the Czech historian František Palacký, but also leaders from Posnania. Many Germans lived in Posnania, but about two-thirds of Posnania's population was Polish. Many Germans in the parliament argued, however, that all areas with a substantial German population should become part of Germany. The parliament agreed that a small part of Posnania did not have to join Germany, but the part they wanted to annex had a large Polish population. In the eyes of German liberals, German nationalism was simply more important than Polish nationalism. The German liberals didn't deny the Polish claim to a Polish state; they merely insisted that areas that were home to both Poles and Germans belonged in a German state. (Many Poles graciously acknowledged the justification for a German state but insisted that areas like Posnania belonged to a Polish state.[11]) The German liberals failed, however, and the Frankfort Parliament did not produce a united Germany. Almost twenty years later the liberal dream of a unified German state was realized, but the new German state was not very liberal. Once the German state was unified, nationalism was used by Bismarck's government to silence its liberal critics and as a justification for its expansionist designs.[12]

The problem of nationalism is rooted in the basic assumption of nationalists that each nation should have its own state. The world is not divided as nationalists envision; the nation–state, which many take to be the leading form of political organization, is mostly a myth. Most states, if not all, are made up of a variety of peoples.[13] The right to self-determination for a people may be a noble sentiment, but few states in the world are nationally homogeneous. Carving out smaller states to meet the boundaries of different nations is probably an impossible task. Some Armenians live in an enclave in the middle of Azerbajani; some Azeris live in Armenia; Russians and Poles live in Lithuania; some Slovaks complained that they were neglected in the framework of the Czechoslovakian state, but they said little about the hundreds of thousands of Hungarians in their midst; over two hundred American Indian nations exist in the United States; India is a patchwork of many different national groups. Even those states that have been relatively homogeneous—Germany, England, and the Scandinavian countries—have seen large increases in immigration from Southern Europe, Africa, and Asia since World War II. Most states are a heterogeneous cluster of many different groups, with a variety of people identifying in myriad ways. If a people is defined in terms of nationality, the right of a people to self-determination often means that others will be denied this very same right.

The myth of the nation–state and the exclusionary potential of nationalism and its expansionary designs lead some to reject nationalism. One historian criticized the intellectual leaders of the 1848 German revolution, maintaining that "the professorial lambs at Frankfurt, bitten by the Pan-German dog, caught rabies." In a well-known study of nationalism, Elie Kedourie argued that nationalism "has created new conflicts, exacerbated tensions, and brought catastrophe to numberless people innocent of all politics." Since 1919, Kedourie declared, the history of Europe has "shown the disastrous possibilities inherent in nationalism."[14]

Absolute condemnations of nationalism, however, are misguided for two reasons. First, to fight against nationalist sentiments in some parts of the world may have worse effects than to accept its existence and to try to work out a compromise between nationalism and liberalism. In some cases, insisting that two peoples live in the same state will lead to considerable bloodshed if there is ample hatred between them. Separation, if this is possible, is sometimes better than integration, to avoid carnage. Second, condemnations of nationalism ignore the role of language. States must use some language in which to conduct their official business. Although states can have more than one official language, the number of public languages cannot be infinite. It is extremely difficult (if not impossible) to use more than two or three main languages in legislatures, public documents, large businesses, and schools. When a language (or languages) is picked to be the official language of a state, those whose first language is different from the official language will be at a disadvantage.

Before the nationalist movements of the nineteenth century, elites in Central and Eastern Europe often spoke and wrote in French or German, not wanting to use a "peasant" language. These "lowly" languages were often modernized by nationalists so they could be used in schools, government, and books on national history.[15] Palacký switched from writing in German to Czech when he wrote his history of the Czech people. Indeed, many see the majority language of a state as defining the majority nation as well; French is spoken in France, German in Germany, Italian in Italy. The problem of language means that liberals cannot simply dismiss nationalism. Liberals must either explain why the establishment of a particular language in a state does not favor one national group over another or why this choice need not trouble liberals.

Public Language, Public Culture, and Public Space

Quebec became part of the British empire after the French and Indian Wars, which ended in 1763. At first the British tried to assimilate the French Canadians, but in 1791 they divided Canada into two provinces: Upper Canada (British and Protestant) and Lower Canada (mainly French and Catholic). Within this division, there was another divide in Lower Canada. The urban areas of Montreal and Quebec City had large Anglo-Protestant populations who were part of the emerging bourgeoisie. In contrast, the rural areas of Quebec predominantly consisted of French Catholic peasants. As long as most French Canadians remained in the rural areas, the role of the French language in Quebec was hardly an issue. English was spoken in business and governmental circles in the cities, but these circles included few French Canadians.

After World War II, however, more and more French Canadians moved to the cities as the farm economy supported fewer people and the urban economy expanded. The French Canadians found that the language of economic advancement in the cities was English; to obtain a good job and a quality university education, one had to speak English. Many French Canadians resented this dominance of English—and the economic dominance of the economy by those with English heritage. Further, most Allophones (immigrants) chose to learn English, not French.[16] Making matters worse for French-Canadian nationalists was the fact that some Francophone parents sent their children to English-speaking schools. They wanted their children to have the opportunity to advance economically; English was the vehicle for this advancement.

The "public face" of Quebec was more English than French. Although the provincial government was bilingual, the federal government used much more English than French, and most businesses used English. This dominance worried the French Canadians not because they did not want to learn a second language but because the predominance of English threatened the survival of French. To survive, speech communities in liberal, industrial nations must be rather large. The world of the peasant, however, is quite small, usually a village and not much else. The peasant must be able to communicate with neighbors, but not with people in other villages. People who live in different villages that are physically close to each other can speak different languages or dialects without much difficulty. This is why many different languages could easily survive in rural France until the nineteenth century. The peasants who lived in these rural areas were isolated from others. It was only when roads, railroads, the military draft, and education decreased the isolation of rural France that French spread to these areas. The isolation of the preindustrial world allowed tremendous linguistic (and cultural) diversity.

The need for large speech communities in industrial society helps clear the ground for nationalist movements. Local dialects and languages fade as one or two public languages emerge, languages spoken by large numbers of people. As the technology of industrial society decreases the distance between people, the citizens of a state are able to feel part of the same nation.

In an elegant argument, Benedict Anderson explains how the printing press helped make nationalism possible. The printing press allowed the mass production of books and newspapers, meaning that thousands or even millions of people wake up in the morning and read about the same events. Although few of these people know each other, they all know about the same events, tying themselves into an imagined community, which can take the shape of a nation. Before the printing press, the huge variety of spoken dialects made it difficult for people who spoke the same language to think of themselves as part of the same speech community. Some dialects were so different that they were not mutually intelligible.

People who spoke very different dialects of German, Spanish, or French and who might not be able to understand each other in conversation, however, could understand each other in print. "In the process, they gradually became aware of the hundreds of thousands, even millions, of people in their particular language-field, and at the same time, *only those* hundreds of thousands, or millions, that belonged." The large number of dialects was slowly reduced by the printing press, with the dialects closer to the print-language dominating the final forms of the print-languages. As different dialects merge and fade, large communities form, tied together by speech, enabling the rise of nationalism.[17]

The needs of an advanced industrial society also encourage the development of a standard language over a vast territory. People who work for IBM in two different cities must be able to communicate, even if they never see each other. People within the large bureaucracies widespread in advanced industrial societies need to be able to communicate with each other. Members of industrial society must be able to "follow the manuals and instructions of a new activity or occupation. In the course of their work they must constantly communicate with large numbers of other [women and] men, with whom they frequently have no previous association."[18] For this communication to take place, people in industrial society receive a generic education in a standard language. By receiving a similar education, citizens can understand each other easily, even if they never meet. Moreover, the government and corporations must be able to communicate with large publics; large industries must reach large markets. The mass media project movies, television shows, and radio broadcasts in only one or two languages. For commercial viability, these shows must have a large enough audience to sustain them; the media will rarely target small speech communities.

One, perhaps two, public languages will emerge in most industrial states. Private languages can coexist with different public languages, but the pressure of an industrial society makes it hard for a private language to last more than two generations. If the children of a French-speaking family attend English-speaking schools, read English books, watch television shows and movies in English, listen to English lyrics on the radio, and speak English in stores, they may not speak French very long. They may become so comfortable in English that when they have children they may speak English to them. When that happens, French will wither away. This process has made it difficult for many private languages to survive in the United States. Many languages of the old country are not spoken by the children and grandchildren of many immigrants. Languages that are not supported by public institutions or in civil society will have a hard time surviving. Those who do not speak the public languages or do so only poorly will have severely restricted opportunities. They will not be able to attend institutions of higher learning or apply for many jobs.

Learning English well was one route to economic opportunity for the French Canadians, but many in Quebec saw an alternative route. They wanted to make French the dominant language in Quebec, putting English in a clearly subordinate position. Toward this end, a variety of laws supporting French were enacted. French-speaking workers now have the right to be spoken to in French; manuals and other technical documents must be written in French. Professional associations now communicate in French only, with entry into many professions granted only after competence in French is established. French is now the main language used by the provincial government, and many public signs can be written only in French. The Quebec government created an office to support, with advice and money, the establishment of French businesses. French-speaking universities were expanded, and Allophone children were forced to attend French-speaking schools. In public life and in civil society, French was established as the dominant language.

These laws passed over the fierce objections of many parts of the Anglophone and Allophone communities. Many Anglophone businesses and professionals left for other parts of Canada, particularly Toronto, when they saw that the Francophones, who made up the majority in Quebec, were intent on imposing French on the public space in Quebec.[19]

These laws and policies worked because most Francophones lived in a fairly contiguous land area and because the Canadian federal government enabled the province of Quebec to institute policies that reinforced French. If Francophones had been evenly spread over Canada or if they had not controlled a part of the government, it would have been difficult to institutionalize French. There must be a large mass of people speaking the same language to support the institutions of civil society and government in the industrial state.

Some language groups are simply too small to support many institutions that use their language. In Switzerland, for example, there are four national languages: French, German, Italian, and Romansch. Romansch, however, is spoken by only a few thousand people, who have primarily been peasants in the twentieth century. Realizing the constraints that a linguistic knowledge restricted to Romansch puts on people, many Romansch parents have successfully pushed to have most of their children's classes taught in German.[20] Fluency in German will allow these children to attend universities; it will also allow them to leave peasant life. As they move to German-speaking cities, the position of Romansch will become increasingly precarious. As its speakers move to cities, the Romansch-speaking community will disperse. Romansch will perhaps be spoken in a few homes, but that is all; the children in these homes will find themselves comfortable and fluent in German. The Romansch are not an isolated example. Many of the speakers of local languages in nineteenth-century France wanted their children to learn French because this knowledge allowed "for mobility, advancement, economic and social promotion, and escape from the restrictive bonds of home."[21]

I cannot supply the magical number of language speakers that are able to support large institutions using their language. This is a matter of particular circumstances. For a language to thrive, it needs a public space that includes the institutions of modern life. Since the 1960s, the public face of Quebec has become increasingly French; the chance for the survival of French has correspondingly been enhanced. The need for a public space is not the same as the need for a state; states can have different public spaces, accommodating different language groups. Although there are limits to this accommodation, Canada can surely support both English and French.

A language that is different from the dominant language and is spoken by large clusters of people living in a fairly contiguous area has a chance to survive in a modern liberal state. Why some languages can survive while others fade away is more a matter of historical accident than of fairness or justice. Some viable languages have been stamped out by oppressive regimes, but in many other cases speech communities have dwindled for other reasons; at other times, government action to end certain speech communities only hastened their inevitable demise. Talk of fairness or justice when it comes to the evolution of dominant languages will sometimes obscure more than it will illuminate. It is hardly fair that English is the dominant language of the United States, but it wouldn't be any fairer if the dominant language was Spanish or Yiddish or Hindu. Some language must dominate in an industrial state (and then some dialect must dominate); there simply are some winners and some losers.

The Liberal Facilitation
of Nationalism

The world may lose something when some languages die out, but retaining cultures for their own sake is a mistake. Cultures are always in flux.[22] There are times, however, when languages can be preserved, as is shown by the case of the French Canadians. French was hardly used by federal government officials or in many large businesses in Quebec in the 1950s, but by the 1980s its use was widespread. With French preserved, so too presumably is French-Canadian culture—at least according to many

Francophone intellectuals. They do not want to preserve French for its own sake but because, they argue, French-Canadian culture is at stake.

Some people argue that language is merely a utilitarian vehicle; we all must speak a language to express ourselves, but which language we use is a relatively unimportant matter. Language simply designates ideas and objects. On this account, many different cultures can easily coexist in the same speech community. The alternative view, however, finds language to be expressive; that is, while language allows us to designate things, it also affects the way we think. Like a face or a piece of art, language cannot be broken down into its parts to see how the whole works or looks. Language is like a web, with its speakers in the middle, unable to step completely outside the web. Language changes and grows organically, through conversations among people. "Language is fashioned and grows not principally in monologue, but in dialogue, or better, in the life of the speech community."[23] The interactions of members of a speech community fashion language; in turn, by making some concepts and categories available, language influences what people think and say. The culture of a speech community and its language are, on this account, intimately linked. Unsurprisingly, it is often members of minority language groups like the Québecois who make this latter argument. Many Francophones argue that the "French language coincides with a society through an historic heritage, which one may regret or exult in, but which is a fact."[24]

Whether this argument is right or wrong is less important than the belief of millions of Québecois that this argument is correct.[25] In Quebec, this feeling is enough to mobilize people to fight for the preservation of French. I also think that there is good reason for the worry that, with the disappearance of French, a distinctive French-Canadian identity would fade, although my argument has little to do with how language shapes thought or how it is embedded in culture. In an ironic way, the forces of industrialization, combined with the effects of liberalism, bolstered Québecois nationalism.

A new, modern French-Canadian nationalism emerged in the 1950s. This massive movement changed French-Canadian culture considerably. Before the 1950s, "the Catholic religion and the culture of French Canada were strongly intertwined." French-Canadian culture was "seen to be spiritualist, in contrast to the materialism of the two philosophies the church found unacceptable, liberalism and socialism." A basic unit of the Catholic church was the parish—"a community of believers living in a defined territory of limited size." The spiritual community of the parish coincided with the economic and social communities in rural areas, but the parish did not work well as the locus of community in cities. When they moved to the cities, many Catholics "lived in communities not easily within the reach of the church's institutions and worked in jobs which the church had difficulty integrating into its life of ritual."[26] Furthermore, many urban Catholics attended vocational and technical schools because they were not satisfied with the traditional education—which emphasized ancient history, Greek, and Latin—supplied by church-controlled schools.

In the 1950s and 1960s, church control over the public schools (there was a separate school system for Protestants, who were mostly Anglophone) was successfully challenged by Québecois nationalists, who wanted the schools to teach math, statistics, computer programming, and so forth. These nationalists wanted schools to prepare the students to work in an advanced industrial society; by the 1970s, Quebec universities produced Francophone engineers, MBAs, architects, and social science graduates in large numbers—the people needed to run an advanced industrial economy. These people would have lacked job opportunities in an Anglophone-dominated economy, but the Quebec government helped establish the Francophone businesses needed to hire them. Quebec's government grew considerably during the 1960s and 1970s, staffed by French-speaking bureaucrats. The outcome of much Québecois nationalist activity was the establishment of a Francophone-run capitalist economy, an economy that is very similar to the economies of English Canada and the United States, except that more French is spoken in Quebec.

The effects of industrialization and liberalism combine to reduce (but not necessarily eliminate) cultural differences. If the Francophones who moved to Montreal could not or did not want to take on jobs other than low-skilled jobs, the move to preserve French would probably not have taken place. The Québecois could have spoken French on the factory floor, while upper management made their business plans in English; middle class government employees could have continued to work in English, translating laws into French. But the Francophones demanded that the liberal idea of equal opportunity be realized. They wanted to take advantage of all of the economic opportunities in an advanced industrial economy. This demand carried with it an important side effect: if the Québecois took advantage of these opportunities in English, the demands of liberal citizenship would have made it hard for the Francophones to retain a distinctive identity. Just as some of the emancipated Jews found it difficult to distinguish themselves from their fellow citizens, Francophones might find it hard to distinguish themselves from their Anglophone counterparts.

The difficulty experienced by Jews and other ethnics in preserving their identity lies in the way boundaries work. By decreasing the differences among people and breaking down boundaries, liberalism makes it difficult to preserve ethnic identities. Because the Québecois do not aspire to a way of life that is much different from that of their English counterparts, the

Québecois need a public marker of their identity to demarcate the boundaries between them and other Canadians and to preserve their Francophone identity. Without this marker, Québecois identity would probably fade; there is little else to distinguish French Canadians from other Canadians. To be sure, there are differences among Canadians besides language. The Québecois are more likely to be Catholic than are other Canadians; they may eat some different foods. But these differences have dwindled over time and are too shallow to support a dynamic and distinctive identity.

Without French, the Québecois might look less like a nation and more like an American ethnic group: with a glimmer of distinctiveness, but for the most part not much different from other Americans. Unlike American ethnic and racial groups, the Québecois live close together; they have a claim to the land that they already occupy. Together with the federal system of government of Canada, which gives them political power in the province of Quebec, the Québecois can successfully implement strategies to establish French-speaking institutions to serve their community. They have both the numbers and the political force to accomplish their goals.

The Francophones want to preserve their particular identity and want to be recognized as different from their English-speaking neighbors. They want to be recognized by Canada and the world community as a distinct group of people. This desire for recognition is hard to capture with the language used by many (particularly liberal and communitarian) contemporary political theorists. Many current debates are about "the right" versus "the good." Should implementing fair procedures be the main concern of the state, or should the state be more concerned with helping its citizens live the good life? Charles Taylor uses this dichotomy in discussing Quebec, arguing that the Francophones, by insisting that French be spoken in Quebec, are trying to organize their society "around a definition of the good life."[27] This language is too strong, however, for the definition of the good life around which many Francophones want to organize their society is rather thin. Most Francophones do not aspire to define the sort of life people in Quebec should lead; they want to live lives quite similar to those of the English speakers of North America, but they want to do so while speaking French. The Francophones want to be recognized as a group of people distinct from English Canada. Recognition and identity are central to the claims of the Francophones; little light is shed on these claims by discussions of the right and the good. This desire for recognition highlights another difference between American ethnic groups and the Québecois. Most American ethnics also want recognition, but they want to be recognized by the polity as equal citizens; when this recognition is given, the cultural differences between particular ethnics and others begin to fade. The Francophones do not simply want to be recognized as equal

Canadian citizens; they want specific recognition as Québecois.

The quest for this recognition and their desire to retain their Francophone identity means that the Québecois need to keep French a vibrant language—*because there is little else they can use to maintain their identity.* Quebec French doesn't mean that the Francophones think differently than do English speakers; rather, Quebec French is a public marker, an easy way to distinguish Francophones from others. Between the 1950s and the 1970s, the defenders of French-Canadian culture decreased their emphasis on traditional church values and increasingly looked to the French language as the harbinger of Québecois culture.[28] If most Québecois had retained their traditional Catholic ways, it wouldn't have mattered if they spoke English—their way of life would still be easily distinguishable from that of their Anglophone neighbors, who are mostly modern Protestants. As the Québecois moved to cities, however, and successfully clamored for entry into middle- and upper-management positions in industry and into the professions, their lives became more like the lives of the Anglophones. In searching for ways to retain their identity, the Québecois had little choice but to settle on language.

The irony here is that, as liberalism (along with industrialization) reduces differences among people, it increases the likelihood of the rise of language-based nationalism. Too many languages have faded over the past two hundred years to think that language-based nationalism is an inevitable outcome of liberalism, but liberalism does facilitate some nationalisms, although it is not a cause of nationalism. Because liberal citizenship breaks down boundaries, liberalism enhances the importance of language as a marker of identity, increasing the likelihood that some nationalist movements based on language will emerge. The rehabilitation of a nearly forgotten language or the protection of a language that seems to be dying (or dead) is integral to many nationalist movements, including those in Wales, Scotland, Israel, the Basque country and Catalonia in Spain, and India.

The use of French must be institutionalized if it is to survive. To succeed, Québecois nationalists had to ensure that Quebec's public face would be French. A political movement was needed, and so modern Quebec nationalism emerged. This movement is about power, among other things. The Francophones resented the power held by the Anglophone community. It was unfair, many French Canadians argued, that they had to speak English to advance economically in a place with a majority of French speakers. For the Francophones to have the same economic opportunities as the Anglophones, the opportunities of the Anglophones had to be reduced. The liberal idea of equal opportunity cannot be fully realized in Quebec. If English remained the dominant language in Quebec, then the Francophones would be at an economic disadvantage because English is their second language. Language difficulties would cause their work to suffer, postponing promotions or causing customers who want to reduce the chances of communication problems to seek out native English speakers. Although the barrier of language need not be a permanent obstacle to opportunity—people do learn second languages, sometimes quite well—it is difficult to reach the fluency of native speakers. In any case, it is much harder for most people to learn a second language (particularly as adults) than it is to learn a first language.

When French became dominant in Quebec, the Anglophones were put at a disadvantage. One speech community will probably have to have more power and opportunity in Quebec than the other. (All this says nothing about the Allophones, who must learn either French or English.) This answer may be unsatisfactory for those who want to find fair solutions to problems, but a solution fair to all cannot be had in Quebec. The language of "the right," of ensuring that fair procedures are implemented, does not help navigate through the problem of equal opportunity. Some people will have more opportunity than others in Quebec until everyone is equally fluent in the dominant language. Talk about the good is not much more illuminating; what is good for one community harms the other. The grizzly fact is that the community with the most power implemented the language policy it wanted in Quebec.

The liberal value of equal opportunity, while damaged by the need for a public language, is not completely lost. To say that one language community will have more power than the other does not mean that the community should be able to use this power in any way it wants. In some cases, it is better to think of equal opportunity in generational terms. Immigrants may speak the language of their new country awkwardly and may not have equal opportunity, but there is no reason why this situation should be inherited by their children. These children may very well be fluent in the dominant language. The liberal state should work toward ensuring that all of its citizens are fluent in the public language. Working toward this goal of equality of opportunity also shows how liberalism and some forms of cultural pluralism clash. Deny ethnic children knowledge of the dominant language and they will undoubtedly retain many aspects of the ethnic culture—and remain economically subordinate. Allophones in Quebec who want to preserve all of the elements of their culture by preventing their children from learning French well and encouraging them to remain fluent in their native language are condemning their children to lives of obstructed economic opportunities. (There are, to be sure, few Allophones who want this.) There is no reason why these children cannot be bilingual; when ethnics learn French, however, they are able to take on parts of the dominant culture relatively easily, weakening the ethnic culture.

Some people bemoan the weakening of their ethnic or national cultures, although it is hard to determine precisely why. Why do some people want to retain their particular identity for themselves and for their children? Why the need to institutionalize French in Quebec? Why the need to remain distinct from the rest of English Canada? One possible but unsatisfying answer is psychological: we all need to be rooted somewhere, and the nation is a natural part of our identity. Liberalism may be seen to help this process along. By reducing the salience of many boundaries and ascriptive identities, liberalism may increase the likelihood that people will attach themselves to national identities, particularly those based on language. In this view, the Québecois nationalist movement, like other nationalist movements, is a way for people to become rooted. A related view argues that the dislocation caused by industrialization led many people to embrace nationalism as a secure identity in an unsettled world.[29] Not all Québecois support the nationalist movement, however; some French capitalists, in fact, fear that English-speaking businesses will leave Montreal, harming the Quebec economy. Few nationalist movements enjoy universal support from members of their nation; dissenters abound in the history of nationalism. The nation is not somehow a natural part of the world but is a relatively recent creation, dating from the late eighteenth century.[30]

Some people feel closely attached to a particular language and culture; they may feel that giving up their language is akin to giving up part of themselves. To prevent this, they may fight to retain their identity. Both Romansch speakers and the Québecois may think they lose part of themselves when they cannot use their native language in many settings, yet few Romansch fight for their language like the Québecois fight for theirs, probably in part because of the high economic cost the Romansch must pay to retain their language. Although the promise of cultural preservation in conjunction with economic health may make some nationalisms more likely than others, some people are willing to forgo economic opportunity to ensure the cultural preservation of their nation. I don't think the question of why some groups fight for their survival while others disappear quietly can be completely answered.

Cultural Preservation

There is a need, some liberals argue, to preserve cultures, a need that may in fact justify special political provisions for certain groups. This need is usually justified because group respect and self-respect are often thought to be intertwined. Avishai Margalit and Joseph Raz explain that "it may be no more than a brute fact that people's sense of their own identity is bound up with their sense of belonging to encompassing groups and that their self-respect is affected by the esteem in which these groups are held. But these facts, too, have important consequences." If a person's group is denigrated, then that person too will feel belittled. Some liberals argue that, to safeguard the self-respect of individuals, society must protect their group as well.

Allen Buchanan argues that, to preserve cultures, we should accord special rights to minority groups. If these group rights in combination with individual, liberal rights cannot preserve a culture, then the need to preserve a cultural identity justifies secession. Secession, Buchanan makes clear, is an option of last resort, but an option nonetheless. Yael Tamir makes a similar argument, saying that "although it cannot be ensured that each nation will have its own state, all nations are entitled to a public sphere in which they constitute a majority." Depending on the circumstances, a state might be needed to preserve a group's cultural identity, but this is not the only way to preserve a culture, and circumstances might dictate a less drastic way. On the other hand, Chandran Kukathas argues that "liberalism views cultural communities more like private associations or, to use a slightly different metaphor, electoral minorities. Both are the product of a multitude of factors, and neither need be especially enduring, although they can be. The possibility that they might be, however, does not justify entrenching the interests they manifest."[31] The preservation of cultures, according to Kukathas, is a purely private affair. Under Kukathas's argument, it is hard to imagine the justification for a nationalist movement to preserve a cultural identity.

As Buchanan and Tamir understand, however, public space in a state is not a neutral setting; only one or two languages can be used publicly.[32] This does not mean that other languages cannot survive, but public languages have a decided advantage over private languages. The very existence of a state with one or two public languages means that choices about what languages will be public must be made. This choice is not simply another private affair for citizens to determine in their homes.

The Québecois disagree with arguments like Kukathas's because these arguments do nothing to protect their speech community; without public measures, French will almost surely fade in Quebec. Yet there are limits to the argument that minority groups should be granted special rights to preserve their culture. Bilingual education will not ensure the survival of Romansch culture; if the speakers of Romansch move to German-speaking cities, their community will have a hard time surviving. If the state forced the Romansch to live near each other, then Romansch culture would probably survive. But this is drastic curtailment of individual liberty, a curtailment that most of the Romansch would find objectionable (or they would not want their children taught in German). To preserve a culture using measures to which the culture's members object is not sensible.

Tamir would not support the preservation of a culture using such measures; it seems doubtful that Buchanan would either.[33] But the Romansch point to a larger issue: some cultures, some language groups, cannot survive in advanced industrial societies. Liberals should not give blanket support to the survival of speech or cultural communities; the conditions for the survival of a language in an advanced industrial society must be in place for liberals to support its survival. What should liberals do if not all cultures and speech communities can survive, but group membership is an important part of the identity of people? At the least, the connection between group respect and self-respect has "negative consequences"; ascriptive group membership should never be the cause of ridicule, discrimination, or persecution. Although the Romansch want to be fluent in German, this does not mean that they cannot also be fluent in Romansch. It may be important for Native American to speak English, but this hardly excuses the old policy of punishing Native American schoolchildren for speaking their native language.[34] The Québecois should not prevent the Allophones from speaking their ethnic languages at home or on the streets. Fluency in the dominant language and mainstream culture need not (and so should not) mean the eradication of the vestiges of all other cultures.

Liberals should not fool themselves, however, into thinking that respect will be enough for some cultures and speech communities to survive. It is not. Some of these communities will disappear in the modern world, regardless of the amount of respect they command. Whether group respect is cause for more positive action—laws promoting a particular language or secession, for example—is harder to answer. There are two elements to language-based nationalist movements that must be in place for liberalism to be *compatible* with nationalism, elements that can be determined only by the particular circumstances surrounding nationalist movements.[35] First, the nationalist movements should center around a speech community that is large enough to support the institutions of an industrial society. Second, the movement must be willing to construct a liberal, pluralistic public space; language-based nationalisms that do not exclude people based on their ancestry or insist that people take on a specific set of values fit this description. Compatibility does not equate with support, but I suggest several reasons why liberals can support—or, at the least, not oppose—efforts to preserve French in Quebec. My argument is an attempt to forge a compromise between liberalism and nationalism, not to justify robust liberal support for nationalism.

French can be supported without restricting the opportunities or the mobility of the Québecois. Furthermore, French can be supported without restricting the opportunities of the children of the Anglophones or the Allophones either—assuming that they learn French. This relatively benign view of culture and nationalism was not always prevalent in Quebec. Until the 1960s, the French-speaking schools infused Catholic doctrine into their curriculum, leading Jews and other non-Catholic Allophones to attend the English schools, where there was little religious emphasis. The English schools were more receptive to Allophone students and added many Allophone teachers to their staffs.[36] This Anglicization of the Allophones worried many Québecois. When the Québecois did insist that Allophone children attend French schools, their schools became less nationalist and more pluralistic. The Québecois could have insisted on teaching traditional Catholic values to the immigrants, but this would have understandably encountered considerable resistance. Because many Francophones were more interested in establishing a Québecois bourgeoisie than in reinforcing the values of the Catholic church, this fight rarely materialized, although there were some important skirmishes in the schools.

By the 1970s, French had officially replaced religion as the cornerstone of French-Canadian culture.[37] With this shift, Québecois culture became more pluralistic. If this shift had not occurred, there would have been cause for vigorous liberal opposition to Québecois nationalism. A nationalism heavily infused with Catholicism would prevent most Allophones and Anglophones from receiving equal citizenship.

Jewish, Haitian, and French Québecois can all speak French to each other in public and in civil society. If the Québecois claim that French is the key to their culture, are they not imposing their culture on those who must speak French to gain equal opportunity? This formula is too strong. Jews can speak French but remain Jewish; Haitians and Italians who come to Quebec will not have the same way of life as those in Haiti or Italy, but neither will they be exactly like the Francophones. Language is one factor in determining a culture, but it is not the only or even the most important factor. Within the parameters set by a particular language, different lifestyles and cultural practices can exist and flourish. English speakers in the United States have many different cultural practices; a similar kind of pluralism can exist in Quebec. As different cultural practices come to Quebec and as the distinctions between Anglophone and Francophone institutions decline, Québecois culture changes and becomes more pluralistic. The immigrants take on certain Québecois practices as they enter the institutions of Quebec. As this happens, Francophones eat at ethnic restaurants, participate in ethnic celebrations, and learn different ethnic practices. Although the Allophones and Anglophones may have distinctive practices, as they learn French the boundaries between them and the Francophones will become blurred. The Québecois want to ensure that any blurring of boundaries is done in French.

Québecois culture will change as it becomes more pluralistic, but this does not mean that it will disappear. The ways in which different cultural practices change, mesh, and are transformed are affected by both the dominant culture and ethnic cultures. Because the dominant culture in the United States is different from that of Quebec, the transformation of U.S. and ethnic cultures when they meet will not duplicate this transformation in Quebec. The interactions among Francophones, Anglophones, and Allophones will produce a culture that is notably Québecois. Anderson's argument about nationalism helps explain why Québecois culture will remain unique—the people in Quebec will share a collective memory that is produced and reproduced by the newspapers, radio, and television. This collective memory does not preclude other, smaller collective memories like those of the Haitian or Jewish Québecois.[38] There will, however, be an overarching memory that ties the people of Quebec into an imagined community.

A language should enjoy widespread support from citizens to become a public language. French has this support in Quebec. The maintenance of French in Quebec probably harms fewer people than would its disappearance and so deserves liberal support.

Some liberals are troubled by the efforts to preserve French in Quebec because these efforts have led to forced Allophone attendance in French-speaking schools. The most controversial law states that Allophone children must attend French-speaking schools, although they can also learn English in them. Other laws insist that many public signs be written only in French; many signs in the workplace can be bilingual, but they must have larger French than English letters. Some Anglophones reacted strongly against these measures, seeing them as threats to their liberty to speak the language of their choice.

Liberals are traditionally hesitant to restrict choice, yet the principles behind these rules are not objectionable, although some of the particular rules may be.[39] If the Allophones sent their children to English schools, if there was no state intervention to create French-speaking businesses, if Anglophones immigrated to Montreal from the rest of Canada, then many Francophone parents might feel that they had little choice but to send their children to English schools as well (just as some Romansch parents feel compelled to send their children to German-speaking schools). Choice, then, is restricted not only by official state policies; a decision by the state to avoid involvement would also restrict choices, but it would restrict the choices of a different set of people.

French is a minority language in North America, as Quebec is surrounded by English-speaking Canada and the English-speaking United States. As the dominant language in these places, English does not need special protection to survive. English has a better chance of surviving in Quebec without legal support than does French. English speakers in Quebec can easily buy magazines and books and see movies in English; they do not have to travel far to be in places where English dominates.[40]

Support for efforts to preserve French does not necessarily translate into support for an independent Quebec. As there are so many more ethnic and national groups than states and as not all these groups can be given states, liberals should work toward ensuring that these groups do not face pressure to abandon their distinctive practices. This means supporting efforts to maintain speech communities when these communities can survive in the modern, industrialized world.[41] If national groups are given the means to protect their culture (when that's possible), then the pressure to create new states will probably decrease. The suppression of nationalist movements may cause these nationalists to turn to violent means to pursue their goals. This does not mean that all nationalist movements should be supported because they may turn violent otherwise. Some nationalist movements will be violent whether they are suppressed or not; some nationalist movements strive for "ethnic purification" in their states. These nationalist movements deserve to be condemned by liberals.

Few Québecois, however, talk about expelling those with the wrong ancestry. The Québecois effort to preserve French is not predicated on doing violence to others; there is no indication that Francophones will violate the rights of others in a Québecois state. I doubt that the Québecois need their own state to retain their identity—there are ways within the context of a federal government to grant Québecois nationalists the recognition they want. There is little cause for strong liberal opposition, however, if the majority of the Québecois insist that they need a state to preserve their culture and they are committed to a pluralistic culture. A new French-Canadian state would almost surely be liberal. A liberal state with French as its official language can hardly be seen as much better or worse than an English-speaking state. Because there is no reason to think that a new Québecois state would violate the rights of its citizens, it is not worth resorting to bloodshed to prevent secession from Canada. If the majority of the Québecois want their own state, they should be able to secede. (Liberals can also support a decision by the majority of the Québecois to remain in Canada.) A Québecois state would hardly constitute a great liberal victory, though. As long as language remains the key to the claims of the Québecois, liberals can support efforts to institutionalize French in Quebec, yet any liberal support for an independent Quebec state should be tepid.

Nationalism and Citizenship

While some nationalisms, like Québecois nationalism, are about cultural preservation, another kind of nationalism is about securing full liberal citizenship. A state that is home to different nationalities that hate each other can sometimes use this hate to oppress its citizens. John Stuart Mill worried that in some multinational states each nation might fear "more injury to itself from the other nationalities, than from the common arbiter, the State. Their mutual antipathies are generally much stronger than jealousy of the government." If several different nationalities live under the same government but hate each other, the state can use one nationality to oppress another. Or members of each nationality might be more interested in how advantaged or disadvantaged members of the other nationalities are than in the government's oppressive measures. Liberty, Mill worried, would take a back seat to concerns about the relative advantages of one's national group. Mill contended that to preserve liberty the creation of nation-states was sometimes needed: "Where the sentiment of nationality exists in any force, there is a prima facie case for uniting all the members of the nationality under the same government, and a government to themselves apart."[42]

For a state's citizens to look out after themselves and to guard the government, they need to have "fellow-feeling": "Among a people without fellow-feeling, especially if they read and speak different languages, the united public opinion, necessary to the working of representative government, cannot exist."[43] To work together, citizens must think of themselves as part of the same public. Mill argued that, in a state of different nationalities, the debates that go on within one community will not be replicated in the other. This allows the government to manipulate each side; it allows misunderstandings to erupt. Mill did not have a picture of citizens all agreeing on every issue, but he did suggest that, when people hate each other because of their group membership, they will not be able to work together on public matters. They will not even be able to disagree constructively. Fruitful dialogue cannot take place when fierce hatred based on nationality makes people deaf to the claims and arguments of others.

Mill's argument here is instrumental: if people of different groups hate each other so much that this hatred takes precedence over interest in their own liberty, then these groups should not coexist in the same state.[44] Under conditions of hatred, each nation should have its own state; within these boundaries, the proper fellow-feeling necessary for a functioning public opinion can emerge. Yet Mill also recognized that the geography of nations does not always lend itself to carving out new nation-states: "There are parts even of Europe, in which different nationalities are so locally intermingled, that it is not practicable for them to be under separate governments." Unfortunately, Mill's recognition of this problem did not lead him to try to resolve it. In creating nation-states, Mill said only that "proper allowance [should be] made for geographical exigencies."[45]

Mill avoided this problem probably because it is rather difficult to address. Still, his argument cannot be completely dismissed. Although the construction of real nation-states is rarely a possibility, hatred between nationalities is sometimes a reason for using nationality as the basis for creating states. Sometimes a government can play different nationalities off each other, manufacturing or fanning the hatreds between different national groups. In the twentieth century a slight twist on this problem has been added; it is quite common for a government to be in the hands of a national group that discriminates against members of other groups. Examples of this abound; one of the better known cases is Israel.

The liberty of the Palestinians in the West Bank and the Gaza Strip is restricted in ways that do not apply to Israeli Jews. The Israeli-Palestinian conflict shows that blanket condemnation of nationalism is sometimes worse than a grudging acceptance of it. First, condemnation of nationalism sentences the Palestinians to an indefinite period of second class citizenship. There is little reason to believe that the Israelis will treat the Palestinians as equal citizens. Second, such condemnation is simply a formula for further bloodshed. The ample hatred between Palestinians and Jews will not disappear with the creation of a binational state.[46] It is unlikely that such a state, in which Palestinians and Jews would have the same political rights, can work without considerable carnage. Nationalism may not be a wonderful solution to a difficult problem, but the current alternatives are much worse. Hand wringing about nationalism as more blood is spilled is not morally acceptable. As long as a binational state is not feasible, a Palestinian state is the best way to stop the killing.

There is a certain symmetry in the case for a Palestinian state. In large part, it is a response to the Jewish state, and Israel is in part a reaction to the creation of nation-states in Europe. With the rise of the nation-state in the nineteenth century, the question of the place of the Jews in Europe became important. The Austrian empire was home to many peoples; the Jews were simply one people among many. In a Polish or German or French state, however, the Jews could not simply be another people and be loyal citizens. Although the French Assembly after the Revolution gave Jews citizenship, this decision did not establish a pattern in Europe (or in France). In many European states Jews were considered to be their own nation and so were thought of as aliens. The status of the Jews in most European states was in flux for most of the nineteenth and part of the twentieth centuries. This uncertainty, combined with pogroms in Russia, the Dreyfus trial in France, the establishment of the International Antisemitic Congress in the late nineteenth century, and the rise of fascism in Germany and elsewhere convinced many Jews that they needed their own nation-state. The French, the Germans, the Italians all had their own states—why shouldn't the Jews? Many Jews argued that they would always be foreigners in the nation-states of others; the best way to live in a place the Jews could call home was to create their own nation-state. In a Jewish state, all Jews would presumably be full citizens, just as Poles are full Polish citizens and the French have equal citizenship in France.

Nation-states, then, beget nation-states, even if they are mythical. The problem is that only some nationalists see the nation-state as mythical and as an instrumental way to prevent oppression; other nationalists seek the creation of a "greater" Israel or a "greater" Italy that has expansive territorial designs. Many nationalists refuse to accept the possibility that some of their fellow nationals may live in an adjoining state. They seek control over areas in adjoining states that are home to their fellow nationals, even if these areas are also home to other nationalities. Nationalisms that are ever expanding should be opposed by liberals. The best roadblock to the power of these nation-states may be another nation-state, assuming that there is land that this group could claim. The creation of new nation-states, though, does not solve the problems of nationalism. If a Palestinian state was created, neither it nor Israel would then become a real nation-state; many Palestinians would still live in Israel, and some Jews would probably live in Palestine. This is not reason enough to disdain the creation of a Palestinian state. Although not all Palestinians would have equal citizenship in this state, many would; surely, equal citizenship for some Palestinians is better than full citizenship for none. Moreover, a Palestinian state could oversee Israeli treatment of Palestinian citizens in Israel, and Israel could oversee Palestinian treatment of Jews in Palestine.[47]

Liberalism and Nationalism

The creation of national states in the face of persecution and hatred does not end the role of liberalism in nationalist movements or states. Liberalism can help ensure that the rights of national minorities are not abused and can curb the excesses of nationalism. Liberalism gives oppressed people a language in which to express their grievances and demand full citizenship. This language can be used by national minorities. The desire to be free from domination and discrimination is often at the root of national movements; this same desire is often held by national minorities. Liberalism, in this view, is a philosophy of resistance rather than the ideology of a dominant majority. The claims of liberalism can be used to battle the exclusiveness of nationalism.

Liberalism can push some nationalisms into less exclusive ways, for example, by trying to make nationalism language-based. Liberals should admit the need for one or two public languages in a state. One or two public languages will not always foster the fellow-feeling that Mill thought was necessary for liberty in a state, but one or two public languages are necessary to reach the goal of equal opportunity. Members of smaller language communities need to learn one of the public languages in their state if they are to be equal to other citizens. One or two public languages may foster a sense of community, giving people an ability to communicate with others in the same state. A public language allows a collective memory among a limited (although possibly large) number of people. This limited number of people may develop a sense of identity with one another, an identity that they do not share with others. I'm hesitant to call this a national identity because it is fluid, changing with the identity of the members of the political community. A political community based on one or two public languages is relatively inclusive, which is why this sort of identity can be compatible with liberalism. Newcomers to the state need learn only a public language to become full members; if they cannot learn the language, their children certainly can. At the same time, however, liberals should insist that the need for a public language need not mean the forcible eradication of other languages in the state; cultural practices (and languages), regardless of their origin, should be allowed to exist if they do not violate liberal principles. Enough people may speak a second or third language for it to emerge as a public language. This will happen rarely, but there is no reason for liberals to oppose this possibility; the identity of the political community may change over time, perhaps dramatically so.

By softening the edges of nationalism, liberalism can point the way to postnationalist states. Liberalism should push states past nationalism because each nation in the world cannot have its own state; therefore, liberals should work toward pluralistic states. When this is not possible or when the push for a pluralistic state would have worse consequences than would a nationalist state, a nationalist movement may be necessary to secure the individual rights of the members of a nation or to preserve a language community. But liberals should not be satisfied with nationalist states.

Nationalism is too exclusive; its potential to treat some people as less than equal should make liberals uneasy. Once a nation-state is established, its worries about its cultural survival decrease. The new worry should then become the survival of the smaller groups within its midst. The dominant cultural groups in the West are certainly not in danger of being persecuted. The contingent circumstances that make nationalism acceptable rarely apply to majorities in established states. In their own countries German, English, and French citizens are not persecuted; smaller cultural communities in all of these states, however, do suffer discrimination. Liberalism's role in these countries is to help ensure the end of discrimination by bringing about pluralistic integration. Since World War II, millions of people from Southern Europe, Africa, Asia, and the West Indies have entered wealthy Western Europe for jobs and safety; some are refugees, fleeing wars and persecution, and others came looking for economic security. The "depluralization" of industrial society is countered by "repluralization" due to the movements of immigrants and refugees.[48] Exclusive forms of nationalism, however, will prevent these immigrants from gaining full citizenship. Liberalism should help ensure that these immigrants receive equal citizenship.

Liberals can support some nationalist movements, but liberalism works toward a world past nationalism, although not a world past culture or a monocultural world. Liberals may want to move past the nation-state, but the state itself should probably continue to exist. Each state can be a locus of different cultural groups and practices, a particular mixture that is not replicated elsewhere, with unique patterns in its dominant culture and in its smaller communities. Cultural differences may be on the decline, but they have not disappeared. State boundaries can protect particular cultural patterns and communities. In the (relatively) small setting of the state, these groups can work for their cultural survival. National groups can demand a public space for their language and culture. They can press for multilingual signs and education; they can demand that the history of their group is taught in schools.[49]

As different national groups push for equal citizenship, they will contribute to the culture of the state in which they live. Their differences will not be as great as the cultural differences of preindustrial societies, but the decline in global cultural pluralism may very well increase the salience of the differences that do exist. The difficulty of maintaining distinctive identities in the liberal, industrialized world may lead members of different groups to adhere more closely to the few markers that distinguish them from others. This is part of the reason why national and ethnic conflict are so prominent in a world that has seen a decline in cultural differences. As differences decline, some people will hang on ever more ferociously to their few remaining cultural markers. Some will demand a state to ease the burdens of cultural maintenance; others will demand laws that will help maintain their language. These laws, however, will increase the opportunities of some and decrease the opportunities of others. Although this may be inevitable, the role of liberalism is to ensure that the maintenance of distinctive identities does not lead to discrimination against others and the relegation of an inherited, permanent minority to the status of second class citizenship.

CHAPTER 8

THE BOUNDARIES OF
CITIZENSHIP

BOUNDARIES HELP DETERMINE identity by marking off who is in a particular group and who is not. These boundaries take many forms: clothing,
food, language, skin color, and economic, social, and political subordination all help determine who is part of a group. Neither liberalism nor the
institutions of modern society abolish these boundaries, but they do work
toward reducing the distinctions among many of them. In the liberal state,
the cultural practices of different groups can be scrutinized and shared by
others. Sometimes this scrutiny will lead to pressure on groups to drop
particular practices that are illiberal; unfortunately, sometimes there will be
pressure to drop practices without this scrutiny. Too often the dominant
group in liberal states demands conformity even though some practices
that may appear unusual do not violate any liberal principles. Even if this
pressure for conformity disappears, as it should, the boundaries between
groups will weaken in the liberal state.

There are, however, important exceptions to this tendency; groups like
the Amish and the Hasidim are not about to become confused with mainstream Americans. These groups remain different by a (voluntary) radical
separation from mainstream culture. It is not accidental that the Amish and
Hasidim, while culturally different from most Americans, are also religious
groups. The maintenance of their groups is heavily dependent on strict
obedience to their leaders, religious leaders who call on God's authority to

demand conformity. Believers are understandably hesitant to depart from the strictures of their leaders. This radical separation and this unstinting belief in religious leaders are not easily achieved in today's world.

The Amish and the Hasidim are noticeably absent from debates about cultural pluralism or the meaning of American citizenship. They don't care if they are part of the collective memories of mainstream America. Few people, however, are able or willing to imitate the Amish or Hasidim to maintain a particular identity; few are willing to retreat into their insular group, keep their distance from mainstream society, and reject bourgeois values. Therefore, fights about identity, collective memories, and citizenship erupt in the places where mainstream society meets—in the schools, legislatures, movies, television shows, books, and newspapers. These places, which are the battlegrounds of identity, are shaped by the contours of the state. Although these fights take place in many countries, their particular shape is different from state to state. The fights in Quebec differ from the conflicts in England, which are different still from the battles in the United States. The state plays a crucial role in these fights by establishing the setting in which they take place.

By establishing boundaries, the state plays a large role in determining identity. American citizenship is established within the boundaries set by the American state. Although the internationalization of the world has made state boundaries less important, boundaries still play an important role in matters of identity and citizenship.

Boundaries and Identity

The state shapes identity by establishing boundaries. What it means to be an American citizen is not only a matter of enjoying the protection of the Bill of Rights. Being an American is also about collective memories and collective arguments; it is about inhabiting the same general space as do other Americans. Not the same exact space, of course, but all Americans are supposed to enjoy the right to move to any state, to any city, to any neighborhood they want (assuming they have enough money to do so). Americans can move to France or Canada or India, but these moves are more difficult. An American cannot simply move to another country; papers must be filled out, questions answered, jobs obtained. None of this is true for those who want to move within the United States. Liberal citizens can and do move a lot. They move to attend college or to get a job, to be with their spouse, or simply for a change of scenery.

The boundaries of the state also matter as a point of reference for members of the political community. When Benedict Anderson talks about the imagined community as a place where millions of the same people read the same things, it is also true that these people read about events that affect each other and that take place within the boundaries of the state. To be sure, Americans read about what happens in other parts of the world, but what happens in the United States dominates the news in the United States. People in other countries may be keenly interested in what happens in the United States, but they too are primarily interested in what happens in their own countries, within the boundaries set by their states. Political matters are discussed by the community that is fenced in by state boundaries. People from all over the United States congregate in Washington, D.C., to protest and voice their opinions about particular issues. Debates in Congress, cases before the Supreme Court, and issues raised by the president all help to shape the collective arguments of citizens in the United States. Some people doggedly avoid politics, but popular culture and mass marketing also help form the political community. The same television shows, movies, stores, and products are watched by and consumed by the same public.

The boundaries of the state help form the political community—when it bestows equal citizenship on its residents. This is a crucial caveat. There are many examples of people living in the same state without forming a political community. Jews and Christians in pre-Enlightenment Europe felt little affinity for each other, shared few memories, and did not share the same space. (Jews had a different educational system and often could not own land or live in certain areas.) Jews easily formed their own collective memories under these circumstances. With the decline of anti-Semitism and the end of legally sanctioned Jewish communities, however, the struggle to maintain Jewish memory and Jewish identity began; there was no longer a Jewish space in the Western states. To ensure the survival of a particular cultural identity, society must carve out a public space for this identity or construct a community that has sanctions over its members. Without the legal authority to fashion boundaries, however, this is difficult. One notable attempt to construct a unified, voluntary Jewish community in New York City earlier in this century was called the Kehillah.[1] The Kehillah failed because the Jewish community was too diverse and because it lacked any coercive power over its members. If some Jews disliked the Kehillah, they could simply ignore it, which is exactly what many did. The experiment fell apart when it became apparent that the divergent demands of different Jews could not be satisfied by the Kehillah.

Although a Jewish public space is not easily constructed in the United States, the situation is quite different in Israel. "A sharp distinction between being a Jew in private and a citizen in public cannot be made when Jews control the public domain of their lives."[2] In a Jewish state, Jewish holidays are not private celebrations but public ones. Jews in Israel do not have to worry much about how to retain their Jewish identity; for most, living in Israel enshrines their identity as Jewish. Because American Jews do not have a public space or the legal authority to draw boundaries and are not economically and socially subordinate, it is harder to maintain a Jewish identity in the United States than in Israel. This lack of boundaries in the liberal state worries many Québecois, leading them to insist on a public space; with a public space the survival of Québecois identity is no longer in question. A nation tied to a particular piece of land that it controls has a good chance of maintaining its identity.

The state is about space and memories; through these commonalities, liberal citizens often develop overlapping memories. Few Americans will have the same collective memories, but the memories of most will overlap. These collective memories will be shaped by the history of the United States, the political and social battles fought here, and popular culture. People won't always agree on the meaning of American history, but then the political community will engage in a collective argument over this history. Fights as well as agreements help form a community.

Apart from collective culture, American citizens have memories that they share with other members of a particular group. Many Black Americans share a collective memory that other Americans do not share; Jewish Americans, too, have their own collective memory, as do some Italian Americans and Irish Americans and Chinese Americans and Japanese Americans. Collective memories are not restricted to members of racial and ethnic groups: women, lesbians and gay men, war veterans, and others may share collective memories. These collective memories help maintain particular identities because they belong to a particular set of people. To maintain their identity, members of ethnic groups may also look outside the United States as a reference point in their lives. Italian Americans may look to Italy, Jews to Israel, and Korean Americans to Korea. Members of these groups, however, will also look to the United States as a reference point. This reference point overlaps the reference points of other Americans.

The state matters, then, as a source of identity for its citizens. Chiseled into the identity of most people will be the imprint of the state in which they live. As long as states exist, the identity of the citizens of these states will differ, even if cultural differences among many of these states decrease, particularly if different languages are used in these states. The boundaries of the state help form the people living within them into a political community. To be sure, because of the internationalization of the world economy the borders of the state do not mean what they used to mean. Some people travel easily from one country to another, but these people are still more the exception than the rule. Most people live their lives within the boundaries of the state, traveling abroad every once in a while for a brief time. Although multinational corporations market their goods in many different countries, they do so in the language of the country where they sell their products; they often slightly alter their products to fit their market better. Yet the imprint of the state is not equally pressed on everyone. Some people opt out of the community and become partial citizens. Others find that liberal citizenship is withheld from them, that they are outsiders, struggling to be included. They have to fight to have their memories and experiences included as part of the collective American memory.

The Tensions of Diversity

The successful effort by some to keep their particular ethnic memories while sharing in a collective American memory is cited by others as proof of the richness of American diversity. Some people breezily celebrate the unity and diversity of the United States. "Our unity and diversity," announces one typical American platitude, "are not opposites; they are necessary complements to each other."[3] It's hard to know what this vague pronouncement precisely means, but the implication that unity and diversity can easily coexist is wrong. Tensions are caused by efforts to maintain ethnic identity and liberal citizenship. These tensions do not mean the end of ethnic identity or reveal liberal citizenship to be irredeemably flawed, but they do show that "unity and diversity" will frequently be hard to reconcile.

For Jews to maintain their identity in the United States, they may have to set themselves apart in certain situations. If they do not distinguish between Jews and non-Jews, it will be hard to remain Jewish. It is, however, sometimes difficult to distinguish efforts to maintain a particular identity from simple discrimination. Those who strive to preserve their ethnic identity must set up boundaries between themselves and others. Since they cannot establish public spaces for their ethnic group, they often try to establish private spaces where their ethnic identity can flourish, where others cannot enter or can enter only and clearly as guests. (This attempt to establish a private space may spill over to civil society, where members of one ethnic group favor their fellow members in a variety of ways.) The extent to which ethnic identity survives in the liberal state heavily depends on the establishment of these boundaries. Maintaining these boundaries will mean that some ethnics must perform a delicate balancing act between being ethnic in private and citizen in public. The difference between the preservation of boundaries and discrimination may be lost on those who find themselves outside the boundary. If a Jewish person shies away from having non-Jewish friends, this may feel like discrimination to non-Jews. This is something about which liberal citizens sometimes complain: if all people are the same, if we all are equal, then why do members of some groups stick together? Do they think they are better than others?

The attempt of some weak ethnics to maintain their ethnic ties and to have their children do the same often causes a predicament for children of first or second generation ethnics who have been deeply affected by liberal citizenship. The children may (and, in this country, often do) meet and fall in love with people from other ethnic groups, to their parents' chagrin. This dilemma can create an impossible choice, a choice between their parents and their lover. Ethnic parents sometimes shun their children for marrying outside the ethnic group. Weak ethnics may feel caught between the traditional world of their parents and the lure of liberal citizenship; as time goes on and as new generations arise, this dilemma will fade. This is little solace, however, for those individual ethnics who are unhappily caught between two worlds, who want to move to one world but feel pulled in by the other.

Conflicts between members of different cultural groups are also created by different cultural styles. Some people are rather reserved in their manners; some ethnics are regarded as loud and boisterous by others; others gesticulate with their hands while speaking. Some of the many different ways in which people speak and act have specific cultural roots. Different styles in talking and relating to others will inevitably cause misunderstandings and conflicts. In some cultures, people touch each other when they talk; in others, people keep their distance. (A conversation between two people from each cultural tradition may literally lead them to walk in circles, with one person reaching out while the other backs away.) Awareness of different cultural styles will help reduce tensions; with so many different cultural traditions represented in the United States, however, it is impossible for everyone to know about every cultural style. Some people may dislike and ridicule the cultural styles of others. Furthermore, cultural stereotypes can often be misleading. Not every American Protestant is reserved, not every Black or Jewish American loud, not every Asian American quiet. The distinction between race and culture makes things more difficult for people trying to be attentive to different cultural styles. Someone may have Asian ancestors and be American; she may have more mainstream American cultural characteristics than Korean or Japanese or Chinese cultural traits.[4] Knowledge of different cultural styles may not be very useful when dealing with particular members of ethnic or racial groups.

Tensions are created by attempts to maintain ethnic identity in the United States, tensions between liberal citizens and tensions between parents and children. Diversity and unity can coexist, but they do so uneasily.

Some of these tensions need not be a tremendous worry. Memories of the old country are hard to keep intact if these memories have not been lived by liberal citizens; these citizens will create their own memories where they live. Most second and third generation Italian Americans will know more about California and Florida than about Rome or Venice. The boundaries of the American state will shape the memories of its citizens into particularly American memories. Some ethnics will strive to be included in the dominant culture, yet they will not want to leave their ethnic identity behind completely. This may lead to an occasional social problem, but sporadic social tensions are not necessarily cause for state involvement. Sometimes tensions between members of different ethnic and racial groups will become severe and occasionally they will turn violent. Members of one group may pervasively discriminate against members of another group; large violations of liberal principles in civil society or the public sphere do in fact call for state involvement.

Some ethnics may find that the achievement of equal citizenship has disturbing effects. The sharing of cultural practices that often accompanies equal citizenship will transform the ethnic identity of some. This does not mean that all ethnics will become like American Protestants, but it does mean that there are many different cultural practices in the United States, practices that can be shared among many. Pluralistic integration means—or should mean—that different cultural practices become diffuse, spreading out across the population. Black and white Americans can learn from Japanese Americans to appreciate the pause before speaking, Protestant Americans can learn to be louder and more expressive, and all Americans can celebrate St. Patrick's Day. Not all ethnic practices will be shared with others (few non-Jews wear yarmulkes), but, as long as some are shared, specific cultural practices will become less attached to their ethnic moorings.

Ethnic practices are easily shared when the desire for equal citizenship leads to the quest for public recognition. When ethnics are recognized and their practices are explained in schools and in the media, when the stores and restaurants they own are accepted and frequented by members of the dominant culture, when politicians recognize them as important political actors, when members of the dominant community share in their celebrations, the distinctive identity of these ethnics will begin to break down. Without this recognition, however, many ethnics will be denied equal citizenship. This is the dilemma that many ethnics face in liberal states, a dilemma that cannot be fully resolved. Those ethnics who strive for equal citizenship do so because they understandably do not want to face discrimination. Acceptance as equal citizens, however, will often lead to a major change in the identity of their groups. Implanted in equal citizenship are the seeds of ethnic transformation; resisting this transformation is possible but not easy.

There is another, related dilemma of public recognition: public recognition may lead to a distortion of ethnic practices caused in part by mainstream culture. Although many of the obvious restrictions on the lives of members of ethnic and racial groups have been overturned, a cultural pull toward the norms set by white Christians (particularly Protestants) remains. The United States is heavily influenced by Christianity. The attachment of many American citizens to prayers in schools and at commencement ceremonies is testimony to this, as is the national celebration of Christmas. The celebration of Christmas is deeply ingrained in this country, woven into its school year and its businesses. Schools are not about to rearrange their calenders to avoid favoring Christmas in holiday schedules; businesses will continue to be open for longer hours before Christmas (and to close on Christmas), touting Christmas time as a great time to buy gifts. This is not cause for complete despair. The Christian character of this country has thinned since its founding (although the fundamentalist revival that began in the 1980s is a worrisome development and may reinvigorate the Christian nature of the United States). The Christian veneer of the United States will remain for a long time, but this does not drastically harm the opportunities and life chances of non-Christians.

Many non-Christians, however, will often have to resist the pull of Christian norms if they want to retain their identity. Schools in the United States have traditionally celebrated Christmas; with the influx of Jewish students in some schools, the search to treat Jewish and Christian students equally began. One way would have been simple: to abolish Christmas celebrations. Nothing in liberal theory insists that schools celebrate Christmas. But bringing Christmas out of the public realm in the United States is not about to happen, no matter what liberal theory says. The role of Christmas in the United States certainly confirms that pluralistic integration probably will not be fully achieved in the near future. To the credit of many educators, they recognized that their Jewish students did not share in Christmas celebrations and they elected to celebrate both Hanukkah and Christmas.

Hanukkah is traditionally a minor Jewish holiday that happens to fall in December, near Christmas. During Hanukkah young children were traditionally given small gifts. But Hanukkah is now celebrated in many schools with Jewish populations as the "Jewish Christmas." Its role in American Judaism has become far more important than its historical place in Judaism. Expensive Hanukkah presents are often given to friends and family, just as gifts are given at Christmas. Just as Christmas songs are sung, so too are Hanukkah songs. There is a traditionally joyous Jewish holiday, a holiday where children dress up in costumes and everyone eats sweets and makes a lot of noise. But this holiday—the holiday of Purim—inconveniently falls in February or March. This inconvenience meant that Hanukkah, not Purim, would become the Jewish holiday that entered the public realm in the United States. And now in some schools the relatively new African-American celebration of Kwanza is also celebrated. It too is celebrated in December, and it too is becoming a holiday of expensive gift giving.

The public schools did not change the meaning of Hanukkah by themselves; many Jewish parents, not wanting their children to feel completely left out of Christmas celebrations and gift giving, abetted in the alteration of Hanukkah. Nobody forced these parents, but the dominance of Christmas pressured them. This pressure could have been resisted—and is resisted by some Jews—but perhaps many liberal citizens are too weak-willed to withstand it.[5] Many Jews have altered their celebrations (more Jews celebrate Hanukkah than Purim) to fit in better with the dominant culture. Because Christmas and other elements of Christianity will not be expunged from the public realm, ethnics themselves must resist the influence of the dominant culture if they want to retain their distinct identity. Ethnics don't always succeed, but they can use some of their cultural resources to resist the strong pull toward conformity in liberal states. The preservation of some ethnic practices is one instrumental way to maintain diversity; it is a resource that some people can call on to resist the temptation to conform.

Liberalism, when its goals are achieved, bestows important benefits on its citizens. Yet these benefits are not without cost. Folded into equal citizenship itself is the possibility of weakening ethnic ties; the pull of the dominant culture makes it hard to maintain a robust ethnic identity. This pull is not unique to liberalism, but liberals do not have a special way to resist this pull. Only some ethnics will have the fortitude to withstand the pressure to change their practices to fit the cast of the dominant culture.

Although many distinctive ethnic cultures are weakened by liberalism, their practices do not necessarily disappear. Sometimes ethnics do try to shed distinctive practices and assimilate to the dominant cultural norms, but this is not the only or even the predominant way in which ethnic cultures change. Ethnic cultures change as they interact with the dominant culture, and this interaction often changes the dominant culture as well. Ethnic cultures become less distinctive not because their cultural practices are lost but because some of their practices are incorporated into the dominant culture. Liberal citizenship provides fertile ground for the sharing of cultural practices. There are clearly tensions of diversity, but there are benefits of diversity as well; the United States is a much more interesting place with a richer culture because of the influence of many ethnics. This influence—festivals, foods, parades, churches, literature—shows that assimilation has not always been the dominant mode here. The alternative to assimilation is not cultural pluralism; because ethnic cultural practices are not expunged does not automatically mean that there will be distinct ethnic cultures. When the goals of liberal citizenship are achieved, ethnic cultures and the mainstream culture are both transformed, with the ethnic cultures frequently becoming less distinct.

It is the weakening of distinctive identities folded into liberal citizenship that sometimes facilitates nationalist movements in liberal states. Some groups see that, without political action designed to confer political status on their group, their identity will weaken. In liberal states, it is no accident that these groups are usually defined in terms of language, for other markers in liberal states are becoming increasingly tenuous as markers of identity. Political boundaries allow groups that feel that their identity is threatened to gain recognition from others in the world. They allow them to be seen as a people. Ethnic and racial groups may also want this kind of recognition, but, without a claim to land, their desire for recognition will be much harder to realize. The plea for self-determination made by some peoples and the related desire to preserve their identity will find a sympathetic ear among some liberals. Yet not every culture or language community can survive in the modern world; certainly not every community can have its own state. In some cases liberals need not oppose language-based nationalisms, but the very large number of languages in the world means that liberals are best off pushing the world past nationalism in most cases and toward pluralistic integration.

Liberal pluralistic integration should mean that there is a relatively wide range of cultural practices in the United States and Canada and a wide range of ways in which people identify with their ethnic or racial group. I've discussed both the maintenance of and the transformation of cultural identity. Cultural identity in the United States cannot be characterized in one single way, although there is a strong tendency toward a weakening of ethnic identity. A few people will live in insular communities, and others —mostly immigrants—will live in ethnic communities, peering into the dominant culture. Their children, though, may become part of this dominant culture, bringing some of their ethnic practices with them. Others will straddle the lines between their cultural community and the dominant culture, living (perhaps a bit uneasily) in both worlds.

Pluralistic Education

The fight for this inclusion occurs in many places, in universities, museums, Congress, and the courts in arguments over policies for immigration, cities, and the economy. One arena that is often in the middle of debates about pluralism, culture, and inclusion is the public schools. The fiercest debates about pluralism in schools usually center around two areas, history and language, although many areas of schools are touched by these debates, even physical education. In Britain, for example, many Hindu and Muslim girls object to wearing shorts because of the "modesty" requirements of their religions. Objectionable as this reason may seem to some liberals, these different cultural practices should be accommodated in schools. Presumably, these girls can wear sweat pants and still partake in gym class. Similarly, a student should not be penalized for not attending class on an ethnic or religious holiday. New immigrants bring different ways of dress and different celebrations with them; within the confines of liberalism, schools should try to provide an atmosphere where ethnics do not feel that they must give up all of their cultural differences. Schools should reach out to the different ethnic communities to discover their practices and observances so they can accommodate the different needs of their students.

The more difficult questions in education arise when the discussion is turned to cultural, historical, and bilingual education. Iris Marion Young argues that public schools should have "bilingual-bicultural maintenance programs" that aim to "reinforce knowledge of the students' native language and culture."[6] An important report by a New York educational committee makes several recommendations for changes in the social studies curriculum. It says that the curriculum should "continually encourage students to ask themselves" these questions: Who am I? What is/are my cultural heritage(s)? Why should I be proud of it/them? Why should I develop an understanding of and respect for my own culture(s), language(s), religion, and national origin(s)? Why should I develop an understanding and respect for the cultures, the languages, the religions, and the national origins of others? What is an American? What holds us together as a nation?[7]

One wonders if students will have time to do anything else after they continually ask themselves these questions. Neither Young nor the committee takes into account the complicated ways in which cultures clash and combine. Furthermore, the implicit assumption behind their announcements is that all aspects of all cultures should be celebrated and reinforced by schools. They do not indicate that there are aspects of every culture in the world in which people should *not* take pride. Many cultural values are inegalitarian and hierarchical and so should not be encouraged in a liberal society. Teachers should not be teaching their students to take pride in illiberal aspects of different cultures. Moreover, Young and the committee spend little time explaining how "native cultures" can survive transplanted in the United States. The cultures of immigrants will be transformed when they arrive in the United States and become severed from their roots. Given this transformation, given the illiberal aspects of many cultures, it is a bad idea simply to charge schools with the task of constructing maintenance programs for native cultures.

Young wants schools to "affirm [the] group-specific identity" of students and reinforce their knowledge of their "native culture," but what if some students do not want to affirm their "group-specific identity"? Some students may not care much about their native culture or their cultural heritage. With the United States as their point of reference, with their memories formed in the United States, their primary culture may be American, even if it is ethnic or racial American—their "native culture" may not seem very native to them. If the students do not care about their ancestral countries, why should schools tell them to care? Moreover, many people in the United States are the products of ethnic and racial intermarriages. They may not have a group-specific identity. They may have multiple ethnic identities, along with nonethnic identities that are important to them. Finally, there is also the matter of logistics and cost. Some large school districts in this country (like New York, Los Angeles, Chicago, and San Francisco) have students from dozens of countries in their classrooms. To design educational programs that reinforce the native culture of every student would be an enormous financial burden on many school districts, a burden that would undoubtedly take funds away from other programs. In a country that rarely spends enough money on education, this would be resources misspent. If students can't read or write well, their bilingual and bicultural education will not do them much good.

The goals of the New York committee, like the goals of many advocates of "multicultural education," are also confused.[8] They argue that all citizens in the United States, "whatever their race or ethnicity, must believe that they and their ancestors have shared in the building of the country and have a stake in its success." (What about those recent immigrants whose ancestors actually had nothing to do with the building of this country?) The goal of this version of multicultural education is inclusion; members of groups that have historically been excluded or denigrated in the curriculum (Blacks, Latinos, Native Americans, women) need to be included, not in an extra picture or sidebar, but as an important part of the narrative in U.S. history textbooks. This is an important goal that liberals should support.

The confusion comes with the next goal: American schooling should not work toward the "erasure of distinctive cultural identities" as it has in the past. "Education," the committee contends, "must respond to the joint imperatives of educating toward citizenship in a common polity while respecting and taking account of continuing distinctiveness."[9] I agree that schools should not work toward erasing cultural identities; however, when schools and their curriculums become more inclusive, they work toward breaking down distinctive cultural identities. The inclusion of the history of the traditionally excluded means that not just Black students but all students will learn about the important antilynching crusade of Ida B. Wells and read the writings of Frederick Douglass. All students can become inspired by the struggles of these two Black Americans and learn that these two people are important parts of American history. Students will no longer be taught a caricature of slavery but will learn about the struggles of slaves to retain their humanity and the culture they developed, a culture apart from the mainstream. All American students should learn about the internment of the Japanese Americans during World War II. This important if ugly chapter in American history should not be part of the collective memory only of Japanese Americans. All Americans should learn about these historical figures and events; they helped shaped the United States into what it is today.

There are good reasons to teach a more inclusive—and more accurate—history in schools. Japanese Americans know about the internment camps during World War II; when this history is ignored, they may feel excluded from the polity. When the history of Blacks is excluded or distorted, many Blacks will feel similarly excluded. If equal citizenship is to become a reality, the role played by members of certain groups cannot be excluded from the history taught in schools. This exclusion all too often tells the excluded that they are not equal citizens and that what has happened to people like them is not important. Nor should history be distorted; if Blacks are shown only as lazy or happy slaves, many Black students will feel embarrassed and marginalized. Blacks know when a distorted history of Black Americans is taught; when this happens, many Black students will feel alienated from school. History should not be taught in a way that denigrates or ignores some groups and celebrates others.

History is rarely a story of the simple good of some people or groups and the simple evil of others. American history cannot be characterized in any one way; it should be taught with all of its complications, including both its glorious and its disgraceful moments. Moreover, American history cannot always be compartmentalized into different ethnic and racial subjects. The lives of Black Americans and white Americans, Japanese Americans and Jewish Americans have been and remain intertwined. The history of slavery, Jim Crow laws, and the nativist movement involves members of many different groups. It's tempting to say that only accurate history should be taught, but history is not only a matter of undisputed facts. There are many disagreements over the interpretations of historical events; disputes too can be discussed, with schoolchildren taught to figure out for themselves who they think is right in historical controversies.

When students learn the same history, even a more inclusive history, there is no reason to think that distinctive cultural identities will be maintained. Part of what enables cultural groups to maintain their distinctive identity is their *particular* collective memories. The goal of the New York committee, however, is to change these particular memories into American collective memories, shared by all students. This removes one of the key components in maintaining cultural identities. When students learn the same history and each other's cultural practices, cultural differences begin to fade. Differences will surely remain between students, but "cultural distinctiveness" is too strong a characterization of the results of a more inclusive curriculum. Inclusiveness does not reinforce distinctiveness, as some multiculturalists seem to think; inclusiveness wears away differences. The New York committee's confusion also lies in the way it assumes that race and ethnicity map onto culture. Racial and ethnic diversity can mean cultural diversity, but not automatically. Members of different racial groups can and do share in the same culture.

Besides the move toward inclusiveness—which liberalism supports—there are two important rationales behind multicultural education. The first is a move away from teaching students a long list of facts and toward teaching how to think critically about history and contemporary events. Materials given to teachers "should be limited and focused, providing teachers with a range of choices, each including diverse perspectives, in order to promote understanding and the development of critical thought."[10] Some people object to this idea; they want the history of the United States to be taught as one glorious triumph after another. Students unable to think critically or to criticize, who are mindless cheerleaders, however, won't make particularly good citizens in a liberal democracy. Several hundred years ago, Montaigne noted that the usual method of teaching was to "bawl into a pupil's ears as if one were pouring water into a funnel, and the boy's business is simply to repeat what he is told."[11] Unhappily, Montaigne's description of teaching is too often still true. Liberal citizens must think about their government, its policies, its traditions and history, so they can make informed judgments when they vote and participate politically in other ways. Encouraging students to think critically is certainly a goal that should be applauded.

The second goal is to enhance the self-respect and self-esteem of students. This goal partly arose out of a reaction to the distorted way many history books portrayed Blacks, Latinos, and others. Certainly, the distortions prevalent in these history books need to change. The goal to enhance self-esteem has led some to advocate teaching nearly every subject through ethnic and racial eyes. This strategy will not suddenly produce better students. Some educators want to show students that what they study today is somehow historically rooted in the achievements of their ancestors because they believe that this will increase the students' self-esteem and their performance in schools. Molefi Kete Asante argues that "surely" one of the elements explaining the high scores of Koreans on international math tests is "the linkage of Korean traditions in mathematics to present mathematical problems. Koreans do not study European theorists prior to their own; indeed they are taught to honor and respect the ancestral mathematicians. This is true for Indians, Chinese and Japanese."[12] Asante seems to assume that the ancestral mathematicians in each country discovered important elements in math that can be studied in each country. Surely, not every country can point to important math discoveries made by its ancestors.[13]

Students with low self-esteem probably won't perform to their potential, but this hardly means that misleading students about their "ancestral traditions" will improve their study habits. Asian-American children in the United States do better on math tests than do members of any other racial or ethnic group, even though they study the same textbooks as do other American schoolchildren. They do not study their "ancestral mathematicians."[14] Teachers should encourage students to believe that they are capable of doing well in school, but distorting history is not a good way of doing this.

Some advocates of bilingual education also couch their arguments in terms of self-respect. When students who speak English poorly are taught only in English, they will have a hard time learning until they know English well and they may feel ashamed of their first language, thinking that it is un-American and somehow wrong to speak. Opponents of bilingual education argue that knowledge of English is important in the United States for people to be able to advance economically. Advocates of bilingual education usually agree. Young, for example, says that "proficiency in English is a necessary condition for full participation in American society."[15] The issues involved in arguments over bilingual education are whether bilingual education inhibits the learning of English and whether the schools should help maintain the first language of students when it is not English. I doubt that schools are necessary to maintain the native language of immigrants. In most of the homes of these students, the native language will be spoken; for the students who live in ethnic communities, their native language will be spoken on the streets and in stores as well. These students, once they learn English, will be bilingual; they'll learn English in schools as well as from television, movies, and music. The priority in bilingual programs must be to teach immigrants English; without good English skills their opportunities here will be severely restricted.[16]

Yet there remains the issue of individual and group respect; just as history textbooks and school policies on dress and days off should not denigrate ethnics, neither should language policies. Immigrant children and nonimmigrant children must be told that there is nothing wrong with speaking languages besides English; in fact, speaking other languages is an advantage. People should be proud of their bilingualism because they can communicate with more people and have a window into more cultures.

In an increasingly international world, multilingualism is all the more important. Bilingualism opens up all sorts of opportunities for people, and not only immigrants should be given the chance to become bilingual. Schools can use immigrant ethnic communities as a resource to teach other Americans another language. If a community has a large number of Spanish-speaking immigrants, the non–Spanish speakers in schools can be taught Spanish with relative ease. Classes can be taught in both Spanish and English with all students required to take courses in each language. Just as Spanish speakers will struggle with English early on, so too will English speakers struggle with Spanish. After a short while, of course, most or all students will be bilingual. I envision students taking classes in both languages all the way through high school. These classes should not just be language courses; all students should spend one hour learning math in Spanish, then another hour learning science in English, then social studies in Spanish, and so on.

There are several reasons why this program deserves support.[17] First, relative to adults, young children pick up languages quickly and easily. If a community has native Spanish speakers, young English speakers will be able to learn Spanish from them. (How many adults today now wish that someone had regularly spoken to them in a second language when they were young?) Second, there will be no shame in struggling with a language. If all students are working to learn a second language, few will feel embarrassed by the few months when they speak this language awkwardly. Third, students can help each other learn the languages. Teachers need not do all the teaching; students should be able to share their knowledge with each other. In fact, students can also help teachers learn more languages. When students realize they have knowledge that they can teach others, their self-esteem may rise. Fourth, schools can look to the immigrant communities to supply teachers for the classes that are not taught in English. This will help ethnic communities become involved in schools; ethnic teachers can help explain the particular practices of their communities to school administrators. They can help reduce misunderstandings between schools and ethnic communities by serving as important links between the two.

Using the resources of immigrant ethnic communities to teach a second language to other Americans will not always be easy or possible. Some immigrant communities will be too small to supply teachers to teach classes in their language; some places may simply lack immigrants. Some places will be home to several different immigrant communities, in which case one or two languages besides English must be picked for use in the schools. The teaching of second languages to Americans beginning in elementary schools probably cannot be a nationwide program, but it can, nonetheless, be instituted in many places. As long as immigration to this country continues, there will be excellent opportunities for many students to learn the languages of others.

Teaching Americans other languages may help increase cultural awareness, but there are limits to what schools can do. Many people see the poverty and racism faced by many American citizens and the drugs and crime in inner cities, and their solution to these problems is to change the curriculum. These problems, however, are beyond the reach of schools. Changes in schools may ease some of the cultural tensions in this country, but these changes won't bring industry back to the inner cities or convince every student to believe in equality or that everyone deserves respect. A Black student who lives in an impoverished home, does not eat enough, has ragged clothes, and views the country as controlled by racist whites will probably not do a lot better in school when taught to honor and respect the ancestral mathematicians. Henry Louis Gates argues that people critical of how Blacks and other minority groups are treated in the United States should acknowledge "that the relation between our critical postures and the social struggles they reflect upon is far from transparent. That doesn't mean there's no relation, of course, only that it's a highly mediated one. In any event, I do think we should be clear about when we've swatted a fly and when we've toppled a giant."[18] Changing the curriculum is important, but people who want to eliminate racism in the United States and alter the face of inner cities and who spend most of their time arguing for curriculum changes are not trying to topple a giant.

Liberalism and Cultural Identity

Liberals need not stand by helplessly in the face of some groups' problems, saying simply that matters of culture and identity are private affairs. This is the usual liberal argument: different cultural practices, liberals say, can flourish in private. In public institutions and the institutions of civil society, liberals often contend that culture and identity simply should not matter. This liberal argument is flawed, however, for at least three reasons.

First, it is deceptive. It is misleading to say that liberalism can accommodate many cultures without noting how difficult it is for distinct cultures to survive in the liberal state. Illiberal practices are discouraged or forbidden, but other practices are shared, loosening the connection between particular cultural identities and particular cultural practices. Liberalism has been called a philosophy of institutions, not a philosophy of people.[19] But these institutions affect the identity of the citizens who inhabit them, something that many liberals do not acknowledge. Moreover, there will be only one or two public languages in a state, meaning that cultural identities heavily dependent on private languages will have a hard time surviving. Indeed, those citizens who are not fluent in a public language will find that the liberal goal of equality of opportunity eludes them, although this goal may be in the reach of their children. Liberalism allows a diversity of cultural practices, but to accept or even encourage different cultural practices does not necessarily mean that many different vibrant cultures will exist in the liberal state.

The second problem with the conventional liberal argument is that it fails to account for implicit cultural norms that typically exist in liberal states. A dominant culture often establishes the cultural tone of many institutions; when others are told that culture and identity are private matters, they are often disarmed by the pressure to conform to the dominant culture. (Why protest this pressure, people may ask, if culture and identity are private matters for all citizens?) Racial and ethnic identity should be public matters until their practices and identity are accepted by the dominant culture. Sometimes Americans must learn to accept the cultures of newcomers, but racism need not be grounded in cultural differences; it is often a matter of prejudice based on perceived biological differences. Indeed, many racist white Americans borrowed from Black-American culture and so reduced the cultural differences between whites and Blacks while the racial gap remained as large as ever. In any case, racial and ethnic communities need to press for acceptance at schools; they need to become visible in politics, in popular culture, on television, in the movies, and in music. Their citizenship must be made visible so others can learn about cultural groups and accept members of these group as full citizens. Visibility alone does not lead to acceptance, however; the status of Black Americans has often been a public matter in the United States, but this was often to keep Blacks in second class citizenship. Members of racial groups must be visible, but not as subjects to the laws and stereotypes of others. This visibility should be an outcome of their fight to become accepted as equal citizens.

The third problem with the typical liberal argument on culture and identity is that it does not recognize the differences between what liberals tolerate and what they want. Although liberals often emphasize laws and procedures, there is a liberalism of tendencies, a liberalism that encourages certain values and practices and discourages others. Liberalism puts obstacles in front of some life choices; liberals can say they tolerate groups like the Hasidim and the Amish, but these groups remain small. Of course, tendencies and obstacles are not the same thing as laws—exceptions to tendencies cannot be jailed or fined. Members of the Amish and Hasidic communities have remained culturally distinct despite liberal pressure toward integration by retaining illiberal practices. Liberals cannot be too happy about their existence. Although the liberal state can simply outlaw some things (like physically harming others), other illiberal practices cannot be declared illegal. The liberal state cannot forcibly change people who insist on living in patriarchal communities that treasure unthinking obedience. This reveals a tension in liberal theory between the requirements of liberal citizenship and the requirements of liberal toleration. This tension is not evidence of a lethal flaw in liberalism; it's not clear that there is a better alternative to trying to muddle through this tension. This does mean, however, that liberals cannot smugly argue that they can easily deal with all problems. Cultural pluralists don't have a better alternative; they would presumably allow these communities to exist, for they encourage distinct cultural communities. Under cultural pluralism, we should expect to have more communities like the Amish and Hasidim, not fewer.

Although the existence of the Amish and the Hasidim can be considered proof of the success of liberal tolerance, this is a rather hollow liberal victory because members of insular groups escape the demands of liberal citizenship. Some may suggest that the liberalism I offer is just too minimal. I have no robust theory of community, although there are liberal virtues; perhaps my argument for the liberal ethos shows that the liberal ethos is rather thin. A liberalism that emphasizes the role of treating fellow citizens with respect may be seen as a rather uninspiring political theory. The United States and other countries, however, would be more inspiring places if liberal tenets were better implemented. As I write, racism is alive and well in the United States and on the increase in Western Europe; in Eastern Europe different nations are at each other's throats, attacking each other; many of the leaders of African states plunder their countries while hanging onto power through the naked use of force; women in many Islamic countries are increasingly told to hide behind their veils. Those who complain that liberalism assumes that people are strangers ought to realize that too many people in the world think they know each other well enough to hate each other. Liberalism tries to temper this hate and work out ways in which these people can at least treat each other civilly. If liberal principles were better realized in liberal states and if they better reached nonliberal states, the world would in fact be a much better place.[20]

The difficulty in implementing liberal ideals, in both liberal and nonliberal states, shows how demanding liberalism can be. The liberal goal of autonomous citizens who are able to evaluate elected officials and participate in politics is a goal that many citizens in liberal states do not meet. The goal of equal citizenship, which can seem so easy to implement in law, is hard to achieve. Some people are denied equal citizenship because of the color of their skin or the way they dress. This denial shows that liberal citizenship is not a lackadaisical role, filled easily by apathetic citizens. Too often the actions of lazy, ignorant, or racist citizens deny equal citizenship to others. Citizens who think that everyone should simply conform to the dominant norms of society are not good liberal citizens. Citizenship is not only about participation; the demands of liberal citizenship show up before citizens arrive at the voting booth or city hall. In fact, calls for more participation in a society filled with racism and prejudice are not necessarily a great victory. When Blacks increase their voter registration in the United States, registration among whites often increases as well, not because a wave of civic virtue has swept over them but because they want to oppose Black political power.[21] I do not oppose an increase in political participation, but citizenship is about more than participation; its demands show up in the institutions of civil society.

The demands of liberal citizenship require that citizens learn to accept those different from them. Treating others with respect in stores, in the classroom, on the factory floor, and in other places where citizens meet is an important part of citizenship. Respect, however, is not enough for equal citizenship. The standards of many institutions often must be revamped so members of racial and ethnic groups are not unfairly discriminated against; hiring policies and admission standards that do not discriminate must be instituted. These revisions cannot take place just once. As different people become members of the state, standards and policies should be revisited to accommodate their particular practices. These standards often have political consequences, as do the dress codes of schools and at the workplace. The standards of many institutions help determine who receives a good education and a good job. They determine the cultural practices that some people have to give up and take on to gain entry to and succeed in these institutions.

My focus here has been on different cultural practices rather than on different cultures. Liberalism does not insist that citizens take on a particular set of cultural practices; it rules out some practices but rarely rules in others. It sets the parameters within which different life choices can be made and ways of life can exist. The liberal state should strive to establish the conditions within which there can be many different ways of living. But this does not mean that liberals need to recognize specific cultures and work toward preserving them. Liberal pluralistic integration emphasizes the acceptance (and sometimes the rejection) of different practices because it recognizes that cultures and identities are often transformed in many different ways. This is an important difference between pluralistic integration and cultural pluralism. Pluralistic integration emphasizes the protection of different cultural practices that are compatible with liberalism. Cultural pluralism, on the other hand, emphasizes the protection of different cultures, regardless of the practices of these cultures. This emphasis ignores how cultures change and too blindly celebrates all cultures.

The changes in liberal theory that I suggest and the problems in liberalism that I tried to raise are grounded in the particular ways that American society (and, to a lesser extent, Canadian society) is constructed. I've relied here less on a particular way to read texts and more on readings of particular societies. Reading and understanding Western political thought is important to reaching an understanding of Western societies, but political theory can't—or shouldn't—always stop there. Each society has its own peculiarities, some of which are not discussed in the canonical texts. The shape of race, ethnicity, and nationality in the United States and Canada is peculiar to these two countries. Few of the classic liberal texts discuss the issues of culture and identity raised by race, ethnicity, and nationality. Liberal theorists, however, should discuss these issues because they are politically important in liberal states. Ignoring these issues reinforces the idea, held by some people in certain racial and ethnic communities, that liberal political theory has nothing to say to them. Exploring racial, ethnic, and national communities and identities highlights new challenges for liberal equality and liberal rights, challenges that liberal theorists must try to meet.

Liberalism cannot solve all of the issues posed by race, ethnicity, and nationality. Liberalism can open the space for members of these communities to fight for their rights and to fight against the misguided social pressures and discrimination they often face. It gives these people the room to protest and organize, to vote, and sometimes to establish their own institutions. The liberal language of rights can be used to protest the discrimination faced by some members of liberal states; it gives people the conceptual space to protest the abuse of power. Although the tools that liberalism accords communities facing discrimination are important, they do not guarantee that the battles of these communities will be successful. Those who oppose the goals of these communities can also organize, protest, and vote. The state establishes the setting in which the arguments over culture, discrimination, language policy, and national identity take place; liberalism establishes the rules for these fights. Yet liberalism does not determine the victor. Liberalism depends on members of the liberal state to act in ways that uphold liberal principles. Without this support, liberal theory will not be matched in practice.

When this support is given, however, cultural boundaries will not remain taut; liberalism does not reinforce different cultures. Some members of cultural groups will be unhappy with the way liberalism works to break down cultural boundaries. They will see liberalism as posing a threat to their identity. Although some groups do remain cohesive in a liberal society, too often the maintenance of group identity is predicated on the political and economic subordination of others. Along with subordination often comes identity; first and second class citizens can define themselves in opposition to each other. When this subordination aligns with racial or national identity, these identities are further reinforced. Impoverished people with no political power may have a secure identity, but this identity rarely offers them much security. The task of liberalism is to give them the security to reach their possibilities, even though cultural bonds may be stretched and broken in the process.

NOTES

Chapter 1. Introduction

1. Palacký, "Letter to Frankfurt," 304.

2. As I explain below, some nineteenth-century liberals supported nationalists.

3. Hobhouse, *Elements of Social Justice,* 199–200. In *Elements of Politics,* 218–19, Henry Sidgwick argued that a world government was ideal but didn't think it was possible any time soon. He speculated, however, that a federation of Western European states might be possible. In *Perpetual Peace and Other Essays,* 112, Immanuel Kant did not argue for one state, but he did contend that the constitution of every state ought to be republican and, therefore, that each state ought to be similar.

4. For convenience, I use the terms *group identity* and *cultural groups* to refer to racial, ethnic, and national groups, even though these terms are not completely accurate.

5. I stand "in the cave, in the city, on the ground." See Walzer, *Spheres of Justice,* xiv. Looking at the practices of communities has long aided theorists in developing their ideas; Aristotle may be the most prominent of this kind of theorist, but he is hardly the only one.

6. The relationship of the philosophes with the despots of their time was rocky. See Gay, *The Enlightenment,* 483–96.

7. Jefferson, *Notes on Virginia,* 198.

8. Hume, "Of National Characters." In a footnote in this essay, Hume opposed slavery but "suspected" that Blacks were inferior to whites.

9. Mill, *Considerations on Representative Government,* 380–88; Acton, *History of Liberty.*

10. Sheehan argues that many German liberals wrongly assumed that all members of the many different German states and principalities would want to shed their political identity and become German. See his *German Liberalism,* 72–73.

11. Mill, *Considerations on Representative Government,* 385.

12. Alter, *Nationalism,* 30.

13. Madison, Hamilton, and Jay, *Federalist Papers,* 91.

14. Mellon, *Early American Views on Slavery,* presents a sympathetic view of Jefferson's views on Blacks. Discussing slavery, Jefferson said, "I tremble for my country when I reflect that God is just." See *Notes on Virginia,* 215. I capitalize *Black* because I use it to indicate a cultural group. I do not capitalize *white* because I use the term only to indicate race, not culture. I capitalize ethnic Americans, like Italian Americans, Japanese Americans, and so on.

15. I discuss the few (though increasing) exceptions later, particularly in chapters 5 and 7.

16. Van Dyke, "Individual, State, and Ethnic Communities," 347–69; Van Dyke, "Collective Entities and Moral Rights," 44.

17. Some critics think that liberalism is structurally sexist or racist and that it cannot be amended to extend real equality to all adults. I hope that my construction of liberal theory indirectly answers these critics. For an argument that liberalism is structurally sexist, see Hirschmann, *Rethinking Obligation*. (Hirschmann barely mentions J. S. Mill, so it's hard to know how comprehensive her criticism really is.) Mackinnon forcefully argues against liberal equality in *Feminism Unmodified*. For a defense against some of the charges aimed at liberalism by Mackinnon and Hirschmann, see Wendell, "(Qualified) Defense of Liberal Feminism," 65–91.

18. The liberal and nonliberal leanings of the Court are discussed by R. Smith, "'American Creed' and American Identity," 225–51.

19. See ibid., 230–40, for an explanation of these two traditions. Smith uses the term *ethnocultural Americanism* instead of *nativism*.

20. The best communitarian arguments are Sandel, *Liberalism and Limits of Justice,* and MacIntyre, *After Virtue*. There are many critiques of communitarianism; perhaps the most comprehensive is Holmes, *Anatomy of Antiliberalism*.

21. Macedo, *Liberal Virtues*, 278–79.

22. Locke, *Letter Concerning Toleration*, 55.

23. Mill, *On Liberty*, 12.

24. When cultural groups have been recognized by nonliberal Western theorists, they have rarely been seen as something to celebrate. In *Politics,* for example, Aristotle argued that non-Greeks—"barbarians"—were fit only for slavery (bk. 1, chap. 6–7). In *Government of Poland* and *Social Contract,* Rousseau argued extensively for the need to make the states' citizens homogeneous.

Chapter 2. The Formation of Identity

1. Spitzer discusses May's life (and his ancestors) in *Lives in Between*.

2. Ibid., 155.

3. Ibid., 159.

4. Ibid., 160.

5. Thernstrom, *Harvard Encyclopedia of Ethnic Groups;* Glazer and Moynihan's important book, *Ethnicity: Theory and Experience,* has chapters on ethnicity, nationality, and race. The very title of Benson's *Ambiguous Ethnicity: Interracial Families in London* shows the uncertainty of these terms.

6. The classic argument is Benedict, *Patterns of Culture*.

7. Sandel, *Liberalism and Limits of Justice,* 55, 179, 59. Holmes discusses how communitarians like Sandel make the puzzling claim that liberalism's theory of agency is both impossible and disastrous in "Permanent Structure of Anti-liberal Thought," 227–53.

8. Spitzer, *Lives in Between,* 162–72.

9. Banton argues that people perceive not racial differences, but phenotypical differences (hair, skin color, etc.); how they interpret phenotypical differences determines the course of racism. This definition, however, does not always apply to Jews very well. Jews have been seen as physically different (curly hair, large noses) but have also been defined according to dress, ancestry, and language. If all Jews

had obvious phenotypical differences from others, the Nazis would not have forced the Jews to wear the yellow Star of David. (Although some Jews could be identified by their dress or looks, many assimilated Jews and progeny of intermarriages could not be easily identified as Jews.) See Banton's "Concepts of Race," 130.

10. There are not, of course, any "pure" races in the world; different peoples of the world have intermingled and intermarried for centuries.

11. Before the Civil War, some states recognized mulattoes as a distinct category.

12. For a history and explanation of the "one drop" rule see F. J. Davis, *Who Is Black?*

13. Degler, *Neither Black nor White.*

14. Quoted in Higham, *Strangers in the Land,* 137. My account of American nativism comes from Higham's masterful book.

15. Ibid., 168, 66, 173.

16. Grant, *Passing of the Great Race.*

17. Fredrickson, *Arrogance of Race,* 205, 210.

18. Orwell, *Road to Wigan Pier,* 124–25.

19. *Dred Scott v. Sanford; Plessy v. Ferguson.*

20. For ethnics in politics generally, see Higham, *Strangers in the Land,* 123–30. Erie discusses Irish-American political machines in six cities in *Rainbow's End.* Pinderhughes describes the restricted access to the political system that Blacks had in Chicago in *Race and Ethnicity in Chicago.*

21. Fields charges that many historians, noting that race is no longer institutionalized in American life as it once was, explain the existence of race today by arguing that it has mysteriously "taken on a life of its own." It is true that race and racism are re-created in American daily life, as Fields argues, in the images and stereotypes projected by the mass media and held by many citizens, in the actions of many citizens, and in the standards of many institutions. But the daily re-creation of race does not come from nowhere; it is rooted in the way the state historically shaped racial identity. See "Slavery, Race and Ideology," 95–118.

22. See L. Levine, *Black Culture and Consciousness,* for a description of this adaptation.

23. Because some ethnic group members think that the hyphen opens up the charge of "dual loyalty," I do not hyphenate ethnic group names when used as nouns.

24. Other scholars make a similar distinction between race and ethnicity. See Banton, "Concepts of Race," 136; Banton, *Racial and Ethnic Competition,* 10, 135; van den Berghe, *Race and Racism,* 21–25.

25. I can further clarify my definition of race here. Black Americans have, like many ethnic Americans, their own set of cultural practices; members of both racial and ethnic groups feel different from others for cultural reasons. In this way, Black and ethnic Americans are quite similar. My arguments in the following chapters about different cultural practices in the liberal state will often apply to both Blacks and ethnics. When I discuss the cultural practices of ethnics, I mean members of racial and ethnic groups with practices that differ from those of mainstream culture. Unlike ethnics, however, Blacks have considerable external constraints imposed upon them, constraints caused by racism. In chapter 6, I discuss how liberalism should respond to these constraints.

26. Sandel, *Liberalism and Limits of Justice*. Taylor makes similar criticisms, but he is more sympathetic to liberalism than is Sandel. See his *Human Agency and Language* and "Cross-Purposes: The Liberal-Communitarian Debate," 159–82.

27. In *Ambiguous Ethnicity* Benson closely examines the lives of the members of several interracial families in London. The children all identified themselves as Black, often because that is how others perceived them.

28. Sowell, *Ethnic America*, 4; Glazer, *Ethnic Dilemmas*.

29. Waters, *Ethnic Options*, 163–65.

30. Seton-Watson, *Nations and States*, 5; Anderson, *Imagined Communities*, 6–7.

31. Black nationalism has faltered at times in the twentieth century at least in part because it could not sustain a claim to a particular piece of land. Black nationalism is currently more concerned with community control over resources than with the establishment of a Black-American nation. Some Black nationalists, however, see this as a prelude to securing sovereignty over land.

32. Fuchs, *American Kaleidoscope*, 1, 363.

33. Some nations, like the Québecois, are made up of the descendants of immigrants. But they no longer consider themselves immigrants. If you are willing to go back far enough, all nations are, in some sense, made up of the descendants of immigrants.

34. I mostly use the term *Black American,* albeit uneasily, because it captures the cultural and racial aspects of being Black. *African American* emphasizes the cultural heritage of Blacks but does not indicate that Blacks are seen as racially distinct from whites as well. Furthermore, the term *African American* excludes those Black Americans who have immigrated here from the Caribbean and see themselves as *Caribbean Americans.* (I sometimes use *African American* when I refer to Black Americans as a cultural group but not as a racial group.) I realize that the terms I am using are all a bit misleading, but other terms that could be used in their stead are also misleading in some way.

35. For white nationalism see Fredrickson, *Black Image in White Mind*, 130–64; for colonization, see Litwak, *North of Slavery*, 20–24.

36. Benson, *Ambiguous Ethnicity*, 45.

37. Gwaltney, *Drylongso*, 18–19.

38. I cannot say that Japanese Americans are representative of all Asian-American groups. It's impossible to know the path that other Asian-American communities will take in the United States. The length of time that the Japanese-American community has been here, however, makes it a good group to examine.

As with Asian Americans, it is hard to discuss Latinos in one breath; there are large cultural, economic, and historical differences among Cuban Americans, Puerto Ricans, Mexican Americans, and other Latino groups. For an introduction to Puerto Ricans, Cuban Americans, and Mexican Americans, see Nelson and Tienda, "Structuring of Hispanic Ethnicity," 49–74.

39. Second generation Japanese Americans are called *Nisei*. The *Issei* are the immigrant generation, the *Sansei* are the third generation, and the *Yonsei* are the fourth.

40. Bonacich and Modell, *Economic Basis of Ethnic Solidarity*, 94.

41. Gene N. Levine and Rhodes argue that, "as Nisei and Sansei have entered the social and economic networks of the larger society, they have willy-nilly moved away from older-style, Japanese American identities. In this respect, they follow the fates of so many noncolored ethnic groups." *Japanese American Commu-*

nity, 146. Their findings are mirrored by other studies of the Japanese-American community. See Bonacich and Modell, *Economic Basis of Ethnic Solidarity;* Montero, *Japanese Americans,* 88; Nee and Sanders, "Road to Parity," 75–93.

42. Only 10 percent of the Nisei intermarried, but half of the Sansei have. For Asian-American marriage patterns, see Lee and Yamanaka, "Patterns of Asian American Intermarriage," 287–305; Kitano et al., "Asian-American Interracial Marriage," 179–89.

Chapter 3. The Demands of Liberal Citizenship

1. Quoted in Kates, "Jews into Frenchmen," 229.
2. Ibid., 224.
3. Rorty, *Objectivity, Relativism, and Truth,* 209; Kukathas, *Fraternal Conceit,* 22.
4. My account of Jewish emancipation comes from Katz, *Out of the Ghetto,* and Ettinger, "Modern Period," 727–1096. It is important to note that Jews in Eastern Europe were not emancipated until the twentieth century.
5. Meyer, *Origins of the Modern Jew,* 12.
6. In nineteenth- and twentieth-century Europe, invitations to the Jews to enter Christian society alternated with an anti-Semitism that was often vicious and that culminated in the Holocaust. Debates arose in European Jewish communities during this time about the nature of anti-Semitism; some argued that it would pass, while others insisted that it was part of the permanent landscape in Europe. For discussions of these debates in three countries, see Poppel, *Zionism in Germany;* Rozenblit, *Jews of Vienna;* Marrus, *Politics of Assimilation.*
7. Marx, "On the Jewish Question," 45. I have removed the emphasis from all quotations from Marx. Although I concentrate here on Marx's criticism of the liberal public/private distinction, in the second part of "On the Jewish Question" Marx equated capitalism (huckstering) with Judaism. The nationality of the Jew, he declared, was the nationality of the trader and the financier. Once capitalism was abolished, Marx argued, the Jews would simply have no reason to exist and so Jewish identity would disappear. Marx provided little evidence for his sweeping (and anti-Semitic) statements about Jews. For a critical exploration of Marx's attitudes toward the Jews, see Carlebach, *Marx and the Radical Critique,* especially 148–86.
8. Marx, "On the Jewish Question," 32, 39.
9. Ibid., 35, 43.
10. Ibid., 39, 34, 28.
11. Locke, *Letter Concerning Toleration,* 34, 31.
12. Ibid., 52.
13. Shklar, *American Citizenship,* 2–3.
14. King, "Letter from Birmingham City Jail," 292–93.
15. Hirschmann, *Rethinking Obligation,* 74–75.
16. Other political theorists have discussed and defined civil society differently than I do. There is no one definitive explanation of civil society; I am more interested in the concept I explain in the next few pages than in what it is called, although I do believe my definition is close to what many people consider civil society to be. For two histories of the concept of civil society, see Seligman, *Civil Society,* and Taylor, "Modes."

17. Karst discusses the Supreme Court's role in outlawing discrimination in many institutions (and criticizes the Court's failures in this regard) in *Belonging to America,* especially 75–78. Most antidiscrimination laws exempt small businesses (usually defined as having fewer than ten employees) from having to comply. These businesses are often family firms.

18. Friedman, *Capitalism and Freedom,* 109–10.

19. Light, *Ethnic Enterprise in America,* 48–52.

20. Smith argued, for example, that merchants "complain much of the bad effects of high wages in raising the price . . . [but] say nothing concerning the bad effects of high profits. They are silent with regard to the pernicious effects of their own gains." See *Wealth of Nations,* 115.

21. Habermas describes the rise of the public role played by these institutions in the eighteenth century and laments their subsequent failure to live up to this role in *Transformation of the Public Sphere.*

22. In *Marsh v. Alabama* and *Amalgamated Food Employees v. Logan Valley Plaza,* the Court upheld the argument that shopping places were the equivalent of public squares. The Court took steps toward reversing these decisions in *Lloyd Corporation v. Tanner* and completed its reversal in *Hudgens v. NLRB.* It did rule, however, in *Pruneyard Shopping Center v. Robbins* that states could demand that shopping places be open to political groups.

23. Gutmann, *Liberal Equality,* 45.

24. Walzer, "Liberalism and Separation," 325; see also Larmore, *Patterns of Moral Complexity,* 129. For criticisms of liberal separation besides Marx, "On the Jewish Question," see MacIntyre, *After Virtue,* chaps. 3 and 15.

25. Rorty, *Objectivity, Relativism, and Truth,* 209.

26. Aristotle, *Politics,* 1257b; Barber, *Strong Democracy,* 4; Beiner, *What's the Matter with Liberalism?;* Walzer, "Idea of Civil Society," 299; Flathman, *Toward a Liberalism,* 107. Political scientists generally conceive of citizenship in terms of participation as well. The classic study on participation is Verba and Nie, *Participation in America.*

27. Having fewer people with racist attitudes does not mean that the United States would be rid of racism. Some racist practices are embedded in institutional practices that will not end if people simply treat each other better. I discuss this issue further in chapter 6.

28. Aristotle, *Nichomachaen Ethics,* 61. Also see Elster, *Ulysses and the Sirens,* 77–85, 103–11.

29. Beiner, *What's the Matter with Liberalism?* 63, 22.

30. In his insightful book, Beiner takes liberalism to task for its neutrality on the good life, using Charles Larmore as his main foil. But Beiner himself recognizes that not all liberals agree that liberalism rests on neutrality. Despite this recognition, Beiner seems to think that liberalism is irrevocably committed to neutrality on the good life. He periodically criticizes something he calls "pure liberal theory," but this is a rather mysterious construct. See Beiner, *What's the Matter with Liberalism?* 61 n. 40, 107.

31. This is a prominent theme in the work of Rousseau, recently echoed by Sandel in *Liberalism and Limits of Justice,* particularly 179–83. See Walzer's criticism of Sandel in "Communitarian Critique of Liberalism," 9.

32. Some evidence from psychology suggests that forced actions may change

beliefs. See Festinger and Carlsmith, "Cognitive Consequences of Forced Compliance," 203–10.

33. Cuddihy, *No Offense,* 34. Cuddihy's other book, *Ordeal of Civility,* explores the effects of democratic manners on Jews.

34. Cuddihy, *No Offense,* 120. This is also a claim about equality: that equality means sameness, that Jews must act like Protestants to be equal in the United States. I discuss this claim in the next chapter.

35. I supply the evidence for this transformation in the next chapter.

36. Kraybill, *Amish Culture,* 218.

37. Quoted in Alba, *Ethnic Identity,* 103.

38. See Alba, *Ethnic Identity,* 79 and chap. 3 generally, for the role of food in ethnicity. Waters reports that "the construction of ethnicity . . . allows an individual to celebrate her Irish identity by eating sauerkraut." See her *Ethnic Options,* 121.

39. A large city without its share of ethnic restaurants is routinely criticized for its lack of culinary options. A columnist wrote the following about the opening of a Chinese restaurant in downtown Detroit: "A big city downtown without a showplace Chinese restaurant doesn't seem like a big city downtown at all." See "Restaurateur Flees to Detroit."

40. Cultural practices can be shared, however, among people or appropriated from one group by another without liberal citizenship. Many white musicians appropriated Black musical practices but did not join with Blacks in making this music. This cultural appropriation took place when liberal citizenship was almost completely denied Blacks. Cultural borrowing in the context of racial hierarchy does not mean that group boundaries will change. Liberal citizenship, however, changes the meaning of cultural borrowing. For example, people with non-German ancestry join those with German heritage to worship in Lutheran churches. People with no Irish ancestry march side by side with Irish Americans in St. Patrick's Day parades. When liberal citizenship is granted, cultural practices are shared on an equal basis, and when this happens the lines between ethnic groups become blurred.

41. hooks, *Feminist Theory,* 56–57. My emphasis.

42. Mill, *Considerations on Representative Government,* 276, 196.

43. Ibid., 198.

44. Hobbes, *Man and Citizen,* 230.

45. Pitkin, "Justice," 347–48. My emphasis.

46. When asked about racial tensions in New York City, former mayor David Dinkins said: "Although I am proud to be an African American, I am the Mayor of *all the people of our city.*" See "Mayor Strongly Attacks Racial Hatred." My emphasis.

47. Locke, *Letter Concerning Toleration,* 55.

Chapter 4. Pluralistic Integration

1. Kallen, "Democracy versus the Melting Pot," 93–94. This chapter originally appeared as an article in *Nation* in 1915. Another early argument for cultural pluralism is Bourne, "Trans-national America," 86–97. For an intellectual history of the debates about assimilation and ethnicity in the early part of the twentieth century, see Mann, *The One and the Many,* particularly chaps. 5 and 6. Mann's criti-

cisms of Kallen are similar to those I offer below. For an intellectual history of cultural pluralism, see Powell, "Concept of Cultural Pluralism."

2. Kallen, *Culture and Democracy*, 115, 119, 106, 124.

3. Ramsey, Vold, and Williams, *Multicultural Education,* 9; Tiendt and Tiendt, *Multicultural Teaching,* 7; Lustgarten, "Liberty in Culturally Plural Society," 101. Ramsey, Vold, and Williams explicitly add Blacks, Hispanics, and Native Americans to their argument, something that Kallen did not do. Lustgarten does make some exceptions to his proposal; the most important one is that the legal autonomy of ethnic groups can be violated to save someone from severe physical abuse. But exceptions to autonomy, Lustgarten insists, should be rare.

4. Young, *Justice and Difference,* 47, 168, 184. Young defines cultural imperialism on 58–61. There she says that to "experience cultural imperialism means to experience how the dominant meanings of a society render the perspective of one's own group invisible." I don't know if Young intends her argument to apply to white immigrants, but her definition of cultural imperialism surely reflects the experience of many ethnics in this country, including white immigrants from Europe. Young makes several references to ethnic groups as oppressed, particularly Jews. See, for example, 59, 160, 175. Much of Young's book is devoted to nonethnic groups, about which I say little.

5. This chapter also touches upon issues that affect Black Americans. I discuss people who have cultural practices that differ from mainstream culture. My arguments apply to members of racial groups to the extent that they have cultural practices that differ from the mainstream. The questions of identity that I raise in the beginning of this chapter, however, do not apply to racial identity.

6. Yancey, Ericksen, and Juliani, "Emergent Ethnicity," 391–403; see also Steinberg, *Ethnic Myth.*

7. Heckmann, "Temporary Labor Migration or Immigration?" 79.

8. In chapter 7 I explain in more detail the effects of advanced industrialized economies on identity.

9. Kallen, " 'Americanization' and the Cultural Prospect." In the early twentieth century, race meant the different immigrant groups in the United States; Italians, Jews, and Poles were often considered to constitute their own races.

10. Quoted in Takaki, *Strangers from a Different Shore,* 468.

11. Young, *Justice and Difference,* 179.

12. Steinberg, *Ethnic Myth,* 43.

13. The high rates of intermarriage are discussed in Lieberson and Waters, *From Many Strands,* 162–246, and Alba, "Americans of European Ancestry," 148–52. To cite one example: of people reporting Italian ancestry in the United States in 1979, 48% were of mixed heritage. Only 6 percent of Italian Americans over the age of 65 had mixed Italian ancestry, yet over 81 percent of children under the age of five were of mixed heritage. This poignantly shows the effect of time on ethnicity. (These figures actually underestimate the amount of intermarriage because there is still some Italian immigration to the United States.)

14. Alba, *Ethnic Identity;* Crispino, *Assimilation of Ethnic Groups;* Sandberg, *Ethnic Identity and Assimilation;* Waters, *Ethnic Options.* (For Japanese Americans, see the citations listed in n. 42 in chap. 2.) These books, which study different ethnic communities, all convincingly show that the straight line theory of ethnicity (that with each generation more and more of ethnic culture is lost) is, for the most part,

accurate. Jews, probably because they are both a religious and an ethnic group, are a partial exception.

15. Gans, "Symbolic Ethnicity," 6.

16. Choosing ethnic identities is the major theme of Waters, *Ethnic Options;* Lieberson discusses the increase of people who do not identify as ethnic in "Un-hyphenated Whites," 159–80.

17. Unlike other cultural pluralists, Young recognizes that boundaries between groups are often obscure. She says that group differences are "ambiguous, relational, shifting without clear borders that keep people straight—as entailing neither amorphous unity not pure individuality." Despite the unclear boundaries of groups, however, Young wants to base politics on group differences (a politics that may work toward reinforcing differences and making them less ambiguous than they are currently). See *Justice and Difference,* 171.

18. In *Hunger of Memory,* in a well-known statement of this flight, Rodriguez tells how he slowly shed his Mexican-American identity as he grew up.

19. Howe, "Limits to Ethnicity," 18. Weber makes a similar argument about the changes in the living conditions of peasants in France in the late nineteenth century: "Many grieved over the death of yesterday, but few who grieved were peasants. Thatched cottages and log cabins are picturesque from the outside; living in them is another matter. Old folk in the Breton commune investigated by Morin had no fond remembrance of the old days. For them as for the Republican reformers of the Third Republic, the past was a time of misery and barbarism, the present a time of unexampled comfort and security, of machines and schooling and services, of all the wonders that are translated as civilization." See *Peasants into Frenchmen,* 478.

20. The pain that erupts from this clash is expressed in Yezierska's autobiographical novel, *Bread Givers.* She paints the conflicts between a traditional Jewish father and a young Jewish woman during her struggle to be free from his demands. As Yezierska shows, not all examples of pain in novels are proof that changes in ethnic cultures are misguided, Young's protest to the contrary notwithstanding. For other examples of the clash between immigrant fathers and their daughters, see Crispino, *Assimilation of Ethnic Groups,* 29; Gibson, *Accommodation without Assimilation.*

21. This is something that the British Labour party does not seem to understand. In the 1980s the party proclaimed its support of schools of every cultural/religious community, leading it to support Muslim schools, which are segregated by sex. These schools educate girls and boys differently. A letter to the *Guardian* from Southall Black Sisters explains the problem with the party's policy: "the Labour party is prepared to abandon the principle of equality where black women are concerned. Instead, they deliver us into the hands of male, conservative, religious forces within our communities, who deny us the right to live as we please." Quoted in Weeks, "Value of Difference," 94.

22. In other words, the story I told in the previous chapter about "Lisa" would probably have been told about a man if this book had been written two or three decades ago.

23. Young, *Justice and Difference,* 86; see also 152–55. Lustgarten, however, would defend the oppression of women in the name of cultural pluralism, unless this oppression meant severe physical abuse. See his "Liberty in Culturally Plural Society."

24. Rieder describes the racism of the white inhabitants of Canarsie in *Canarsie.*

Rieder comments on the real pull of ethnic attachments in Canarsie: "most talk of a united Canarsie was hype or hyperbole." I argue below that ethnic communities can exist without strict control over the composition of their neighborhoods.

25. Young, *Justice and Difference,* 119.

26. Higham, *Send These to Me,* 239.

27. Raban, *God, Man and Mrs Thatcher,* 16–17.

28. Gibson, *Accommodation without Assimilation,* 144, 164.

29. Mill, *On Liberty,* 90.

30. Ibid., 9.

31. Ibid., 81, 70.

32. Mackinnon, *Feminism Unmodified,* 22; Young, *Justice and Difference,* 164.

33. Rawls is another liberal who recognizes that coercion may come from "public opinion and social pressure." See *Theory of Justice,* 202.

34. Cuddihy, *Ordeal of Civility* and *No Offense.*

35. Young, *Justice and Difference,* 86, 152.

36. Locke, *Second Treatise,* par. 142.

Chapter 5. The Ethnic Rejection of Liberal Citizenship

1. *Wisconsin v. Yoder.*

2. The idea that liberalism encourages people to be self-reflective and autonomous is endorsed by many liberals. An incomplete list would include Gutmann, *Democratic Education;* Herzog, *Happy Slaves;* Macedo, *Liberal Virtues;* and R. Smith, *Liberalism and American Constitutional Law.*

3. One prominent theorist who takes this view is Larmore, *Patterns of Moral Complexity.* In *Political Liberalism,* John Rawls often says he takes this view as well, but he qualifies his position. I discuss both Larmore and Rawls below.

4. My account of the Amish comes from Hostetler, *Amish Society,* and Kraybill, *Amish Culture.*

5. Kraybill, *Amish Culture,* 25; *Wisconsin v. Yoder;* Kraybill, *Amish Culture,* 95.

6. See Kraybill, *Amish Culture,* chap. 11, and Hostetler, *Amish Society,* pt. 4, for an explanation of how these decisions are made.

7. Hostetler, *Amish Society,* 153, 155, 157.

8. Ibid., 84. A person who declines baptism in the Amish community will not be shunned or excommunicated (for he was never Amish) and can continue to have relations with Amish people.

9. *Wisconsin v. Yoder,* 222.

10. Locke, *Letter Concerning Toleration,* 23, 25, 30. Locke suggested, however, that the state need not tolerate Catholics or atheists. Catholic allegiance to the Pope made their loyalty to the state suspect, whereas atheists could not be trusted because they did not believe in God.

11. Locke might not be enthralled with the pacifism of the Amish. If there came a time for the Amish to oppose the state, the Amish's opposition might not be effective.

12. Locke, *Second Treatise,* par. 131, 124–25, 225, 208–9. Some liberals still assert that protecting property is a main duty of government. See Nozick, *Anarchy, State and Utopia,* and Friedman, *Capitalism and Freedom.*

13. Larmore, "Political Liberalism," 346. For other arguments that place neutrality at the center of liberalism, see Larmore, *Patterns of Moral Complexity,* particularly chaps. 3 and 4; Dworkin, "Liberalism"; Ackerman, *Social Justice.*

14. Constant, *Political Writings,* 327. This theme also looms large in the work of J. S. Mill. Gaus discusses the role of the cultivation of individual talents in modern liberal thought in *Modern Liberal Theory of Man.*

15. Larmore, "Political Liberalism," 344.

16. Macedo, *Liberal Virtues,* 80. I borrow the term *liberal virtues* from Macedo.

17. Rawls, *Political Liberalism,* 50, 78, 199.

18. Ibid., 122.

19. Ibid., 200. Unlike Rawls, Galston is apparently unaware of the tension in his thought between two versions of liberalism. Galston, although critical of liberal neutrality, protests the emphasis on choice by modern liberals, arguing that liberalism is "about the protection of diversity, not the valorization of choice." Galston argues that liberal citizens ought to be able to live their lives in an uncritical fashion, as the Amish do. Yet Galston also argues that it is "essential" that liberal citizens have the "capacity to evaluate the talents, character, and performance of public officials, and the ability to moderate public desires in the face of public limits." Liberal citizens, he declares, ought to have the "critical reflection needed to understand, to accept, and to apply liberal principles of justice" to many of their commitments—the same capacities citizens need to have to promote their self-development. His protestations about contemporary liberalism notwithstanding, Galston is quite close to the liberals he criticizes. See *Liberal Purposes,* 329, 246, 294.

20. *Wisconsin v. Yoder,* 211.

21. Kymlicka, *Liberalism, Community and Culture,* 165.

22. Ibid., chap. 8.

23. Ibid., 195, 196.

24. Svensson discusses the incompatibility of liberal rights and American-Indian culture in "Liberal Democracy and Group Rights," 421–39.

25. At the basis of Kymlicka's argument is a foundationalist argument about individual rights. Kymlicka argues that these rights are inalienable for all people. I don't want to revisit the debate about foundationalism, which has raged in the academy in recent years. Instead, I want to point out here that the consequence of at least one strong version of foundationalism is the probable destruction of some cultures. Kymlicka *is* troubled by the possibility that his argument will destroy American-Indian culture, yet he offers no clear way out of this problem, saying only that it is complex. Kymlicka is hesitant to give the United States authority over the American Indians, considering the record of U.S. treatment of American Indians. Yet, if the American-Indian leadership want their communities to remain theocracies, who will tell them otherwise? Kymlicka says he is concerned only with liberal principles, not with who will enforce those principles. But important principles of sovereignty and authority are at stake here, principles that he skips over. See *Liberalism, Community and Culture,* 197–98.

26. Ibid., 197.

27. Kymlicka's argument that everyone needs membership in a secure cultural structure is confusing because in his book it seems to apply to American and Canadian Indians, the Amish, and weak ethnics. But to what "cultural structure" do weak ethnics belong? Danley argues that Kymlicka's argument cannot be ap-

plied to weak ethnics in "Aboriginal Rights and Cultural Minorities," 168–85. In a later article Kymlicka clarifies matters by distinguishing between immigrant groups (who "do not constitute cultures") and nations. Without examining the claim that immigrant groups do not have their own culture, Kymlicka would probably agree that the Amish have their own culture; it's hard to see how he could persuasively argue otherwise. See "Politicalization of Ethnicity," 239–56.

28. Native Americans also have U.S. citizenship. As long as Native Americans remain impoverished—the result of U.S. policy—this arrangement of dual citizenship seems fair. If Native American communities ever achieve economic prosperity, however, it might be appropriate to force Native Americans to choose one citizenship.

29. This is an important difference between the Amish and Native Americans, who are properly thought of as nations, not as ethnics. Because the Native Americans are nations with a legitimate claim to sovereignty, the United States has less authority to intrude into their community than it has when it comes to the Amish. The Native Americans are not partial U.S. citizens; rather, they have citizenship in their own sovereign communities.

30. Mill, *On Liberty*, 128–29; *Subjection of Women*, 479.

31. Testa paints a very romantic picture of the Amish; he does not even point out that some Amish values may be troublesome. At one point Testa describes an Amish man's report of a discussion he had with a college student. The man's wife couldn't figure out why the student was majoring in philosophy to discover the meaning of life. She asked, "Don't they read the Bible in college?" After replying that it was rare, Testa recounts that he felt like "the official spokesperson for the outside world. Deep in my heart I am ashamed of the culture I am asked to interpret." I am puzzled, however, as to where this shame comes from. Why should people read the Bible to discover the meaning of life? This example of soppy sentimentalism about the Amish permeates Testa's book. Even his title is overdramatic; the Amish of Lancaster County are alive and well. See his *After the Fire*, 93.

32. Zook, "Amish in America," 29–33.

33. Berns argues against *Yoder* on constitutional grounds in *First Amendment*, 37–42.

34. I'm less worried about partial citizenship being a second class citizenship, as long as it is chosen. There is perhaps some resemblance between partial citizenship and Schuck and Smith's suggestion that children of citizens be allowed to renounce their citizenship while living in the United States as permanent resident aliens. This status does not fit the Amish well because it doesn't recognize the Amish as a community in which people live their entire lives; it doesn't indicate that the Amish have an ambiguous relationship with the state. Rather, their suggestion seems only to allow people to protest their U.S. citizenship, something that may be important to some people but doesn't capture the status of groups like the Amish. See Schuck and Smith, *Citizenship without Consent*, 122–26.

35. I am troubled by the exemption of the Amish from paying social security taxes. People exempted from social security taxes must be self-employed and members of a religious body that provides for its own dependent members. If this exemption remains narrow and the Amish take care of their elderly, then this exemption may be acceptable. If this exemption, however, gives the Amish a business advantage over their economic competitors, it ought to be repealed.

36. *Mozert v. Hawkins,* 1062. For a detailed description of the *Mozert* case, along with some useful historical background, see Stolzenberg, " 'Circle That Shut Me Out,' " 581–667.

37. *Mozert v. Hawkins,* 1067. The court explicitly rejected *Yoder* as applicable in this case.

38. One of the plaintiffs in the case said that the word of God in the Bible represented the "totality of [her] beliefs." This is a worrisome prospect because some of what the Bible teaches can be interpreted in drastically illiberal ways. For example, Deuteronomy 13 says that, if you find a person who teaches that there are gods other than the God of the Bible, "you shall surely kill him. . . . You shall stone him with stones until he dies."

39. Gutmann, *Democratic Education,* 30.

40. There may be other groups in the United States that can be considered partial citizens, but I do not know of any. Of course, other groups of partial citizens may arise in the future.

41. Rogers Smith has suggested to me that it is possible that the Supreme Court should not be the final arbiter in cases like *Wisconsin v. Yoder.* The difficult issue of what to do with the Amish may best be treated as public policy rather than as a constitutional issue. For a defense of the political community deciding on hard cases instead of the courts, see Walzer, "Philosophy and Democracy," 379–99.

42. There are about one hundred thousand members of Old Order Amish communities.

43. Quoted in "Birth of a Voting Bloc." Hasidic voters are hardly the only ones to vote as someone tells them to vote. Union members, for example, sometimes vote as the leaders of the union suggest. But within unions there are often debates and discussions about who to endorse; different members run for union offices. Union leaders do not have the sanction of God when they are elected and when they speak. Moreover, union members can disregard their leaders and still remain union members. But there's little room for dissent among Hasidim. A Hasid who disobeys the rebbe won't last long as a Hasid.

44. The Lubovitcher rebbe even influences Israeli politics. In 1989 he ordered the Lubovitch political party in Israel to refrain from entering a coalition with the liberal Labor party because the Labor party was not religious enough. The party obeyed, enabling the Likud party, led by Yitzhak Shamir, to form a government. The rebbe has never been to Israel, but he once mentioned that he might visit there one day. At this mention, his followers built an exact duplicate of his Brooklyn house in a field near the main Israeli airport so, if he does visit, his time in Israel will be as comfortable and familiar as possible. The house currently stands empty.

45. For a democratic argument against prohibiting private schools, see Gutmann, *Democratic Education,* 115–17. Gutmann points out that most private schools in the United States are religious (and most of these are Catholic). She reports that "private schools are more segregated than public ones by religion, but not by class, race or academic talent."

46. Page, "At Issue."

47. One danger that must be fought against here is the possibility of arguments about the Hasidim's political influence turning into anti-Semitic arguments.

Chapter 6. Race and the Failure of Liberal Citizenship

1. Dench, *Minorities in the Open Society*, 124.

2. Two oral descriptions of the Black community are Gwaltney, *Drylongso*, and Blauner, *Black Lives, White Lives*. Boston in *Race, Class and Conservatism* discusses the effects of racial discrimination in the labor market. Schuman, Steeh, and Bobo in *Racial Attitudes in America* measure racial attitudes from the 1960s through the early 1980s, showing that, although racism has declined, it is far from extinct.

3. For Black culture generally, see L. Levine, *Black Culture and Consciousness*. For the creation of Black Christianity, see Raboteau, *Slave Religion*.

4. In fact, I am uncomfortable with my use of the term *Black culture* here because it is increasingly difficult to speak of a single Black culture in late twentieth-century America. All Black Americans face racism, but racism itself is not necessarily enough to form the basis of a culture. Wealthy and poor Blacks may have very different ways of life; Black immigrants from the Caribbean often think of themselves as Caribbean Americans, with cultural practices distinct from those of African Americans. I use the term *Black culture* (or *African-American culture*) because it identifies a cultural community that is still fairly cohesive, although it may not be in a few decades.

5. The effects of the legacy of racism on the Black poor, as opposed to current discrimination, is discussed in Wilson, *Declining Significance of Race*.

6. *Regents of the University of California v. Bakke*.

7. As Banton says, "good racial relations would be ethnic relations." See *Racial and Ethnic Competition*, 397.

8. Quoted in Oakes, *Slavery and Freedom*, 72.

9. Many liberals do not embrace the Lockean justification for property rights. Mill, for example, argued extensively that society as a whole should decide how to distribute property. He complained that people worship "an imaginary idol called the Rights of Property." See *Collected Works*, 920; see also *Principles of Political Economy*, 233. Hume argued that "any idea of property" has its origin "in the artifice and contrivance of man." See *Treatise of Human Nature*, 542.

10. *Dred Scott v. Sanford*.

11. Locke, *Second Treatise*, par. 6. As with property rights, not all liberals believe in a law of nature.

12. Oakes, *Slavery and Freedom*, 158–66.

13. Rodgers, *Contested Truths*, 133, 70.

14. Williams, *Alchemy of Race and Rights*, 164, 159. Williams's emphasis. Williams argues that the contention of many Critical Legal Studies scholars that the formal structure and language of rights should be replaced by more informal structures is mistaken. Another Black legal scholar, Crenshaw, similarly criticizes the CLS critique of liberal rights in "Race, Reform and Retrenchment," 1356–66.

15. Calhoun, *Disquisition on Government*; Fitzhugh, *Cannibals All!*

16. Rogers Smith argues against the popular idea that the United States is essentially a liberal society that has had some marked deviations from its liberal core since its founding, deviations that will eventually be eradicated. Instead, Smith maintains that the United States is marked by multiple traditions, including a liberal one, but also including racist and sexist traditions that are deeply American. One of the lessons drawn from this by Smith is that liberals cannot complacently expect

liberal ideas to triumph; U.S. history already shows that liberal ideas have suffered many defeats. Liberal ideas will triumph only through long, laborious struggles. See "Beyond Tocqueville, Myrdal, and Hartz," 549–66.

17. Smith expands upon this argument in "Beyond Tocqueville, Myrdal, and Hartz."

18. Locke, *Second Treatise,* par. 208. During the Civil Rights Movement, liberals often endorsed nonviolent methods of change, but Locke clearly supports the right of people to protect or regain their rights forcibly (even if he thinks such force is futile). Compare Malcolm X's argument for self-defense, which made many liberals uneasy: "The only thing that I've ever said is that in areas where the government has proven itself either unwilling or unable to defend the lives and the property of Negroes, it's time for Negroes to defend themselves." See *Malcolm X Speaks,* 43.

19. Locke, *Second Treatise,* par. 208.

20. Madison, Hamilton, and Jay, *Federalist Papers,* 321; see also 127 (nos. 51 and 10).

21. The tensions between democracy and liberalism exposed by the issue of race are explored in Hochschild, *New American Dilemma.*

22. Another problem for court action is that often Black plaintiffs must prove that they faced intentional discrimination, but intent is difficult to prove. It is also unclear why intent should always matter. It is small comfort to know that the people making a policy had no racist intentions but that the policy has racist effects anyway. For criticism of the intent standard, see Brooks, *Rethinking the American Race Problem,* 84–86.

23. But not all American laws. Until the Civil War, slavery was enshrined in the Constitution; women did not receive the vote until 1919. Effective laws prohibiting discrimination did not appear until the 1960s. The fight to establish equality as an important principle in the United States has been long and is not over.

24. DuBois, *Dusk of Dawn,* 221.

25. King, *Where Do We Go from Here?* 89.

26. Douglass, "What Does the Black Man Want?" 159, 158, 162. Despite its title, Douglass's essay supported the enfranchisement of women in this essay.

27. For a discussion of the way whites have tried to decrease the electoral strength of Black voters, see C. Davis, *Minority Vote Dilution.* The essay by Parker, "Racial Gerrymandering," is particularly informative.

28. Farley et al., "Chocolate City, Vanilla Suburbs," 319–44.

29. Creating a Black majority may sometimes decrease Black political influence. In some districts, Blacks ally with liberal whites to elect representatives who are responsive to the needs of Blacks. When districts are carved out so that Blacks are the majority in one or two districts instead of being a substantial minority in three or four, Blacks are unable to influence as many representatives. Until whites agree to live near Blacks, however, the symbolic importance of Black representation along with the greater (although not absolute) assurance that Black representatives will better represent Blacks mean that Black majority districts should be constructed.

30. Browning, Marshall, and Taub, *Protest Is Not Enough,* show that Blacks and Hispanics gained political power in California cities only when they worked in coalitions with liberal whites.

31. There are some districts with large numbers of both Black and white voters. Perhaps the most prominent is the Georgia district that sent the 1960s civil rights leader John Lewis to Congress. In 1986 Lewis ran against another civil rights leader, Julian Bond, in a district where white voters, making up 40 percent of the electorate, were the swing vote.

32. King, *Where Do We Go from Here?* 9.

33. Head Start is a program that feeds young, poor children and gives them additional educational support.

34. King, *Where Do We Go from Here?* 5.

35. Bluestone and Harrison, *Deindustrialization of America,* 54–55.

36. I've skipped over many of the important issues in constructing a democratic workplace that does not replicate more conventional enterprises. Carnoy and Shearer, *Economic Democracy,* is a good introduction to the issues involved, particularly chaps. 3 and 4. Mill argued that liberalism was best supported by workplace democracy in *Principles of Political Economy,* bk. 4, chap. 7. A more recent argument is Walzer, *Spheres of Justice,* 295–303.

37. For differences in the role of food in the businesses of immigrants and Blacks, see Light, *Ethnic Enterprise in America,* 11–12. Wright describes the killing of his uncle by whites who had "long coveted his flourishing liquor business" in *Black Boy,* 63.

38. Higham, *Send These to Me,* 149, 151. Higham's emphasis.

39. Nagel, *Equality and Partiality,* 29.

40. King, *Where Do We Go from Here?* 128.

41. Ibid., 37. The title of Carmichael and Hamilton's book, *Black Power: The Politics of Liberation in America,* is telling. Malcolm X also discussed the need for Blacks to organize to defend themselves against violence and help themselves economically, although at the end of his life Malcolm said that whites could help as allies in this struggle. See *Malcolm X Speaks* and *Autobiography of Malcolm X.*

42. Mazrui equates the importance of Black cultural rights with political and economic rights in "Multiculturalism and Comparative Holocaust," 41–44.

43. The classic polemic against the Black middle class is Frazier, *Black Bourgeoisie.*

44. Landry, *New Black Middle Class,* 186–89.

45. Some Blacks accuse others of acting or thinking "white." For an argument against these accusations, see Carter, *Affirmative Action Baby.*

46. The number of Black-white married couples tripled between 1970 and 1990, from 65,000 to 211,000. The percentage of married Black people married to whites rose 190 percent during this time. (The jump between 1970 and 1980 was much more marked than was that between 1980 and 1990.) These numbers are computed from the *U.S. Statistical Abstract.*

47. Dawson, *Behind the Mule,* chap. 4.

Chapter 7. Language and Nationality

1. Geertz, "Uses of Diversity," 105.

2. Ibid., 114.

3. Berlin, *Against the Current,* 337. Nairn maintains that the "theory of national-

ism represents Marxism's great historical failure." But not only Marxism: "Idealism, German historicism, liberalism, social Darwinism, and modern sociology have foundered as badly as Marxism here." See *Break-up of Britain,* 329. Although many English liberals expected nationalism to fade (see chap. 1, n. 3), this characterization does not quite fit many French and German liberals. Many were enthusiastically nationalistic and did not discuss the inevitable decline of nationalism. Yet these liberals rarely came to terms with the illiberal aspects of nationalism, which I discuss below.

4. Hobsbawm, *Nations and Nationalism since 1780,* 183. Hobsbawm wrote this before the breakup of the old Soviet Union and Yugoslavia. The owl of Minerva has not yet flown.

5. My focus here is on two types of nationalism that are common in the West. I do not pretend that my arguments in this chapter apply around the globe. Provocative discussions of nationalism in other parts of the world are Anderson, *Imagined Communities,* and Chatterjee, *Nationalist Thought.*

6. My argument here about the number of failed nationalisms is taken directly from Gellner, *Nations and Nationalism,* 43–45.

7. Weber, *Peasants into Frenchmen,* 66.

8. Gellner, in *Nations and Nationalism,* 43, suggests that nationalism is weak.

9. In one typical document the General Assembly declares that "all peoples have the right to self-determination; by virtue of that right they freely determine their political status and freely pursue their economic, social and cultural development." Quoted in Buchanan, *Secession,* 48.

10. Nairn, *Break-up of Britain,* 348. See also Anderson, *Imagined Communities,* 159.

11. Tamir is too kind to nineteenth-century liberal nationalists by ignoring the hard political decisions that liberal nationalists had to make. She quotes one Polish nationalist as saying that every nation has a right to exist. This nationalist's lofty words, however, wouldn't have done much to soothe the feelings of the Germans in Posnania if they had become part of Poland. Tamir says that liberal nationalism is polycentric, but the center and periphery of each nationalism matter a lot—and typically clash, even between liberals—when boundaries are drawn up. She argues that the claim of one person to the right of having her national culture preserved need not negate the claim of another person. But what happens when they live next door to each other? One will get his own state, while the other one will not; it is exactly this sort of situation that often becomes bloody and that even a polycentric theory of nationalism cannot solve. See *Liberal Nationalism,* 92, 101.

12. Namier critically discusses German nationalism of the mid–nineteenth century in *1848.* Alter gives a brief but good history of many European nationalisms in *Nationalism.* Sheehan's *German Liberalism* is an excellent account of nineteenth-century German nationalism and liberalism.

13. In 1970 Walker Connor reported that only 10 percent of all states are really nation-states; in 30 percent the principal ethnic group did not account for the majority of the population; in 40 percent there were five or more important ethnic groups. Since Connor's article was written, immigration has reduced the number of real nation-states even further. See "Ethnic Nationalism," 94.

14. Namier, *1848,* 57; Kedourie, *Nationalism,* 138. Hobsbawm also is critical of nationalism in *Nations and Nationalism since 1780.*

15. Hobsbawm, *Nations and Nationalism since 1780,* 51–63, 93–100, and Anderson, *Imagined Communities,* chap. 5, discuss how languages were constructed and modernized by different national movements.

16. Allophones are residents of Quebec who are neither native French Canadians (Francophones) nor descendants of the British (Anglophones). Most Allophones are Jews or are from Italy, Greece, or Haiti.

17. Anderson, *Imagined Communities,* 44. Anderson's emphasis. I do not think that the printing press made nationalism inevitable, but it did make the rise of nationalism more probable.

18. Gellner, *Nations and Nationalism,* 35.

19. A good account of the Quebec independence movement is Coleman, *Independence Movement in Quebec.* Marc V. Levine, in *Reconquest of Montreal,* pays particular attention to the effects of the independence movement on businesses in Montreal.

20. Schmid, *Conflict and Consensus in Switzerland,* 33.

21. Weber, *Peasants into Frenchmen,* 84.

22. I defend these arguments in chapter 4.

23. Taylor, *Human Agency and Language,* 234. My explanation of the two views of language comes from Taylor's essay (where he defends the expressive argument), "Language and Human Nature," 215–47.

24. Quoted in Knopff, "Language and Culture," 70.

25. As similar technologies spread to Western countries, their languages are becoming increasingly similar. Coleman notes: "French, in becoming an improved medium for technological and scientific discussion, is also moving away more and more from its traditional roots and becoming more like the language of advanced capitalism in North America, English." See *Independence Movement in Quebec,* 209.

26. Coleman, *Independence Movement in Quebec,* 46, 49, 54, 62.

27. Taylor, *Multiculturalism,* 59. Elsewhere, however, Taylor argues that groups like the Francophones are striving for recognition, not for a version of the good life. See "Why Do Nations Have to Become States?"

28. The new nationalist movement also looked toward history and literary accomplishments to buttress its nationalism. These tools, however, are more inclusive than religion; it is easier to read a history book than to become Catholic. And learning history need not interfere heavily with one's way of life, the way Catholicism can.

29. Nash makes this argument about both ethnic and national groups (although he does not distinguish between the two) in *Cauldron of Ethnicity,* 90.

30. Modern day nations are not creations of nature but are the result of a particular set of processes that include the rise of the printing press, the establishment of extensive systems of roads and education, and other products of the industrialization that reduced the variety of languages and dialects in different places. Modern day nations do have roots in smaller, preexistent cultures, but as the nations emerged these cultures were transformed in the process. Leaders of many national movements often talk about the long, glorious history of their nation; as their nation didn't exist until recent times, however, this history is mostly mythical.

31. Margalit and Raz, "National Self-determination," 449; Buchanan, *Secession,* 61; Tamir, *Liberal Nationalism,* 150; Kukathas, "Are There Any Cultural Rights?" 115. Buchanan adds one important caveat to his justification for secession: "The

culture in question must meet minimal standards of justice (unlike Nazi culture or the culture of the Khmer Rouge)."

32. See particularly Tamir, *Liberal Nationalism*, 53–56.

33. Ibid., 56.

34. Debo, *History of the Indians*, 288. Debo reports that in 1885 the federal superintendent of Indian schools said his task was to "recreate" the American Indian and "make him a new personality."

35. I know that I have repeated this admonishment—liberal support is contingent on particular circumstances—several times already. I can note only that others who have written about nationalism have repeated this same admonishment as endlessly as I have. See Walzer, "New Tribalism"; Buchanan, *Secession;* Margalit and Raz, "National Self-determination."

36. In 1970, only 2 percent of elementary school teachers in the French sector were Allophones, compared to 23 percent in English schools. See M. C. Levine, *Reconquest of Montreal*, 58.

37. In the 1950s a Quebec government commission issued the Tremblay Report, which maintained that the Catholic religion was a key component of French-Canadian culture. (Other important elements were Quebec's classical educational system, its church-controlled social welfare system, and its rural heritage— all elements that fell by the wayside during the 1960s and 1970s.) In 1978 a report prepared for the Minister for Cultural Development in Quebec proclaimed language as the cornerstone of French-Canadian culture. The differences between these reports are discussed in Coleman, *Independence Movement in Quebec*, 134, 171–72.

38. It does mean, however, that some members of the smaller ethnic communities in Quebec may struggle with issues of identity; some may feel estranged from the dominant community as they try to maintain their separate identity. There's only so much, however, that can be done about this, as Tamir notes: "even if governing institutions respect a wide range of rights and liberties and distribute goods and official positions fairly, members of minority groups will unavoidably feel alienated to some extent." See Tamir, *Liberal Nationalism*, 163.

39. Some of the laws do approach the absurd. Mandating larger French letters on signs in the workplace raises the specter (and frequently the reality) of Québecois bureaucrats wandering the halls of Anglophone businesses with measuring tapes, ensuring that this law is followed.

40. A former Quebec minister asks: "Which is more important, the ever-diminishing number of students in English schools or the impact of cable television with American television channels? . . . Which is more important, the principle of unilingual signs or the impact of Boy George or Michael Jackson on the Quebec recording industry? What does it mean for Québecois that English is the language of international technology, for example, of most computer software?" Quoted in M. C. Levine, *Reconquest of Montreal*, 226.

41. This is a major theme of Tamir's book. See *Liberal Nationalism*, especially 72–77.

42. Mill, *Considerations on Representative Government*, 382, 381.

43. Ibid., 382.

44. It is not only different nations that can hate each other, however. Hatreds can often arise between people with different powers and privileges. Class antago-

nisms can be quite deep among people who share a nationality. Members of the many secret services of the former nations of the East Bloc often did rather nasty things to their fellow citizens. It's not a viable solution to say that whenever members of two different groups hate each other they should get their own state; this frequently won't be possible.

45. Mill, *Considerations on Representative Government*, 384–85. Walzer makes a similar, vague argument in *Spheres of Justice*, 62. He has, however, since become more attentive to the difficulties of nation-states and nationalism; see "New Tribalism," 164–71.

46. The hatred between Israeli Jews and Palestinian and other Arabs is vividly expressed in Grossman's *Yellow Wind* and Shipler's *Arab and Jew*.

47. I wrote this before the signing of the remarkable Palestinian-Israeli agreement, which means that the creation of a Palestinian state is no longer a fanciful dream. The agreement may also usher in an era of considerable Israeli-Palestinian cooperation.

48. These terms are Moore's in "Production of Cultural Pluralism," 30. Although immigration "repluralizes" a society, as Moore suggests, the cultures of the immigrants, as I've pointed out in earlier chapters, will drastically change as they settle in their new land.

49. My argument here is not all that different from that of Tamir, who suggests that we work toward large regional organizations with economic, ecological, and strategic powers while smaller nations within their umbrella have cultural and political autonomy. The larger the economic organization, however, the more likely it is that smaller nations will get lost and have a harder time retaining their cultural identity.

Chapter 8. The Boundaries of Citizenship

1. Goren, *New York Jews*.

2. Hartman, "Public Space, Private Values," 63.

3. Sobol, "Understanding Diversity." Sobol is the New York Commissioner of Education; this memo accompanied the report of the New York Social Studies Committee that I cite below. Fuchs also easily celebrates unity and diversity. The subtitle of one of his chapters is revealing: "How the Hyphen Unites." See *American Kaleidoscope*, particularly chap. 4.

4. Many Asian Americans report that other Americans often remark on how well "they speak English" or express surprise that they do not speak any Asian languages. These remarks are insulting, for they imply that Asian Americans are somehow less attached to the United States than are others.

5. Rousseau thought so: "Social man lives always outside himself; he knows how to live only in the opinion of others." *Discourse on Inequality*, 136. Nietzsche maintained that modern democracies are characterized by a "herd mentality" in *Beyond Good and Evil*.

6. Young, *Justice and Difference*, 181.

7. New York State Social Studies Review and Development Committee, *One Nation, Many Peoples*, 9.

8. While the New York committee's report is an important statement of multi-

cultural education, it is far from the only one; *multiculturalism* and *multicultural education* are widely used terms with many meanings, too many to discuss here.

9. New York Social Studies Committee, *One Nation, Many Peoples*, 1, 4.

10. Ibid., 23.

11. Montaigne, *Essays*, 54.

12. Asante and Ravitch, "Multiculturalism," 271.

13. This also assumes that there is an ancestral homeland. As I argued in chapter 7, the rise of the nation-state is a modern phenomenon. The ancestral homeland for many people is mostly mythical if one goes back more than two or three hundred years. Asante maintains that he wants curriculums to present accurate information—a goal with which I agree. Unhappily, his specific recommendations about the curriculum belie his general advice.

14. Diane Ravitch points this out in Asante and Ravitch, "Multiculturalism," 267–76.

15. Young, *Justice and the Politics of Difference*, 184.

16. There is also the issue of cost. In the Los Angeles school district, over sixty different languages are spoken. The financial burden of supplying bilingual education to all of these speech communities may simply be too great for the school districts in the area to bear.

17. These programs have been successfully tried in a few school districts. See Porter, *Forked Tongue*, 249–52.

18. Gates, *Loose Canons*, 20.

19. Larmore, *Patterns of Moral Complexity*, 129.

20. Many of the participants in bloody disputes around the world would do well to learn from Locke's *Letter Concerning Toleration*.

21. Teixeria, "Registration and Turnout," 12–13, 56–58.

BIBLIOGRAPHY

Ackerman, Bruce. *Social Justice in the Liberal State*. New Haven: Yale University Press, 1980.

Acton, Lord. *Essays in the History of Liberty*. Edited by J. Rufus Fears. Vol. 1, *Nationality*. Indianapolis: Liberty Classics, 1985 [1862].

Alba, Richard D. *Ethnic Identity: The Transformation of White America*. New Haven: Yale University Press, 1990.

———. "The Twilight of Ethnicity among Americans of European Ancestry: The Case of the Italians." In *Ethnicity and Race in the U.S.A.: Toward the Twenty First Century*, edited by Richard D. Alba, 134–58. London: Routledge, 1989.

Alter, Peter. *Nationalism*. Translated by Stuart MacKinnon-Evans. London: Edward Arnold, 1989.

Amalgamated Food Employees v. Logan Valley Plaza 391 U.S. 308 (1968).

Anderson, Benedict. *Imagined Communities: Reflections on the Origins and Spread of Nationalism*. 2d ed. London: Verso, 1991.

Aristotle. *Nichomachaen Ethics*. Translated by David Ross. Revised by J. L. Ackrill and J. O. Urmson. Oxford: Oxford University Press, 1984.

———. *Politics*. Translated by Carnes Lord. Chicago: University of Chicago Press, 1984.

Asante, Molefi Kete, and Diane Ravitch. "Multiculturalism: An Exchange." *American Scholar* (Spring 1991): 267–77.

Banton, Michael. "Analytical and Folk Concepts of Race." *Ethnic and Racial Studies* 2 (April 1979): 127–38.

———. *Racial and Ethnic Competition*. Cambridge: Cambridge University Press, 1983.

Barber, Benjamin. *Strong Democracy: Participatory Politics for a New Age*. Berkeley: University of California Press, 1984.

Beiner, Ronald. *What's the Matter with Liberalism?* Berkeley: University of California Press, 1992.

Benedict, Ruth. *Patterns of Culture*. Boston: Houghton Mifflin, 1932.

Benson, Susan. *Ambiguous Ethnicity: Interracial Families in London*. Cambridge: Cambridge University Press, 1981.

Berlin, Isaiah. *Against the Current*. London: Hogarth Press, 1979.

Berns, Walter. *The First Amendment and the Future of American Democracy*. New York: Basic Books, 1976.

"Birth of a Voting Bloc: The Hasidim and Orthodox Organize." *New York Times* (2 May 1989): B1.

Blauner, Rob. *Black Lives, White Lives: Three Decades of Race Relations in America.* Berkeley: University of California Press, 1989.

Bluestone, Barry, and Bennett Harrison. *The Deindustrialization of America: Plant Closings, Community Abandonment and the Dismantling of Basic Industry.* New York: Basic Books, 1982.

Bonacich, Edna, and John Modell. *The Economic Basis of Ethnic Solidarity: Small Business in the Japanese American Community.* Berkeley: University of California Press, 1980.

Boston, Thomas D. *Race, Class and Conservatism.* Boston: Unwin Hyman, 1988.

Bourne, Randolph. "Trans-national America." *Atlantic Monthly* (July 1916): 86–97.

Brooks, Roy L. *Rethinking the American Race Problem.* Berkeley: University of California Press, 1990.

Browning, Rufus P., Dale Rogers Marshall, and David H. Taub. *Protest Is Not Enough: The Struggle of Blacks and Hispanics for Equality in Urban Politics.* Berkeley: University of California Press, 1984.

Buchanan, Allen. *Secession: The Morality of Political Divorce from Fort Sumter to Lithuania and Quebec.* Boulder, Colo.: Westview Press, 1991.

Calhoun, John C. *A Disquisition on Government.* Edited by C. Gordon Post. Indianapolis: Bobbs-Merrill, 1953 [1853].

Carlebach, Julius. *Karl Marx and the Radical Critique of Judaism.* London: Routledge & Kegan Paul, 1978.

Carmichael, Stokely, and Charles Hamilton. *Black Power: The Politics of Liberation in America.* New York: Vintage, 1967.

Carnoy, Martin, and Derek Shearer. *Economic Democracy.* New York: Sharpe, 1980.

Carter, Stephen L. *Reflections of an Affirmative Action Baby.* New York: Basic Books, 1991.

Chatterjee, Partha. *Nationalist Thought in the Colonial World: A Derivative Discourse.* Tokyo: United Nations University, 1986.

Coleman, William D. *The Independence Movement in Quebec: 1945–1980.* Toronto: University of Toronto Press, 1984.

Connor, Walker. "Ethnic Nationalism as a Political Force." *World Affairs* 133 (Sept. 1970): 91–98.

Constant, Benjamin. *Political Writings.* Translated by Biancamaria Fontana. Cambridge: Cambridge University Press, 1988.

Crenshaw, Kimberlé William. "Race, Reform and Retrenchment: Transformation and Legitimization in Antidiscrimination Law." *Harvard Law Review* 101 (May 1988): 1331–87.

Crispino, James. *The Assimilation of Ethnic Groups: The Italian Case.* New York: Center for Migration Studies, 1980.

Cuddihy, John Murray. *No Offense: Civil Religion and Protestant Taste.* New York: Seabury Press, 1978.

———. *The Ordeal of Civility: Freud, Marx, Lévi-Strauss and the Jewish Struggle with Modernity.* 2d ed. Boston: Beacon Press, 1987.

Danley, John R. "Liberalism, Aboriginal Rights, and Cultural Minorities." *Philosophy and Public Affairs* 20 (Summer 1991): 168–85.

Davis, Chandler, ed. *Minority Vote Dilution*. Washington, D.C.: Joint Center for Political Studies, 1984.

Davis, F. James. *Who Is Black? One Nation's Definition*. University Park: Pennsylvania State University Press, 1991.

Dawson, Michael. *Behind the Mule: Race and Class in African American Politics*. Princeton: Princeton University Press, 1994.

Debo, Angie. *A History of the Indians of the United States*. Norman: University of Oklahoma Press, 1970.

Degler, Carl N. *Neither Black nor White: Slavery and Race Relations in Brazil and the United States*. Madison: University of Wisconsin Press, 1986 [1971].

Dench, Geoff. *Minorities in the Open Society: Prisoners of Ambivalence*. London: Routledge & Kegan Paul, 1986.

Douglass, Frederick. "What Does the Black Man Want?" In *The Life and Writings of Frederick Douglass*, edited by Philip Foner, vol. 4, 157–64. New York: International Publishers, 1955.

Dred Scott v. Sanford 60 U.S. 393 (1857).

DuBois, W.E.B. *Dusk of Dawn*. New York: Harcourt Brace, 1940.

Dworkin, Ronald. "Liberalism." In *Public and Private Morality*, edited by Stuart Hampshire, 113–43. Cambridge: Cambridge University Press, 1978.

Elster, Jon. *Ulysses and the Sirens: Studies in Rationality and Irrationality*. 2d ed. Cambridge: Cambridge University Press, 1984.

Erie, Steven P. *Rainbow's End: Irish Americans and the Dilemmas of Urban Machine Politics, 1840–1985*. Berkeley: University of California Press, 1988.

Ettinger, S. "The Modern Period." In *A History of the Jewish People*, edited by H. H. Ben-Sasson, 727–1096. Cambridge: Harvard University Press, 1976.

Farley, Reynolds, Howard Schuman, Suzanne Bianchi, Dian Colasanto, and Shirley Hatchett. "Chocolate City, Vanilla Suburbs: Will the Trend toward Racially Separate Communities Continue?" *Social Science Research* 7 (March 1978): 319–44.

Festinger, Leon, and James M. Carlsmith. "Cognitive Consequences of Forced Compliance." *Journal of Abnormal and Social Psychology* 58 (March 1959): 203–10.

Fields, Barbara Jeanne. "Slavery, Race and Ideology in the United States of America." *New Left Review*, no. 181 (May/June 1990): 95–118.

Fitzhugh, George. *Cannibals All! or Slaves without Masters*. Edited by C. Vann Woodward. Cambridge: Harvard University Press, Belknap Press, 1960 [1856].

Flathman, Richard. *Toward a Liberalism*. Ithaca: Cornell University Press, 1989.

Frazier, Franklin E. *Black Bourgeoisie*. New York: Free Press, 1957.

Fredrickson, George. *The Arrogance of Race*. Middletown, Conn.: Wesleyan University Press, 1988.

———. *The Black Image in the White Mind*. New York: Harper Torchbooks, 1971.

Friedman, Milton. *Capitalism and Freedom*. Chicago: University of Chicago Press, 1962.

Fuchs, Lawrence H. *The American Kaleidoscope: Race, Ethnicity, and the Civic Culture*. Middletown, Conn.: Wesleyan University Press, 1990.

Galston, William. *Liberal Purposes: Goods, Virtues, and Diversity in the Liberal State*. Cambridge: Cambridge University Press, 1991.

Gans, Herbert J. "Symbolic Ethnicity: The Future of Ethnic Groups and Cultures in America." *Ethnic and Racial Studies* 2 (Jan. 1979): 1–20.

Gates, Henry Louis. *Loose Canons*. New York: Oxford University Press, 1992.

Gaus, Gerald. *The Modern Liberal Theory of Man*. New York: St. Martin's, 1983.

Gay, Peter. *The Enlightenment: The Science of Freedom*. New York: Norton, 1969.

Geertz, Clifford. "The Uses of Diversity." *Michigan Quarterly Review* 25 (Winter 1986): 105–23.

Gellner, Ernest. *Nations and Nationalism*. Ithaca: Cornell University Press, 1983.

Gibson, Margaret. *Accommodation without Assimilation: Sikh Immigrants in an American High School*. Ithaca: Cornell University Press, 1988.

Glazer, Nathan. *Ethnic Dilemmas, 1964–1982*. Cambridge: Harvard University Press, 1983.

Glazer, Nathan, and Daniel Moynihan, eds. *Ethnicity: Theory and Experience*. Cambridge: Harvard University Press, 1975.

Goren, Arthur A. *New York Jews and the Quest for Community: The Kehillah Experiment, 1908–1922*. New York: Columbia University Press, 1970.

Grant, Madison. *The Passing of the Great Race*. New York: Scribner's Sons, 1916.

Grossman, David. *The Yellow Wind*. Translated by Haim Watzman. New York: Farrar, Straus & Giroux 1988.

Gutmann, Amy. *Democratic Education*. Princeton: Princeton University Press, 1989.

———. *Liberal Equality*. Princeton: Princeton University Press, 1980.

Gwaltney, John Langston. *Drylongso: A Self-Portrait of Black America*. New York: Random House, 1980.

Habermas, Jurgen. *The Structural Transformation of the Public Sphere: An Inquiry into a Category of Bourgeois Society*. Translated by Thomas Burger and Frederick Lawrence. Cambridge: MIT Press, 1991 [1962].

Hartman, David. "Public Space, Private Values." *Jerusalem Report* (20 June 1991): 63.

Heckmann, Friedrich. "Temporary Labor Migration or Immigration? 'Guest Workers' in the Federal Republic of Germany." In *Guests Come to Stay: The Effects of European Labor Migration on Sending and Receiving Countries*, edited by Rosemarie Rogers, 69–84. Boulder, Colo.: Westview Press, 1985.

Herzog, Don. *Happy Slaves: A Critique of Consent Theory*. Chicago: University of Chicago Press, 1989.

Higham, John. *Send These to Me: Immigrants in Urban America*. Rev. ed. Baltimore: Johns Hopkins University Press, 1984.

———. *Strangers in the Land: Patterns of American Nativism, 1860–1925*. New York: Atheneum, 1955.

Hirschmann, Nancy J. *Rethinking Obligation: A Feminist Method for Political Theory.* Ithaca: Cornell University Press, 1992.

Hobbes, Thomas. *Man and Citizen.* Edited by Bernard Gert. Indianapolis: Hackett, 1991 [1642].

Hobhouse, L. T. *The Elements of Social Justice.* London: George Allen & Unwin, 1922.

Hobsbawm, Eric. *Nations and Nationalism since 1780: Programme, Myth and Reality.* Cambridge: Cambridge University Press, 1990.

Hochschild, Jennifer L. *The New American Dilemma: Liberal Democracy and School Desegregation.* New Haven: Yale University Press, 1984.

Holmes, Stephen. *The Anatomy of Antiliberalism.* Cambridge: Harvard University Press, 1993.

―――. "The Permanent Structure of Anti-liberal Thought." In *Liberalism and the Moral Life,* edited by Nancy Rosenblum, 227–54. Cambridge: Harvard University Press, 1989.

Hooks, Bell. *Feminist Theory: From Margin to Center.* Boston: South End Press, 1984.

Hostetler, John. *Amish Society.* 3d ed. Baltimore: Johns Hopkins University Press, 1980.

Howe, Irving. "The Limits to Ethnicity." *New Republic* (25 June 1977): 17–19.

Hudgens v. NLRB 424 U.S. 507 (1976).

Hume, David. "Of National Characters." In *Essays: Moral, Political and Literary,* edited by Eugene Miller, 197–215. Indianapolis: Liberty Classics, 1987 [1777].

―――. *A Treatise of Human Nature.* Edited by Ernest C. Mossner. Harmondsworth, England: Penguin, 1985 [1739, 1740].

Jefferson, Thomas. *Notes on the State of Virginia.* In *The Portable Thomas Jefferson,* edited by Merrill Peterson, 23–232. Harmondsworth, England: Penguin, 1983 [1787].

Kallen, Horace. "Americanization and the Cultural Prospect." In *Culture and Democracy in the United States: Studies in the Group Psychologies of the American Peoples,* 176–77. New York: Boni & Liveright, 1924.

―――. *Culture and Democracy in the United States: Studies in the Group Psychologies of the American Peoples.* New York: Boni & Liveright, 1924.

―――. "Democracy versus the Melting Pot." In *Culture and Democracy in the United States: Studies in the Group Psychologies of the American Peoples.* New York: Boni & Liveright, 1924.

Kant, Immanuel. *Perpetual Peace and Other Essays.* Translated by Ted Humphrey. Indianapolis: Hackett, 1983 [1795].

Karst, Kenneth. *Belonging to America: Equal Citizenship and the Constitution.* New Haven: Yale University Press, 1989.

Kates, Gary. "Jews into Frenchmen: Nationality and Representation in Revolutionary France." *Social Research* 56 (Spring 1989): 213–32.

Katz, Jacob. *Out of the Ghetto: The Social Background of Jewish Emancipation, 1770–1870.* Cambridge: Harvard University Press, 1973.

Kedourie, Elie. *Nationalism.* London: Hutchinson, 1961.

King, Martin Luther, Jr. "Letter from Birmingham City Jail." In *A Testament of Hope: The Essential Writings and Speeches of Martin Luther King, Jr.*, edited by James M. Washington, 292–93. New York: HarperCollins, 1991.

———. *Where Do We Go from Here? Chaos or Community?* Boston: Beacon Press, 1967.

Kitano, Harry H. L., Wai-Tsang Yeung, Lynn Chai, and Herbert Hatanaka. "Asian-American Interracial Marriage." *Journal of Marriage and the Family* 46 (Feb. 1984): 179–89.

Knopff, Rainer. "Language and Culture in the Canadian Debate: The Battle of the White Papers." *Canadian Review of Studies in Nationalism* 6 (Spring 1979): 66–82.

Kraybill, Donald B. *The Riddle of Amish Culture.* Baltimore: Johns Hopkins University Press, 1989.

Kukathas, Chandran. "Are There Any Cultural Rights?" *Political Theory* 20 (Feb. 1992): 105–39.

———. *The Fraternal Conceit: Individualist versus Collectivist Ideas of Community.* Centre for Independent Studies, Occasional Paper Series. St. Leonards, Australia: The Centre, 1991.

Kymlicka, Will. *Liberalism, Commmunity and Culture.* Oxford: Oxford University Press, 1989.

———. "Liberalism and the Politicalization of Ethnicity." *Canadian Journal of Law and Jurisprudence* 6 (July 1991): 239–56.

Landry, Bert. *The New Black Middle Class.* Berkeley: University of California Press, 1987.

Larmore, Charles. *Patterns of Moral Complexity.* Cambridge: Cambridge University Press, 1987.

———. "Political Liberalism." *Political Theory* 18 (Aug. 1990): 339–60.

Lee, Sharon M., and Keiko Yamanaka. "Patterns of Asian American Intermarriage and Marital Assimilation." *Journal of Comparative Family Studies* 21 (Summer 1990): 287–305.

Levine, Gene N., and Colbert Rhodes. *The Japanese American Community: A Three Generation Study.* New York: Praeger, 1981.

Levine, Lawrence. *Black Culture and Consciousness: Afro-American Folk Thought from Slavery to Freedom.* Oxford: Oxford University Press, 1977.

Levine, Marc V. *The Reconquest of Montreal: Language Policy and Social Change in a Bilingual City.* Philadelphia: Temple University Press, 1990.

Lieberson, Stanley. "Unhyphenated Whites in the United States." In *Ethnicity and Race in the U.S.A.: Toward the Twenty First Century,* edited by Richard D. Alba, 159–80. London: Routledge, 1989.

Lieberson, Stanley, and Mary Waters. *From Many Strands: Ethnic and Racial Groups in Contemporary America.* New York: Russell Sage Foundation, 1988.

Light, Ivan. *Ethnic Enterprise in America.* Berkeley: University of California Press, 1972.

Litwak, Leon F. *North of Slavery: The Negro in the Free States, 1790–1860.* Chicago: University of Chicago Press, 1961.

Lloyd Corporation v. Tanner 407 U.S. 551 (1972).

Locke, John. *Letter Concerning Toleration*. Edited by James Tully. Indianapolis: Hackett, 1983 [1689].

———. *Second Treatise of Government*. Edited by C. B. Macpherson. Indianapolis: Hackett, 1980 [1690].

Lustgarten, L. S. "Liberty in a Culturally Plural Society." In *Of Liberty*, edited by A. Phillips Griffiths, 91–108. Cambridge: Cambridge University Press, 1983.

Macedo, Stephen. *Liberal Virtues: Citizenship, Virtue and Community in Liberal Constitutionalism*. Oxford: Oxford University Press, 1990.

MacIntyre, Alaisdair. *After Virtue*. 2d ed. Notre Dame, Ind.: Notre Dame University Press, 1984.

Mackinnon, Catherine. *Feminism Unmodified*. Cambridge: Harvard University Press, 1987.

Madison, James, Alexander Hamilton, and John Jay. *The Federalist Papers*. Edited by Issac Kramnick. Penguin: Harmondsworth, 1987 [1788].

Mann, Arthur. *The One and the Many: Reflections on the American Identity*. Chicago: University of Chicago Press, 1979.

Margalit, Avishai, and Joseph Raz. "National Self-determination." *Journal of Philosophy* 87 (Sept. 1990): 439–61.

Marrus, Michael. *The Politics of Assimilation: A Study of the French Jewish Community at the Time of the Dreyfus Affair*. Oxford: Oxford University Press, 1971.

Marsh v. Alabama 326 U.S. 501 (1946).

Marx, Karl. "On the Jewish Question." In *The Marx-Engels Reader*. 2d ed. Edited by Richard Tucker, 26–32. New York: Norton, 1978.

"Mayor Strongly Attacks Racial Hatred." *New York Times* (26 Sept. 1991): B7.

Mazrui, Ali. "Multiculturalism and Comparative Holocaust: Educational and Moral Implications." In *One Nation, Many Peoples: A Declaration of Cultural Interdependence*, 41–44. Albany: New York State Social Studies Review and Development Committee, 1991.

Mellon, Matthew T. *Early American Views on Negro Slavery*. New York: Bergman Publishers, 1969 [1934].

Meyer, Michael A. *The Origins of the Modern Jew: Jewish Identity and European Culture in Germany, 1749–1824*. Detroit: Wayne State University Press, 1967.

Mill, John Stuart. *Collected Works*. Edited by John M. Robson. Vol. 24, *The Condition of Ireland*. Toronto: University of Toronto Press, 1986 [1846].

———. *Considerations on Representative Government*. In *Three Essays*, edited by Richard Wollheim, 145–243. Oxford: Oxford University Press, 1981 [1859].

———. *On Liberty*. In *Three Essays*, edited by Richard Wollheim, 5–141. Oxford: Oxford University Press, 1981 [1861].

———. *The Principles of Political Economy*. Edited by Sir W. J. Ashley. London: Longmans, Green, 1926 [1848].

———. *The Subjection of Women*. In *Three Essays*, edited by Richard Wollheim. 427–548. Oxford: Oxford University Press, 1981 [1869].

Montaigne, Michel. *Essays*. Translated by J. M. Cohen. Harmondsworth, England: Penguin, 1958 [1580].

Montero, Darrel. *Japanese Americans: Changing Patterns of Ethnic Affiliation over Three Generations*. Boulder, Colo.: Westview Press, 1980.

Moore, Sally Falk. "The Production of Cultural Pluralism as a Process." *Public Culture* 1 (Spring 1989): 26–48.

Mozert v. Hawkins County Board of Education 827 F.2d 1062 (6th Cir. 1987).

Nagel, Thomas. *Equality and Partiality*. Oxford: Oxford University Press, 1991.

Nairn, Thomas. *The Break-up of Britain: Crisis and Neo-nationalism*. London: Verso, 1981.

Namier, Lewis. *1848: The Revolution of the Intellectuals*. Oxford: Oxford University Press, 1943.

Nash, Manning. *The Cauldron of Ethnicity in the Modern World*. Chicago: University of Chicago Press, 1989.

Nee, Victor, and Jimy Sanders. "The Road to Parity: Determinants of the Socioeconomic Achievements of Asian Americans." In *Ethnicity and Race in the U.S.A.: Toward the Twenty First Century*, edited by Richard D. Alba, 75–93. London: Routledge, 1989.

Nelson, Candace, and Marta Tienda. "The Structuring of Hispanic Ethnicity: Historical and Contemporary Perspectives." In *Ethnicity and Race in the U.S.A.: Toward the Twenty First Century*, edited by Richard D. Alba, 49–74. London: Routledge, 1989.

New York State Social Studies Review and Development Committee. *One Nation, Many Peoples: A Declaration of Cultural Interdependence*. Albany: The Committee, 1991.

Nietzsche, Friedrich. *Beyond Good and Evil*. Translated by Walter Kauffman. New York: Vintage, 1966 [1886].

Nozick, Robert. *Anarchy, State and Utopia*. New York: Basic Books, 1974.

Oakes, James. *Slavery and Freedom: An Interpretation of the Old South*. New York: Knopf, 1990.

Orwell, George. *The Road to Wigan Pier*. New York: Harcourt Brace Jovanovich, 1958 [1937].

Page, Clarence. "At Issue: Who's the Greater Victim?" *Chicago Tribune* (25 Aug. 1991): sect. 5, p. 3.

Palacký, Franktíšek. "Letter Sent by Franktíšek Palacký to Frankfurt." *Slavonic Review* 26 (April 1948): 303–8.

Parker, Frank R. "Racial Gerrymandering and Legislative Reapportionment." In *Minority Vote Dilution,* edited by Chandler Davis, 85–118. Washington, D.C.: Joint Center for Political Studies, 1984.

Pinderhughes, Diane. *Race and Ethnicity in Chicago Politics: A Reexamination of Pluralist Theory*. Urbana: University of Illinois Press, 1987.

Pitkin, Hanna Fennichel. "Justice: On Relating Private and Public." *Political Theory* 9 (Aug. 1981): 327–51.

Plessy v. Ferguson 163 U.S. 537 (1896).

Poppel, Stephen M. *Zionism in Germany, 1897–1933: The Shaping of a Jewish Identity*. Philadelphia: Jewish Publication Society of America, 1977.

Porter, Rosalie Pedalino. *Forked Tongue: The Politics of Bilingual Education*. New York: Basic Books, 1990.

Powell, James Henry. "The Concept of Cultural Pluralism in American Social Thought, 1915–1965." Ph.D. diss., University of Notre Dame, 1971.

Pruneyard Shopping Center v. Robbins 447 U.S. 74 (1980).

Raban, Jonathan. *God, Man and Mrs. Thatcher*. London: Chattus & Windus, 1989.

Raboteau, Albert J. *Slave Religion: The "Invisible Institution" in the Antebellum South*. New York: Oxford University Press, 1978.

Ramsey, Patricia G., Edwina Battle Vold, and Leslie R. Williams. *Multicultural Education: A Source Book*. New York: Garland, 1989.

Rawls, John. *Political Liberalism*. New York: Columbia University Press, 1993.

———. *A Theory of Justice*. Cambridge: Harvard University Press, Belknap Press, 1971.

Regents of the University of California v. Bakke 438 U.S. 265 (1978).

"Restaurateur Flees to Land of Low Taxes, Low Wages and Little Traffic—Detroit." *Detroit News* (26 May 1991): D1.

Rieder, Jonathan. *Canarsie: The Jews and Italians of Brooklyn against Liberalism*. Cambridge: Harvard University Press, 1985.

Rodgers, Daniel T. *Contested Truths: Keywords in American Politics since Independence*. New York: Basic Books, 1987.

Rodriguez, Richard. *Hunger of Memory: The Education of Richard Rodriguez*. Boston: Godine, 1981.

Rorty, Richard. *Objectivity, Relativism, and Truth: Philosophical Papers I*. Cambridge: Cambridge University Press, 1991.

Rousseau, Jean-Jacques. *A Discourse on Inequality*. Translated by Maurice Cranston. Harmondsworth: Penguin, 1984 [1754].

———. *The Government of Poland*. Translated by Willmoore Kendall. Indianapolis: Bobbs-Merrill, 1972 [1772].

———. *The Social Contract*. Translated by Maurice Cranston. Harmondsworth: Penguin, 1968 [1762].

Rozenblit, Marsha L. *The Jews of Vienna, 1867–1914: Assimilation and Identity*. Albany: State University Press of New York, 1983.

Sandberg, Neil. *Ethnic Identity and Assimilation: The Polish-American Community*. New York: Praeger, 1974.

Sandel, Michael. *Liberalism and the Limits of Justice*. Cambridge: Cambridge University Press, 1982.

Schmid, Carol L. *Conflict and Consensus in Switzerland*. Berkeley: University of California Press, 1981.

Schuck, Peter H., and Rogers M. Smith. *Citizenship without Consent: Illegal Aliens in the American Polity*. New Haven: Yale University Press, 1985.

Schuman, Howard, Charlotte Steeh, and Lawrence Bobo. *Racial Attitudes in America*. Cambridge: Harvard University Press, 1985.

Seligman, Adam. *The Idea of Civil Society*. New York: Free Press, 1992.

Seton-Watson, Hugh. *Nations and States*. Boulder, Colo.: Westview Press, 1977.

Sheehan, James. *German Liberalism in the Nineteenth Century*. Chicago: University of Chicago Press, 1978.

Shipler, David. *Arab and Jew: Wounded Spirits in the Promised Land*. New York: New York Times Books, 1986.

Shklar, Judith. *American Citizenship: The Quest for Inclusion*. Cambridge: Harvard University Press, 1991.

Sidgwick, Henry. *Elements of Politics*. 2d ed. London: Macmillan, 1897.

Smith, Adam. *An Inquiry into the Nature and Causes of the Wealth of Nations*. Edited by R. H. Campbell, A. S. Skinner, and W. B. Todd. Indianapolis: Liberty Classics, 1981 [1776].

Smith, Rogers. "The 'American Creed' and American Identity: The Limits of Liberal Citizenship in the United States." *Western Political Quarterly* 41 (June 1988): 225–51.

———. "Beyond Tocqueville, Myrdal, and Hartz: The Multiple Traditions in America." *American Political Science Review* 87 (Sept. 1993): 549–66.

———. *Liberalism and American Constitutional Law*. Cambridge: Harvard University Press, 1985.

Sobol, Thomas. "Understanding Diversity." Memo to the New York Board of Regents, 12 July 1991.

Sowell, Thomas. *Ethnic America*. New York: Basic Books, 1981.

Spitzer, Leo. *Lives in Between: Assimilation and Marginality in Austria, Brazil, West Africa, 1780–1945*. Cambridge: Cambridge University Press, 1989.

Steinberg, Stephen. *The Ethnic Myth: Race, Ethnicity and Class in America*. Boston: Beacon Press, 1981.

Stolzenberg, Nomi Maya. "'He Drew a Circle That Shut Me Out': Assimilation, Indoctrination and the Paradox of a Liberal Education." *Harvard Law Review* 106 (Jan. 1993): 581–667.

Svensson, Frances. "Liberal Democracy and Group Rights: The Legacy of Individualism and Its Impact on American Indian Tribes." *Political Studies* 27 (Sept. 1979): 421–39.

Takaki, Ronald. *Strangers from a Different Shore*. Boston: Little, Brown, 1989.

Tamir, Yael. *Liberal Nationalism*. Princeton: Princeton University Press, 1993.

Taylor, Charles. "Cross-Purposes: The Liberal-Communitarian Debate." In *Liberalism and the Moral Life*, edited by Nancy Rosenblum, 159–83. Cambridge: Harvard University Press, 1989.

———. *Human Agency and Language: Philosophical Papers I*. Cambridge: Cambridge University Press, 1985.

———. "Language and Human Nature." In *Human Agency and Language: Philosophical Papers I*, 215–47. Cambridge: Cambridge University Press, 1985.

———. "Modes of Civil Society." *Public Culture* 3 (Fall 1990): 95–118.

———. *Multiculturalism and "The Politics of Recognition,"* edited by Amy Gutmann. Princeton: Princeton University Press, 1992.

———. "Why Do Nations Have to Become States?" In *Philosophers Look at Cana-*

dian Federation, edited by Stanley French, 19–35. Montreal: Canadian Philosophical Association, 1979.

Teixeria, Ruy A. "Registration and Turnout." *Public Opinion* (Jan./Feb. 1989): 12–13, 56–58.

Testa, Randy-Michael. *After the Fire: The Destruction of the Lancaster County Amish.* Hanover, N.H.: University Press of New England, 1992.

Thernstrom, Stephan, ed. *Harvard Encyclopedia of Ethnic Groups.* Cambridge: Harvard University Press, Belknap Press, 1980.

Tiendt, Pamela L., and Iris M. Tiendt. *Multicultural Teaching: A Handbook of Activities, Information and Resources.* 3d ed. Boston: Allyn & Bacon, 1990.

U.S. Statistical Abstract. Washington, D.C.: U.S. Bureau of Census, 1990 & 1992.

van den Berghe, Pierre. *Race and Racism.* 2d ed. New York: John Wiley & Sons, 1978.

Van Dyke, Vernon. "Collective Entities and Moral Rights: Problems in Liberal Democratic Thought." *Journal of Politics* 44 (Feb. 1982): 21–40.

———. "The Individual, the State, and Ethnic Communities in Political Theory." *World Politics* 29 (April 1977): 347–69.

Verba, Sidney, and Norman Nie. *Participation in America: Political Democracy and Social Equality.* Chicago: University of Chicago Press, 1972.

Walzer, Michael. "The Communitarian Critique of Liberalism." *Political Theory* 18 (Feb. 1990): 6–23.

———. "The Idea of Civil Society." *Dissent* (Spring 1991): 293–304.

———. "Liberalism and the Art of Separation." *Political Theory* 12 (Aug. 1984): 315–29.

———. "The New Tribalism." *Dissent* (Spring 1992): 164–71.

———. "Philosophy and Democracy." *Political Theory* 9 (Aug. 1981): 379–99.

———. *Spheres of Justice.* New York: Basic Books, 1983.

Waters, Mary. *Ethnic Options: Choosing Identities in America.* Berkeley: University of California Press, 1990.

Weber, Eugen. *Peasants into Frenchmen: The Modernization of Rural France, 1870–1914.* Stanford: Stanford University Press, 1976.

Weeks, Jeffrey. "The Value of Difference." In *Identity: Community, Culture, Difference,* edited by Jonathan Rutherford. London: Lawrence & Wishart, 1990.

Wendell, Susan. "A (Qualified) Defense of Liberal Feminism." *Hypatia* 2 (Summer 1987): 65–91.

Williams, Patricia. *The Alchemy of Race and Rights.* Cambridge: Harvard University Press, 1991.

Wilson, William Julius. *The Declining Significance of Race: Blacks and Changing American Institutions.* 2d ed. Chicago: University of Chicago Press, 1980.

Wisconsin v. Yoder 406 U.S. 205 (1972).

Wright, Richard. *Black Boy.* New York: Harper & Row, 1937.

X, Malcolm. *The Autobiography of Malcolm X.* New York: Ballantine Books, 1964.

———. *Malcolm X Speaks.* Edited by George Breitman. New York: Grove Weidenfeld, 1965.

Yancey, William L., Eugene P. Ericksen, and Richard N. Juliani. "Emergent Ethnicity: A Review and Reformulation." *American Sociological Review* 41 (June 1976): 391–403.

Yezierska, Anzia. *Bread Givers*. New York: Persea Books, 1975 [1925].

Young, Iris Marion. *Justice and the Politics of Difference*. Princeton: Princeton University Press, 1990.

Zook, Lee. "The Amish in America: Conflicts between Cultures." *Journal of American Culture* 12 (Winter 1989): 29–33.

INDEX

abolitionists, 116
Acton, Lord, 8
affirmative action, 9, 121
Africa, 29, 30, 144, 165
African Americans, 16, 27, 29, 80; and dominant culture, 114; and mainstream culture, 115. *See also* Black Americans
African identity, 15
agency, 17, 26
Alba, Richard, 195nn. 37–38, 196nn. 13–14
Albanians, 28
Alter, Peter, 189n. 12
American Creed, 118
American culture, 52, 65, 74
American identity, 61
American Indians, 65, 96, 144, 199n. 25, 199n. 27. *See also* Native Americans
Amish, 4, 13, 16, 50–51, 87–108, 112, 138, 167–68; and children, 100, 102, 105; and choice, 99–105; and citizenship, 95–99; and civil society 99, 107; community, 88–92, 95; and conformity, 95; and cultural pluralism, 103, 185; and diversity, 104; and education 87, 102, 105; and equality, 91; and family, 91; and individual rights, 91; and liberal state, 98–99, 102–4, 107–8; and liberal values, 92; and mainstream culture, 101–2; and mainstream society, 98, 102, 108; Old Order, 89, 103–4; and political participation, 56; and private sphere, 98, 99; and public/private distinction, 90; and public sphere, 98, 107; Swartzentruber, 104; teen-agers, 101; and toleration, 103
Ammann, Joseph, 88–89
Anabaptists, 88–89, 101
ancien régime, 33
Anderson, Benedict, 27–28, 146, 168
Anglo-Saxons, 20, 60
Arabs, 19
Aristotle, 46–49
Armenia, 144
Asante, Molefe Kete, 181
Asia, 144, 165
Asian Americans, 23–24, 56, 75, 118, 129, 131, 172, 181; and discrimination, 31–32
assimilation, 10, 21, 23, 60, 77, 84, 107, 176

Austria, 18
Austrian empire, 162
Austro-Hungarian empire, 142
Azerbajani, 144

Banton, Michael, 190n. 9, 191n. 24, 202n. 7
Basques, 8, 28–29, 154
Beiner, Ronald, 48
Benedict, Ruth, 190n. 6
Benson, Susan, 190n. 5, 192nn. 27 and 36
Berlin, Isaiah, 204n. 3
Berns, Walter, 200n. 33
Bill of Rights, 168
Bismarck, Otto von, 143
Black American community, 24
Black American representation, 124
Black Americans, 9, 10, 13, 29, 30, 32, 63, 75, 86, 113–39, 170, 172, 173, 179; and businesses, 42; and citizenship, 22, 122–28, 134, 137; and civil society, 122, 128–33; and conformity, 114, 122, 134; cultural practices of, 195n. 40; culture, 114–15, 122, 125, 134–37, 139, 184; and discrimination, 39, 41, 47, 113–15, 118–19, 121, 125, 136; and equal citizenship, 125–28, 134, 137; and economy, 135; inequality of, 136; middle class, 22, 129, 137; oppression of, 11, 113–15; political thought of, 135; and power, 134, 136; and reason, 116; and rights, 118; and segregation, 139; and skin color, 20, 24. *See also* African Americans; race; racial identity; racism
Black identity, 113, 122; and civil society, 138; and liberal state, 137–39; and political system, 124. *See also* discrimination; racial identity
Black nationalism, 28, 192n. 31
Black nationalists, 30
Blackmun, Harry A., 115
Blauner, Rob, 202n. 2
Bluestone, Barry, 204n. 35
Bobo, Lawrence, 202n. 2
Bonacich, Edna, 192nn. 40–41
Boston, Thomas, 202n. 2
boundaries. *See* ethnic groups; identity; liberalism

223

Brazil, 18, 20, 22
Breton, 8
Britain, 2, 9, 54, 74–76, 85, 176
British empire, 145
British Americans, 75
Brixton, 30
Brooklyn, 71
Brooks, Roy, 203n. 22
Brown v. Board of Education, 117
Browning, Rufus, 203n. 30
Buchanan, Allen, 156–57
Burger, Warren, 91, 95, 105, 108

Calhoun, John, 117
California, 18, 25, 76, 83, 173
Cambodia, 31
Canada, 29, 149, 152, 155, 159–60, 168, 176, 187; French, 28; upper, 145. *See also* Quebec
Canadian Indians, 96, 199n. 27. *See also* American Indians; Native Americans
capitalism, 37
Carnoy, Martin, 204n. 36
Carter, Stephen, 204n. 45
Catalonia, 154
Catholic church, 41, 80, 150–51
Catholics, 145, 153
Chatterjee, Partha, 205n. 5
China, 21, 28
Chinese Americans, 170
Chinese traits, 172
Christian Fundamentalists, 106–7, 111
Christian Scientists, 99
Christianity, 14, 74, 174–75
Christians, 35, 45, 52, 75, 92, 101, 114
Church of Scotland, 74
citizens, character of, 93; French, 36; German, 36
citizenship, 11, 39; defined, 33; and education, 106; and ethnicity, 171–72; and ethnics, 52; French, 33; full, 75, 76, 82, 98; German, 63; partial, 95–99, 100, 103, 105–8, 200n. 34; and participation, 46; and poverty, 130; and Supreme Court, 44; universal nature of, 37; and the vote, 123; and whites, 125. *See also* civil society; equal citizenship; liberal citizenship; Locke; nationalism; nondiscrimination
civic republicanism, 11
civil society, 6, 7, 39–45, 72, 78, 85; and citizenship, 43–44, 98; defined, 40–41, 193n. 16; and ethnics, 56; and identity, 57, 183–84; and Marx, 37; and race, 134
Civil Rights Laws, 122
Civil Rights Movement, 42, 117, 120, 137–38
Civil War, 20–22, 118, 127
class, 60; and race, 20, 129
Clermont-Tonnerre, 33–34, 108

Coleman, William, 206nn. 19 and 26, 207n. 37
colonization, 30
communitarianism, 12, 17, 152
conformity, 167, 186; and identity, 10. *See also* ethnicity; immigrants; mainstream culture
Congress, 20, 41, 56, 124, 169
Connor, Walker, 205n. 13
consent, 2
Constant, Benjamin, 94
constitutional rights, 117
Crenshaw, Kimberlé, 202n. 14
Crispino, James, 197n. 20
Croats, 143
Cuddihy, John Murray, 49
cultural identity, 5, 176; and education, 179–80; and liberalism, 183–88; preservation of, 156–57. *See also* identity
cultural pluralism, 5, 7, 13, 61, 176, 185, 187; and Amish, 168; compared with pluralistic integration, 76; and economic subordination, 137; and gender, 70; and Hasidim, 168; and liberalism, 62, 154; limits of, 62–68, 69; and oppression, 63; and segregation, 137
cultural pluralists, 62, 63, 67, 70, 197n. 17; and Amish, 104
culture: changes in, 65, 76–77; Christian, 10; and class, 65; and food, 52; and heritage, 69, 178; and identity, 7, 17, 64; and immigrants, 65, 83; and language, 142, 145–50, 158; and liberalism, 9, 34, 62, 95–97, 125, 165, 184; membership in, 96; and national movements, 160; popular, 169, 170, 184; public, 75, 145–49; and religion, 65; roots of, 63–64; of slaves, 24, 114, 179; and special rights, 156. *See also* dominant culture; ethnicity; mainstream culture; nationalism; race
Czechoslovakia, 144
Czechs, 8

Daley, Richard, 109
Davis, Chandler, 203n. 27
Davis, F. J., 191n. 11
Dawson, Michael, 139
Debo, Angie, 207n. 34
Degler, Carl, 191n. 13
democracy. *See* liberal democracy
Dench, Geoff, 202n. 1
desegregation, 127, 137. *See also* segregation
Dinkins, David, 52, 72
discrimination, 23–24, 43, 47, 81, 173, 187; and citizenship, 6, 10–11, 39; and civil society, 57, 115; and the courts, 12; and cultural preservation, 71; and cultural values, 24; gender, 11, 49, 72; and group membership, 157; and homogeneity, 49; and

identity, 10, 71–73, 171–72; legal penalties for, 119; and liberal laws, 121; and liberal state, 44; and liberalism, 118, 166; and the market, 42–43; and neutrality, 85; and the poor, 49; private, 45; and public sphere, 115; racial, 129; and wealth, 132. *See also* Asian Americans; Black Americans; nondiscrimination

districts: at-large, 123–24; Black, 124, 203n. 29; single-member, 123

diversity, 84, 96; benefits of, 175; and civil society, 128; co-existence with unity, 171–72; and conflict, 58–59; in Jewish community, 35; and liberal society, 48; in liberal state, 78–79; racial, 48, 180; and sharing cultural practices, 52–53; tensions of, 171–77; in West, 140. *See also* ethnicity; liberalism; Locke

dominant culture, 10, 25, 173, 176; and children, 154; and ethnic cultures, 76; and ethnic identity, 78–79, 175; and Quebec, 159. *See also* mainstream culture

Douglass, Frederick, 123, 179

Dreyfus, Alfred, 2; trial of, 163

DuBois, W.E.B., 122

Dukakis, Michael, 57

Dworkin, Ronald, 199n. 13

education: bilingual, 177, 181; and ethnics, 23; and immigrants, 183; in industrial society, 147; and liberalism, 5, 94, 99–100; and parents, 100, 107; pluralistic, 177–83. *See also* Amish; multiculturalism

Elster, Jon, 194n. 28

England, 2, 21, 81, 144, 168

English, 146–48, 157

Enlightenment, the, 5, 141

equal citizenship, 6, 10, 38, 39–45, 49, 73, 179; and boundaries, 169; and class, 129; denial of, 186; and ethnic identity, 6, 173, 175; ethos of, 48; and immigrants, 73; realization of, 122–25. *See also* citizenship; liberal citizenship

equal opportunity: and civil society, 40; generational, 154; and language, 154, 184; and liberalism, 11, 184; in Quebec, 153–54; and the Québecois, 151; and race, 122, 137

equality, 65; and family, 99; formal, 57, 113, 119; gender, 70; and liberal institutions, 49; and liberalism, 3–8, 10, 12, 49–50, 69, 79, 81, 117–20

Estonians, 28

ethnic groups: and boundaries, 151–52; and equality, 50; and liberal citizenship, 6, 46–56; and liberalism, 2–3, 6–8, 9, 12, 68–72, 80, 85–86, 178–79, 184–88; tensions between, 1, 85–86, 171–76, 177; tensions within, 76

ethnic identity: transformation of, 49–56, 62–68, 74. *See also* liberal citizenship; liberal state

ethnicity: and choice, 99–105; compared with nationality, 28; compared with race, 25, 27; and conformity, 26, 78, 80, 82, 84–86, 175; and culture, 52, 58, 68, 73, 180; defined, 16–17, 25–27; and diversity, 28, 48, 56–59, 180; and gender, 69; and liberal citizenship, 58, 59, 64, 88; and mainstream society, 126; and political power, 23; and prejudice, 23, 27; resiliency of, 58; symbolic, 67–68

Ettinger, S., 193n. 4

Europe, 8–9, 57, 118, 145, 162, 169; Eastern, 35, 145, 185; Southern, 144, 165; Western, 10, 140, 165, 185

Farley, Reynolds, 203n. 28

Federalist Papers, 9

Fitzhugh, George, 117

Flathman, Richard, 47

Florida, 173

France, 2, 8, 36, 145, 163, 168

Frankfurt Parliament, 1, 143

Frazier, Franklin, 204n. 43

Fredrickson, George, 191n. 17, 192n. 35

French, 142, 146–49, 158–60

French Assembly, 33, 162

French Canadians, 13, 145–46, 148–155; culture of, 158, 160; and identity, 150. *See also* Quebec; Québecois

French Revolution, 1, 33–34, 162

Friedman, Milton, 18

Fuchs, Lawrence, 28–29

Galston, William, 199n. 19

Gans, Herbert, 67

Gates, Henry Louis, 183

Gaus, Gerald, 199n. 14

Gay, Peter, 189n. 6

gays and lesbians, 52, 62, 72

Gaza Strip, 162

Geertz, Clifford, 140

Gellner, Ernest, 205n. 6, 205n. 8, 206n. 18

gender. *See* cultural pluralism; discrimination; equality; ethnicity

German Americans, 52, 75

German culture, 63

German unification, 143

Germany, 1, 2, 63, 144–45, 163; Nazi, 19

Gibson, Margaret, 76, 83

Glazer, Nathan, 27, 190n. 5

Goren, Arthur, 208n. 1

Grant, Madison, 21

Greeks, 57

Grossman, David, 208n. 46

group representation, 68

groups, oppressed, 62
guest workers, Turkish, 63
Gutmann, Amy, 194n. 23, 201n. 39
Gwaltney, John Langston, 192n. 37, 202n. 2
Gypsies, 19

Habermas, Jürgen, 194n. 21
Hamilton, Alexander, 9
Hanukkah, 174–75
Hartman, David, 208n. 2
Hasidic Jews, 4, 35, 107, 108–12, 167–68, 185;
    and citizenship, 109; and discrimination,
    110; and mainstream society, 110; political
    activity of, 109, 112
Heckmann, Friedrich, 196n. 7
Hegel, George Wilhelm Friedrich, 141
Herzog, Don, 198n. 1
Higham, John, 20, 73
Hindu, 29, 149, 176
Hirschmann, Nancy, 190n. 17, 193n. 15
Hitler, Adolf, 18
Hobbes, Thomas, 54–55
Hobhouse, L. T., 2
Hobsbawm, Eric, 141
Hochschild, Jennifer, 203n. 21
hooks, bell, 52–53
Hostetler, John, 198n. 4, 198nn. 6–7
Howe, Irving, 68
Hume, David, 8, 202n. 9
Hungarians, 142, 144

identity, 110, 174–75, battlegrounds of, 168;
    and biology, 16; and boundaries, 167,
    168–71, 176; of children, 74, 88; and com-
    munitarianism, 17–18; creation of, 14–18;
    group, 61, 156, 178; and Israel, 170; liberal,
    4; and liberal institutions, 37, 45; and lib-
    eralism, 17–18, 26, 34, 57, 188; and mem-
    ories, 65–66; and politics, 55–56; and pri-
    vate sphere, 34, 37; socially constructed,
    16–17; and the state, 170. See also Black
    identity; ethnic identity; racial identity
illiberal practices, 68–73, 75, 88, 184–85
illiberal values, 7, 112
immigrants, 52, 69–71, 85, 132, 144; Asian,
    20; and assimilation, 60, 66; children of,
    182; Chinese, 22; and conformity, 74; and
    culture, 178; and equal opportunity, 154;
    Japanese, 22; and liberal values, 80; and
    pluralism, 165; in Quebec, 158; and
    schools, 181; Sicilian, 25. See also culture;
    education
immigration, 20–25, 31, 52, 62–64, 73, 74,
    177
India, 28, 29, 64, 144, 154, 168
Indians, 181
industrialization, 62, 140, 155
integration, 9, 71–72, 104–5, 126, 131, 145

intermarriage, 19, 23, 27, 32, 66–67, 138, 178,
    196n. 13
International Antisemitic Congress, 163
Irish Americans, 23, 25–27, 29, 30, 46–47, 52,
    66, 72, 75, 170
Islamic countries, 185
Israel, 154, 162, 169–70
Italian Americans, 9, 16, 18, 23, 25, 46–47, 63,
    65–66, 170, 173
Italians, 20–22, 71
Italy, 68, 145, 170

Jamaica, 30
Japan, 21
Japanese Americans, 9, 31–32, 52, 132, 170,
    173, 179
Jay, John, 9
Jefferson, Thomas, 5, 9, 14
Jewish community, 37, 41, 50; antagonism
    within, 25; before emancipation, 35; and
    Kehillah, 169
Jews, 2, 9, 10, 13, 16, 20, 22, 43, 47, 62, 63,
    80–82, 84, 131, 158; American, 170, 172,
    179; and citizenship, 34, 36, 108; and dis-
    crimination, 18, 19, 132; and emancipa-
    tion, 10, 33–6, 50, 81; French, 33; Ger-
    man, 25; identity of, 36–37, 46, 49–51,
    57–59, 151, 169–71; and nationalism,
    162–63; and Purim, 175. See also Hasidic
    Jews
Jim Crow, 22, 179
Judaism, 18, 35, 37, 49, 58, 74, 108, 174

Kallen, Horace, 13, 60–65, 81
Kant, Immanual, 2, 94
Karst, Kenneth, 193n. 1, 194n. 17
Katz, Jacob, 193n. 4
Kedourie, Elie, 144
King, Martin Luther, Jr., 39, 125, 129, 134–35
Kitano, Harry, 193n. 42
Knopff, Rainer, 206n. 24
Korea, 170
Korean Americans, 170
Koreans, 181
Kraybill, Donald, 195n. 36, 198nn. 4–6
Kukathas, Chandran, 156, 193n. 3
Kwanza, 175
Kymlicka, Will, 95–97, 103–4

Landry, Bert, 204n. 44
language: and advanced industrial society, 147;
    and civil society, 147–48; community, 164;
    and culture, 150; and identity, 7, 153, 155;
    in liberal state, 154; and nationalism,
    145–60, 161, 176; and power, 154; public,
    11, 145–49, 159, 184; survival of, 146, 156.
    See also culture; Québecois
Laos, 64

Larmore, Charles, 94, 199n. 13, 199n. 15, 209n. 19
Latin, 151
Latinos, 23–24, 27, 31, 53, 56, 75, 118, 129, 131, 178, 181, 192n. 38
Lebanon, 28
Lee, Sharon, 193n. 42
Levine, Gene, 192n. 41
Levine, Lawrence, 191n. 22, 202n. 3
Levine, Marc, 206n. 19, 207n. 36, 207n. 40
liberal character, 49
liberal citizens, 53, 74–75, 97; and children, 99, 111; equality among, 49; and ethnic practices, 79; and ethnics, 72, 86; identity of, 48; and immigrants, 70–71; and self-respect, 81
liberal citizenship, 11, 45, 46–47, 75–78; and Black Americans, 113, demands of, 6, 46–49, 53–54, 56, 62, 94, 104, 120; and ethnic identity, 51, 171; failures of, 11–12, 113; full, 106; goals of, 176; and Marx, 36–37; and participation, 6; political considerations of, 93; requirements of, 88; and social roles, 50; tensions in, 57; theory of, 37; virtues of, 94. See also citizenship; equal citizenship; ethnic groups; ethnicity
liberal democracy, 13, 110; and citizenship, 39, 106–7, 180; and factions, 119; and participation, 43; problems of, 119; requirements of, 7, 93; and rights, 121; and workplace democracy, 130
liberal neutrality, 48; and equality, 84; and the good life, 47, 93; problems with, 10, 79, 93, 121
liberal rights, 36, 118; and cultures, 96; and racism, 120
liberal separation, 45
liberal state, 4, 90; and citizenship, 38, 74; demands of, 47, 109; and equal opportunity, 129; and ethnic identity, 50, 112; and ethnic practices, 79; ethos of, 48; industrial, 78; and inequality, 45; and liberal principles, 69; and minority cultures, 96; and partial citizenship, 97, 107–8; and power, 10; and private sphere, 46, 69; rejection of cultural practices, 70; and tolerance, 93, 185; and United States, 11. See also Black identity; discrimination
liberal tradition, 11
liberal values, 74, 99; and children, 105, 111; and culture, 103; rejection of, 97; and religion, 105
liberal virtues, 7; and children, 111; and citizenship, 97–99, 106–7; and political virtues, 95
liberalism: American, 113; attitude toward identity, 8; and Black American culture, 122; and boundaries, 151, 155, 167, 188;

changes in, 92–95; and children, 99; and civility, 185; comprehensive, 94; criticism of, 17; critics of, 10–11, 40, 45–46, 48, 113, 190n. 17; and cultural differences, 177; and cultural identity, 4, 13, 183–88; and cultural norms, 7; and cultural practices, 80, 83, 86, 186; defined, 3–8; demands of, 37, 75, 92, 186; and democracy, 5; and diversity, 13, 59; and education, 5; and emancipation, 36; and ethnic cultures, 74; failures of, 10; and family, 112; flaws of, 118–22; and group identity, 6–7, 10, 12; and groups, 2, 4, 9, 13, 34; and individual rights, 2, 4, 117; and individuality, 13; and industrialization, 151; and institutions, 184; and law, 12; Lockean, 116; and neutrality, 7; and oppression, 163; and pluralism, 47; political, 94; and power, 12, 81, 121; and progress, 9; and Protestantism, 79–80; Rawlsian, 17; and reason, 116; and Reformation, 79; strengths of, 12–13; and United States, 11; universalism of, 110; weaknesses of, 13; and world government, 189n. 1. See also cultural pluralism; culture; equality; ethnic groups; identity; Locke; Mill; nationalism; public/private distinction; race
liberals: English, 141; German, 144
libertarians, 40–41
liberty, 3, 8; and equality, 6, 43; and nationality, 61. See also nationalism
Lieberson, Stanley, 196n. 13
Light, Ivan, 194n. 19, 204n. 37
Lithuania, 144
Litwak, Leon, 192n. 35
Locke, John, 6; and citizenship, 38, 92–93; and diversity, 12–13, 58–59; and equality, 84; Letter Concerning Toleration, 2, 12, 38, 92; and oppression, 118–19; and property rights, 116; Second Treatise on Government, 93, 116
Los Angeles, 83, 178
Louisiana, 21
Lustgarten, L. S., 61, 63
Lutheran church, 52

Macedo, Stephen, 190n. 21, 198n. 1, 199n. 15
machine politics, 23
MacIntyre, Alaisdair, 190n. 20, 194n. 24
MacKinnon, Catherine, 79, 190n. 17
Madison, James, 9, 119
Magna Carta, 20
mainstream culture, 167; and Black Americans, 113–14; and Black culture, 135, 139; conformity to, 26–27; and ethnic cultures, 85, 176; and power, 7. See also culture; dominant culture
Mann, Arthur, 195n. 1

Pueblos, 96
Punjab, 29

Quebec, 145–60, 168; Allophones, 148, 154, 157–59; Anglophones, 151, 153, 158–59; Francophones, 148, 150–53, 159. *See also* Canada; French Canadians
Québecois, 28–29; and culture, 149–60; Haitian, 158; and identity, 152–53, 160, 170; Jewish, 158; and language, 150–55, 160; survival of, 156–60. *See also* equal opportunity; French Canadians

Raboteau, Albert, 202n. 3
race: and culture, 114–15, 138, 180; defined, 16–17, 19–25, 29–30, 191n. 25; and identity, 113; and liberalism, 12, 113–39; and liberals, 9; and liberty, 21; and power, 21; and skin color, 20; and social roles, 24; and state, 22, 24; and status, 21; in United States, 6. *See also* African Americans; Black Americans
racial categories, 20, 24
racial groups, 31; antagonism between, 1; and culture, 24
racial identity, 15, 184; and citizenship, 39; defined, 19–25; and skin color, 27; in United States, 17. *See also* Black identity
racism, 63, 122, 126, 129, 185; biological, 14–15; and Black viewpoint, 138; changes in, 114; and cultural rights, 135; and identity, 16, 18, 22; and liberal citizens, 47; and liberalism, 9–11, 16, 115–22; and "linked fate," 139; and market system, 42; and nationalism, 29–30; and power, 21, 136; and state, 22–23. *See also* Black Americans; white Americans; whites
Ramsey, Patricia, 196n. 3
Ravitch, Diane, 209n. 12, 209n. 14
Rawls, John, 17, 94–95, 198n. 33
Raz, Joseph, 155
Reconstruction, 118
Reformation, the, 79
religion. *See under specific religions*
revolution, 58
Rieder, Jonathan, 197n. 24
rights. *See* liberal rights; liberalism
Rodriguez, Richard, 197n. 18
Romanians, 143
Romansch, 148–49, 155–56, 157, 159; and culture, 156
Rome, 143, 173
Rorty, Richard, 34, 46
Rousseau, Jean-Jacques, 190n. 24, 208n. 5
Rozenblit, Marsha, 193n. 6
Russia, 163

San Francisco, 178
Sandel, Michael, 17, 26, 194n. 31

Sanders, Jimy, 193n. 41
Saratoga, 132
Sardinians, 25
Scandinavia, 144
Scandinavians, 62, 64
Schmid, Carol, 206n. 20
Schuck, Peter, 200n. 34
Schuman, Howard, 202n. 2
Scotland, 154
Scott, Dred, 22, 116
secession, 156
segregation, 124, 129. *See also* desegregation
self-determination, 28, 142, 144, 176. *See also* nationalism
Seligman, Joseph, 132
separatism, 131
Seton-Watson, Hugh, 27
sexism, 11
Shearer, Derek, 204n. 36
Sheehan, James, 189n. 10, 205n. 12
Shiites, 28
Shipler, David, 208n. 46
Shklar, Judith, 193n. 13
Sidgwick, Henry, 189n. 3
Sierra Leone, 14
Sikh Americans, 46, 76, 78
Sikhs, 28–29, 70, 82, 85–86
slavery, 21; and inequality, 121; justification for, 116–17; and liberalism, 116–18
Slavs, 19, 143
Slovaks, 143–44
Smith, Adam, 42
Smith, Rogers, 190n. 18, 200n. 34, 201n. 41, 202n. 16, 203n. 17
Sobol, Thomas, 208n. 3
South Africa, 19
sovereignty, 27–28
Soviet Union, 28, 81
Sowell, Thomas, 27, 192n. 28
Spain, 28–29, 154
Spanish, 147, 149, 182
Spitzer, Leo, 18, 190n. 1
St. Patrick's Day, 52, 72, 173
state of nature, 2
Steinberg, Stephen, 66
Stolzenberg, Nomi Maya, 201n. 37
Strauss, Nathan, 132
suburbs, 26
Supreme Court, 11, 22, 56, 88, 169; and democratic debate, 44; and slavery, 116; and voting, 123
Svensson, Frances, 199n. 24
Swiss, 143
Switzerland, 148

Takaki, Ronald, 196n. 10
Tamir, Yael, 156, 205n. 11, 207nn. 32, 33, 38, and 41, 208n. 49
Taney, Roger, 116

LIBRARY OF CONGRESS CATALOGING-IN-PUBLICATION DATA

Spinner, Jeff.
    The boundaries of citizenship : race, ethnicity, and nationality in the liberal state /
Jeff Spinner.
        p.   cm.
    Includes bibliographical references (p.   ) and index.
    ISBN 0-8018-4812-1 (hc : acid-free paper)
        1. Ethnic groups—Civil rights. 2. Minorities—Civil rights. 3. Citizenship.
    4. Liberalism.   I. Title.
JF1061.S65   1994
323.1´73—dc20   93-46089